Preface books

A series of scholarly and critical studies of major writers intended for those needing modern and authoritative guidance through the characteristic difficulties of their work to reach an intelligent understanding and enjoyment of it.

General Editor: MAURICE HUSSEY

Available now:

A Preface to Wordsworth   JOHN PURKIS
A Preface to Donne   JAMES WINNY
A Preface to Milton   LOIS POTTER
A Preface to Coleridge   ALLAN GRANT

A Preface to Yeats

Edward Malins

CHARLES SCRIBNER'S SONS
New York

821
X41 gm 144

Printed in Great Britain
Library of Congress Catalog Card Number 74–11930
ISBN 0–684–14076–4

To Tom Henn

1 3 5 7 9 11 13 15 17 19 I/C 20 18 16 14 12 10 8 6 4 2

Contents

In a compendium such as this book is, the work of scholars is its source, and in particular I should like to show my complete sense of obligation to Professor Ellmann, Dr Henn, Professor Jeffares, Jon Stallworthy and Dr F. A. C. Wilson, whose work is the foundation for all Yeats studies.

I should also like to thank Francis Warner and John Purkis for valuable advice given after reading parts of the manuscript; Sir John and Lady Wheeler Bennett and Miss Rosemary Hovenden for information about Garsington Manor and Stone Cottage respectively; Colin Smythe for access to Gregory MSS and photographs, and to Gabrielle Holmwood for assistance in typing.

The General Editor would like to thank Mr Michael Murphy and Mr John O'Beirne-Ranelagh for their assistance with Irish linguistic and historical matters.

EDWARD MALINS published two shorter studies of Yeats in *The Yeats Centenary Papers, 1965* (Dolmen Press, Dublin) and has since provided Forewords for *Coole* by Lady Gregory (Dolmen Press, 1971), and *A Book of Saints and Wonders* by Lady Gregory (Colin Smythe, 1971). He is widely known for his *English Landscaping and Literature 1660–1840* (OUP), and in 1974 a further study in this subject, *Lost Demesnes, A History of Irish Landscaping* (Irish University Press), written in collaboration with the Knight of Glin.

vi

List of illustrations

Foreword

A reader's impressions of the poetry of a period as long as a half a century are too subjective and sensitive to be likened to the plotting of a map. Two names, however, clamour for near-equal representation for one such period: is the half-century up to about 1945 the age of the Anglo-American, T. S. Eliot or the Anglo-Irishman, W. B. Yeats? Or is it, after all, the period of an older native, now in the 1970s, returning in some strength, Thomas Hardy? Probably the cosmopolitan nature of the Modern Movement in the arts that attained a peak in the 1920s will ensure that Eliot and Yeats, with their compression of the widest range of reference and symbol, are not superseded in general acclaim. Edward Malins in this Preface Book examines the lengthy career of W. B. Yeats, to whose poetry he has devoted a lifetime of study, teaching and writing.

After an assessment of several elements in the poet's biography and intellectual growth Mr Malins selects a small group of poems written between the 1890s and the 1930s as the chart on p.2 demonstrates. Crucial to the entire development of the poet and, much more significantly, to the resurgence of the Irish nation, were the events of Easter 1916 in Dublin. The political background of Irish nationalism is therefore given close attention, along with the history of the country and an explanation in some detail of its mythology, subjects which for the non-Irish reader may be sources of misunderstanding when they are used in the poetry. At the beginning of his career Yeats was most familiar for his excursions into sagas, myths and legends of the ancient world, the Orient and, above everything else, the Celtic race. At that time, as an early reviewer wrote, Yeats's 'special vice' was 'indefiniteness'. But later, as the result of living through a major change of feeling, Yeats revised his early work considerably and attained a mastery of symbol, tone and lyricism, all running together, notably above his earlier grasp. Of the utmost importance here, in the 'Great Period' is the 1928 volume, *The Tower*, source of 'Leda and the Swan' (see p.89) and many other most distinguished pieces.

The scholarly library dealing with the work of Yeats has proliferated, as our selective bibliography shows, to an unprecedented extent in the last quarter-century. Even so, the assistance offered to readers in the present book will enlighten, delight and even astound those who have had considerable contact with the poetry. The entire study is documented from a great range of writers who either knew Yeats personally or have established particularly close links with his work. In the words of a distinguished present-day critic, who nevertheless prefers the claims of T. S. Eliot, the poems of Yeats indeed pose 'the insistent questions of the place, part and possibility of the major artist in modern civilization' (F. R. Leavis, *Lectures in America*). To help readers form their own assessment of this major artist is the purpose of this Preface Book.

MAURICE HUSSEY
General Editor

Introduction

Like others in this Preface series, this volume is primarily concerned with the background to the poet's life and poetry. In the case of Yeats, even though he is near to us in time, this background is as important to understand as it is difficult to acquire. Firstly, the average English-speaking man or woman knows little about Irish history, life and thought; and secondly, he is not equipped educationally to grasp the language of myth. Therefore the outline of Irish history and the study of magic and myth occupy two chapters of this book, for these may open the doors to the visionary land in which Yeats's poetry flowers. In comparison, the Critical Survey in Part Two is short, for there would be little point in adding here to the cairn of scholarly books and Ph.D. theses lying at the top of the mountain of literary criticism. As can be seen, this section deals sometimes with lesser known poems, chosen to shed light on his consistent development as a poet during his long life, or to show the close connections between his poetry and his plays. But this section must be regarded as prolegomena, even though it is reinforced by critical examination of poems in the Reference section, under both 'Family, friends and acquaintances' and the Gazetteer.

One reason for the growing number of students of English literature in colleges and universities today must be the realization that the relationship of poetry to values in life is of first importance; and some may have sensed that those poets in touch with the wisdom of the ages through the archetypes of myth and its imagery may be able to give us, through the incantations of their verse, something which can no longer be said by priest and philosopher, if indeed it ever could be—and certainly not in a magically self-contained artefact like a poem. In a world which is dashing down the Gadarene slope of materialistic chaos at the expense of the spiritual, 'Things fall apart; the centre cannot hold.'

It was the realization of Yeats's awareness of this which prompted T. S. Eliot, the other major poet of this century, to say in his memorial tribute to Yeats:

> There are some poets whose poems can be considered more or less in isolation, for experience and delight. There are others whose poetry, though giving equally experience and delight, has a larger historical importance. Yeats was one of the latter. He was one of the few whose history was the history of our own time, who are part of the consciousness of our age, which cannot be understood without them.

Yet, on the whole, Yeats held unpopular views: his mixture of Neoplatonism, magic and spiritualism, set out in *A Vision*, is beyond the scope of formal literary criticism, so by some he is called 'escapist' (whatever that may mean), and others see the poetry as stronger if divorced from his magical system. But as magic and myth are inherently expressed in images and symbols it is our fault and not the poet's if we do not reach the core of the matter to find reality as he saw it. This accounts for the somewhat forbidding list of names heading the subsections of chapter 3 'The Poet's Reading'; it is hoped that, brief though this section is, it may help the reader to trace some of the common links which the poet himself found, for example, in Neoplatonism, the Occult, the Hindu *Upanishads*, William Blake and Nietzsche. In two other ways also the poet's views are unpopular: in his scepticism of modern science, irrationally based on his own empirical judgments; and in his political views, in which he reveals an intense admiration for what the best of the Protestant aristocracy of eighteenth-century Ireland stood for—a long way from the chill climate of modern Irish democracy.

W. H. Auden has defined poetry as 'memorable speech', adding that 'No poetry . . . which when mastered is not better heard than read is good poetry.' This is especially so in the case of Yeats. Did he not compose his verse in this way, repeating aloud again and again variants on lines until they sounded right? No other modern poet is so packed with memorable verse, whether in the gentle lyrical strain of 'She bid me take life easy as the grass grows on the weirs', or the sure statement of 'A lonely impulse of delight/Drove to this tumult in the clouds', or the savagely prophetic 'And what rough beast its hour come round at last/Slouches towards Bethlehem to be born?' Eloquence like this has to be heard to receive the full incantations of 'articulated sweet sounds together' as he called them. And through such superb poetic statements as these and many others we begin to see Yeats as a poet in the great tradition of Milton, Blake, Coleridge and Shelley, all of whom find their imagery from *Anima Mundi*, the source of life, according to Plato.

As a mature poet, Yeats, like those others, is concerned with the interpretation of the spiritual and the material, and the study of the migration of the soul. An examination of his reading, prose writing and thinking can often help more than analysis of a poem under a literary microscope, for the whole organism of the poem may thereby be unified rather than disorientated as is sometimes the case in analyses. The learning of the imagination (a tradition not usually taught in schools) will open up the visionary world to all who pass beyond the confines of material viewpoints, until 'soul clap its hands and sing'. Blake has shown us the way, which Yeats followed:

> I give you the end of a golden string,
> Only wind it into a ball,
> It will lead you in at Heaven's gate
> Built in Jerusalem's wall.

EDWARD MALINS
St Peter's College, Oxford

List of abbreviations

Part One

Historical and Literary Background

The Yeats family

Jervis Yeats
Dublin merchant
d. 1712

Benjamin = Hannah Warren
Dublin merchant

Benjamin   = Mary Butler (inheritor of lands in Co. Kildare)
Dublin linen draper
1750–1795   1751–1834

Rev. John, M.A. = Jane Taylor
Rector of Drumcliffe, Co. Sligo (1811–1846)
1774–1846

Rev. William Butler, B.A.   = Jane Corbet   Thomas, M.A.   Matthew   Mary ('Aunt Mickey')
Rector of Tullylish, Co. Down   of Sandymount   of Sligo,   of Sligo   of Sligo
1806–1862   1811–1876   1808–1872   Land agent   1821–1891
                                                                 1819–1885

John Butler, B.A. = Susan Pollexfen
artist   of Sligo
1839–1922   1841–1900

William Butler = Georgie Hyde-Lees   Susan Mary   Elizabeth   Robert   John Butler
poet   ('Lily')   ('Lolly')   1870–1873   ('Jack')
1865–1939   1866–1949   1868–1940   1871–1957

Anne Butler   Michael Butler
artist   senator
1919–   1921–

Lord Dunboyne, in his *Butler Family History* (1966) p.29, with reference to Pierce, 8th Earl of Ormond (d. 1539), writes 'the 8th Earl of Ormond's two eldest brothers, Edmund and Theobald, both of whom were deemed illegitimate. From Edmund, numerous Butlers of Neweholme and elsewhere in Co. Kilkenny descended, including Mary Butler who in 1773 married a Dublin linen draper called Benjamin Yeats.'

2

Middleton and Pollexfen relatives of the poet

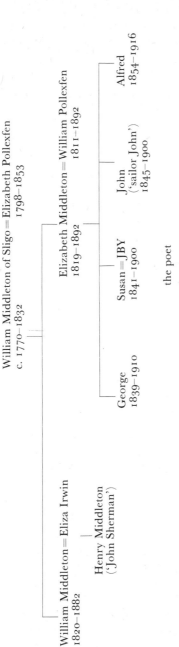

William Middleton of Sligo = Elizabeth Pollexfen
c. 1770–1832   1798–1853

William Middleton = Eliza Irwin
1820–1882

Henry Middleton
('John Sherman')

Elizabeth Middleton = William Pollexfen
1819–1892   1811–1892

George
1839–1910

Susan = JBY
1841–1900

John
('sailor John')
1845–1900

Alfred
1854–1916

the poet

The genealogy is confusing because the poet's grandmother, Elizabeth Middleton Pollexfen, had husband, brother and fath[er] were all named William.

There were many other children in each generation; for example, Henry Middleton and the poet's mother [were] brothers and sisters. Only the ones who concerned the poet are mentioned above.

For further details see William M. Murphy, *The Yeats family and the Pollexfens of Sligo*, with drawings by J[...] Dolmen Press, Dublin, 1971.

3

Biographical summaries

Chronological table

1858 Foundation of Irish Republican Brotherhood.

1862 The Rev W. B. Yeats (grandfather) dies at Sandymount Castle, Dublin.

1863 John B. Yeats (father) marries Susan Pollexfen at Sligo.

1865 13 June. Yeats born in Dublin.

1866 Susan Mary (Lily) born near Sligo.

1867 The Yeatses move.to London.

1867 The Fenian Rising. Execution of the 'Manchester Martyrs'.

1868 John (Jack) and Elizabeth
–73 (Lolly) born in London.

1873 Home Rulç League founded.

1876 The Yeatses move to Bedford Park, Chiswick.

1875 Publication of Standish O'Grady's *Bardic History*.

1877 Yeats at Godolphin School,
–80 Hammersmith. Holidays with cousins in Sligo.

1877 Charles Stewart Parnell chairman of Home Rule League.

1879 Foundation of Irish Land League by Irish National Party of Parnell.

1880 The Yeatses return to Ireland to live.

4

1881 Yeats attends the Erasmus
–83 Smith High School,   1882 Murder of Lord Frederick
     Harcourt Street, Dublin.   Cavendish and Mr Burke
                                      in Phoenix Park.
                                      Irish Land League
                                      suppressed.

1884 A pupil at Metropolitan
–85 School of Art, Dublin.
     Meets George Russell (AE).
1885 Two lyric poems published
     in *The Dublin University
     Review*. First meets Katharine
     Tynan.

1886 Founding of the Dublin   1886 Alliance of Gladstone and
     Lodge of the Hermetic   Parnell for Home Rule.
     Society.   First Home Rule Bill
     First meets John O'Leary.   defeated. Riots in Belfast.

1887 Yeatses move back to
     Chiswick Park.
     Yeats meets Pre-Raphaelites.

1888 (summer) At his grandparents
     in Sligo.

1889 *The Wanderings of Oisin and
     other Poems* published. First
     meets Maud Gonne.

1890 'The Lake Isle of Innisfree'
     published in Henley's
     National Observer.

1891 The Rhymers Club meets at
     the 'Cheshire Cheese' in Fleet
     Street. Yeats working on an
     edition of William Blake.
     Foundation of the Irish
     Literary Society.

1892 Part of *The Countess Kathleen*
     appears in *Various Legends
     and Lyrics*. Pollexfen
     grandparents die.

5

1893 Gladstone's second Home Rule Bill passed in Commons, defeated in Lords. Foundation of Gaelic League by Douglas Hyde.
Arrest of Oscar Wilde.

1894 Feb. Visit to Paris; meets Verlaine with Arthur Symons. March. *The Secret Rose* (short stories) published. *The Land of Heart's Desire* produced in London. (autumn) Sligo staying with George Pollexfen. Two visits to Lissadell House. (winter) Yeats visits Wilde's house with letters of sympathy.

1895 *Poems* published. Moves to the Temple.

1896 Yeats contributes to *The Savoy* (successor to *The Yellow Book*). Moves to Woburn Buildings. Visits Aran Islands. First meets Lady Gregory. Visits Paris, Meets J. M. Synge there.

1897 Stays at Coole; plans Irish National Theatre.

1897 The Queen's Diamond Jubilee.

1898 Meets James Connolly at Maud Gonne's house in Dublin.

1898 Wolfe Tone Centenary.

1899 Visits Maud Gonne in Paris. *The Wind among the Reeds* published.

1899 The Boer War breaks out. Arthur Griffith founds the United Irishman. (Sinn Fein.)

1900 The poet's mother dies.

1901 22 Jan. Death of Queen Victoria.

1901 Yeats first meets Hugh Lane, at Coole.

6

1902 Dun Emer Press (later Cuala Press) established by Lily Yeats. Maude Gonne in *Cathleen ni Houlihan*.

1902 End of Boer War.

1903 *Ideas of Good and Evil* (essays) and *In the Seven Woods* published. Maud Gonne marries Seán MacBride. Irish Players in London. (winter 1903–4) Poet lectures in U.S.A.

1905 Abbey Theatre founded.

1906 Nov. Yeats's *Deirdre* produced there.

1907 Yeats's father goes to New York (never returns to Ireland). The *Playboy* riots at the Abbey Theatre. *Collected Works* (eight vols) published. Visit to Northern Italy with Lady Gregory and her son, Robert.

1903 December. Visits Maud Gonne (now separated from her husband) in Paris.

1909 March. J. M. Synge dies.

1909 April. Swinburne dies.

1910 George Pollexfen dies. May. Visits Maud Gonne in Normandy. *The Green Helmet and other Poems* published.

1910 May. Edward VII dies.

1911 Tour in U.S.A. with Abbey Players.

1912 First meets Georgie Hyde-Lees (his future wife). Works with Rabindranath Tagore on translation of *Gitanjali* from Bengali. (winter) Controversy over the Hugh Lane pictures.

1913	August. Joins Ezra Pound at Stone Cottage, Coleman's Hatch, Sussex.
1914	January–March. Lecture tour in U.S.A. and Canada.
1915	Yeats refuses a knighthood. Hugh Lane drowned in the *Lusitania*.
1916	*The Hawk's Well* produced in London. *Responsibilities* published. 'Easter, 1916' written.
1917	Yeats buys Thoor Ballylee. *The Wild Swans of Coole* published. 20 October, Yeats and Miss Hyde-Lees married in London.
1918	January and February, Oxford. Robert Gregory killed on active service. Ireland with Mrs Yeats.
1919	February. Anne Yeats born. (summer) Thoor Ballylee. (winter) Lecture tour in U.S.A.
1920	(autumn) Oxford. 'All Souls' Night' written. *Michael Robartes and the Dancer* published.
1921	*Four Plays for Dancers* and *Later Poems* published. August, Michael Yeats born.

1914	Third Home Rule Bill receives royal assent. 4th August. Outbreak of First World War.
1916	April. Easter Rising of Irish Republican Brotherhood. 3–9 May. Fifteen leaders executed.
1918	11 November, Armistice signed.
1918 –21	The Troubles (Black and Tans).
1920	Lloyd George's Amending Act. (Six counties in Ulster vote themselves out.)
1921	King George V opens the Northern Parliament at Stormont. December, Anglo-Irish Treaty signed. Civil War breaks out.

8

1922	February, Yeats buys 82 Merrion Square, Dublin. J. B. Yeats dies in New York. Bridge at Thoor Ballylee blown up by Republicans. September, Yeats made a Senator. D.Litt. from Trinity College, Dublin.	1922 Arthur Griffith, first president of Irish Free State dies. Michael Collins killed in an ambush.
1923	'Leda and the Swan' written. Yeats awarded the Nobel Prize for Literature.	1923 de Valera orders Republicans to cease fire.
1924	*Meditations in Time of Civil War* published. (winter) Visits Italy and Sicily.	
1926	Writes 'Sailing to Byzantium' and 'Among School Children' June. Made Chairman of the Seanad Committee on the new Irish coinage.	
1927	October. Ill with congestion of the lungs in Spain and south of France. General breakdown of health.	1927 July. Assassination of Kevin O'Higgins, Minister of Justice.
1928	February. Rapallo, Italy. July. *The Tower* published. Last speech in Seanad. Writing *Words for Music Perhaps*.	
1929	(summer) Last time at Thoor Ballylee. (winter) Rapallo. Finishes *A Vision* and 'Byzantium'.	
1930	(spring) Recuperating from Malta fever at Portofino Vecchio, Gulf of Genoa. November. *The Words upon the Window Pane* produced at the Abbey.	

9

1931 Doctor of Letters, Oxford.
Buys 'Riversdale',
Rathfarnham, Dublin.

1932 May. Lady Gregory dies.   1932 de Valera and Fianna
October. Lecture tour in   fail in office.
U.S.A. *The Winding Stair
and Other Poems*.

1934 June. Rapallo. First meets
Dorothy Wellesley.

1935 George Russell (AE) dies.
November. Majorca.
Translates Hindu *Upanishads*.
A Full Moon in March
published.

1936 Edits *Oxford Book of Modern Verse*.
June. 'Riversdale',
Rathfarnham.

1937 (winter) Mentone.
–38 Writes *On the Boiler*.

1938 January. *New Poems* (last book
seen through the Cuala Press
by Yeats).
August. Dublin, for a
performance of *Purgatory*.
(last public appearance).
Olivia Shakespear dies.
The Death of Cuchulain
finished. Writes 'The Black
Tower', his last poem.

1939 28 January. Yeats dies at   1939 September. Outbreak of
Cap Martin. Buried at   Second World War.
Roquebrune.

1941 Coole Park razed to the
ground.

1948 September. Yeats's body
reinterred in Drumcliffe
churchyard, County Sligo.

Education

Yeats was largely self-educated. In *Reveries over Childhood and Youth* (*AU*), written in 1915, he reveals the chief influences on his childhood. At Sligo for his first eight years he received hardly any formal education. His outstanding memories were of his grandparents and many relations, both Yeatses and Pollexfens, and they filled his mind; particularly his fear of his seafaring grandfather, old William Pollexfen, with the great scar on his hand made by a whaling hook, his brute strength, intolerable silences and violent temper. Yeats as a small boy sailed model boats, listened to sailors' tales, walked the country roads, visited cousins, or heard the family history from his great-aunt Mickey. His father was mostly an absentee in London. His mother, a silent figure, was happiest listening to the tales of cottagers or fishermen's wives; yet Yeats thought she was 'the right kind of mother for a poet or dreamer'. As was customary at the time, the children seemed to have spent much time with nurses.

In 1872 his father wrote from London to his wife in Sligo, concerning Willie's development. The letter reveals as much about his father as Willie:

> I think Willie [aged seven] was greatly disimproved by being at Merville [the large Pollexfen house outside Sligo]. He was coming on from being so much with his mother and away from his grandfather and dictatorial aunts. From his resemblance to Elizabeth [one of his Pollexfen aunts] he derives his nervous sensitiveness. I wish he could be made more robust—by riding or by other means —*not by going to school*. I was very sorry he could not have the pony more, but perhaps he might ride that donkey about which he used to tell me . . .
> Tell Willie not to forget me.

The Yeatses had little money, so were both envious of the Pollexfens' wealth acquired through trade, and conscious of the hard physical qualities which enabled them to keep it. They did not wish their children to appear to be lacking in either physical vigour or wealth, and on this occasion J. B. Yeats evidently wished Willie to become 'more robust' on a pony which was presumably lent them by the Pollexfens. J. B. Yeats also had eccentric ideas about schooling for children; he was not a very good father for a young child, tyrannizing over Willie, having little patience with his difficulties and not really understanding his dreamy turn of mind. However, he used to read much to him, often from Walter Scott's works, and to tell him the plots of Balzac novels, which do not sound very suitable at Willie's age. Some of his aunts attempted to teach him to read, without much success; then his father also tried when he returned from

11

W. B. Yeats, aged 10½. Drawing by his father. Inscribed 'W. B. Yeats' in Lily Yeats's handwriting.

12

London, but with even less success as he had less patience. There were few books in the Pollexfen household which he could have read. The so-called library at 'Merville' must have resembled the Petkoffs' library in Shaw's *Arms and the Man*, 'a single fixed shelf stocked with old paper covered novels, broken backed, coffee stained, torn and thumbed'.

On one occasion when his father had come back from London, he discovered that Willie had that morning been taught to sing at a dame's school:

> Little drops of water,
> Little grains of sand,
> Make the mighty ocean
> And the pleasant land.

From that moment Willie was forbidden to continue at the school, and except for visits to an old gentlewoman who laboured to teach him spelling (evidently with total failure) and some grammar, he received no formal education. Yet these years at Sligo were obviously happy ones, even if he could not read well at the end of them. Much worse was to come.

The family moved to London in 1876, and on 26 January 1877, Willie, aged 10½, entered the chilled Victorian portals of the Godolphin School in Iffley Road, Hammersmith, about a mile and a quarter from his home in Bedford Park, Chiswick. He describes the school in *AU*, p.32:

> It was a Gothic building of yellow brick; a large hall full of desks, some small classrooms, and a separate house for boarders, all built perhaps in 1860 or 1870. . . .
>
> For some days, as I walked homeward along the Hammersmith Road, I told myself that whatever I most cared for had been taken away. I had found a small, green-covered book given to my father by a Dublin man of science; it gave an account of the strange sea creatures the man of science had discovered among the rocks at Howth or dredged out of Dublin Bay. It had long been my favourite book; and when I read it I believed I was growing very wise, but now I should have no time for it nor for my own thoughts. Every moment would be taken up learning or saying lessons, or in walking between school and home four times a day, for I came home in the middle of the day for dinner. But presently I forgot my trouble, absorbed in two things I had never known, companionship and enmity. After my first day's lesson, a circle of boys had got around me in a playing-field and asked me questions, 'Who's your father?' 'What does he do?' 'How much money has he?' Presently a boy said something insulting. I had never struck anybody or been struck, and now all in a minute, without any intention upon my

13

side, but as if I had been a doll moved by a string, I was hitting at the boys within reach and being hit. After that I was called names for being Irish, and had many fights and never, for years, got the better in any of them; for I was delicate and had no muscles.

The academic life at the Godolphin must have been as unpleasant for Willie as the social. He never won any prizes; he was weak in Mathematics, eighth out of a class of thirty-one in Latin at Christmas 1878; his French was 'faible, sans énergie'; and he was reported on by his form master with the usual pedagogic clichés which reveal but little insight: 'A very good boy. Tries to do as well as he can. He does best in Latin and History; with perseverance he will do better. Conduct very good.'

His hunger for Ireland and his hatred of London were mitigated by regular visits once or twice a year to his relations in Sligo. When he had embarked amid the bustle of Clarence Basin, Merseyside, on one of his grandfather's boats, the S.S. *Sligo* or the S.S. *Liverpool*, he would forget London; and when he awoke next morning to hear the Gaelic of the sailors, and then saw the cliffs of Donegal he knew he was nearly home again. After thirty hours at sea the boat would dock alongside the quays of Sligo where his cousins awaited him. As he grew older, life at Sligo became more exacting, bringing with it more independence. Fishing for trout in the loughs with Jim Healy, the stable boy, climbing Knocknarea and Ben Bulben, riding his 'red' (chestnut?) pony past his great-grandfather's rectory at Drumcliffe, past the waterfall thrown back by the wind at Glencar, past the Holy Well of St Patrick and the monastery of St Columba—through a countryside filled with Christian pilgrimage and Pagan myth, the very blood of his poetic inspiration. Fortunately, after three years at the Godolphin school, J. B. Yeats decided to move the family back to Dublin, and Willie was enrolled in the Erasmus Smith High School in Harcourt Street at the beginning of the academic year of 1881. This turned out to be in striking contrast to the Godolphin. He goes on in *AU*, p.56:

> I was now fifteen; and as he did not want to leave his painting my father told me to go to Harcourt Street and put myself to school. I found a bleak eighteenth-century house, a small playing-field full of mud and pebbles, fenced by an iron railing, and opposite a long hoarding and a squalid, ornamental railway station. Here, as I soon found, nobody gave a thought to decorum. We worked in a din of voices. We began the morning with prayers, but when class began the headmaster, if he was in the humour, would laugh at Church and Clergy. 'Let them say what they like', he would say, 'but the earth does go round the sun.' On the other hand there was no bullying and I had not thought it possible that boys could work so hard. Cricket and football, the collecting of

moths and butterflies, though not forbidden, were discouraged. They were for idle boys. I did not know as I used to, the mass of my school-fellows; for we had little life in common outside the class-rooms. I had begun to think of my school work as an interruption of my natural-history studies, but even had I never opened a book in the school course, I could not have learned a quarter of my night's work. I had always done Euclid easily, making the problems out while the other boys were blundering at the blackboard, and it had often carried me from the bottom to the top of my class; but these boys had the same natural gift and instead of being in the fourth or fifth book were in the modern books at the end of the primer; and in place of a dozen lines of Virgil with a dictionary, I was expected to learn with the help of a crib a hundred and fifty lines. The older boys were able to learn the translation off, and to remember what words of Latin and English corresponded with one another, but I, who, it may be, had tried to find out what happened in the parts we had not read, made ridiculous mistakes; and what could I, who never worked when I was not interested, do with a history lesson that was a column of seventy dates? I was worst of all at literature, for we read Shakespeare for his grammar exclusively.

Luckily, his father had read him Shakespeare with a different end in view, and had undoubtedly initiated in him a lifelong love of his plays. Blake's poetry read by his father also stayed with him. But his father's teaching methods were severe though well-intentioned, and he tried unsuccessfully to improve his Latin by regular coaching each evening. Perhaps it was as a result of this that the poet later decided that his son, Michael, should do Greek rather than Latin at school; although when he wrote *AU* he evidently saw the value of classical studies:

He [his father] would have taught me nothing but Greek and Latin and I would have been a properly educated man, and would not have to look in useless longing at books that have been, through the poor mechanism of translation, the builders of my soul, nor face authority with the timidity born of excuse and evasion.

Convincing his father that neither his Latin nor his mathematics was up to the standard of the Trinity College entrance examination, he enrolled in the Metropolitan School of Art in Kildare Street, where he attended classes from May 1884 to July 1885. He showed no special ability at drawing, though his water-colours and pastel drawings are pleasant, sensitive work in a sort of early Turner tradition. In fact, Turner's 'The Golden Bough' was then his favourite picture. Painted in 1834 (now in the Tate Gallery) it is Turner at his most

Claudean—a landscape, with classical temples and dancing figures, with the Bay of Baiae near Naples in the distance. The Sibyl in the foreground is part of the legend, telling the story of her power to enable man to return from the underworld; art in alliance with poetry, as in the Pre-Raphaelite painters whom Yeats also much liked. His tastes were not in the least affected by contemporary art—by the French Impressionists. *AU*, p.81 makes this clear:

> We had no scholarship, no critical knowledge of the history of painting, and no settled standards. . . . No influence touched us but that of France, where one or two of the older students had been already and all hoped to go. Of England I alone knew anything. Our ablest student had learnt Italian to read Dante, but had never heard of Tennyson or Browning, and it was I who carried into the school some knowledge of English poetry, especially of Browning, who had begun to move me by his air of wisdom. I do not believe that I worked well, for I wrote a great deal and that tired me, and the work I was set to bored me.

A month or two at the Royal Hibernian Art School at the beginning of 1886 finished his formal education. During his last years at school he had written much verse, and in 1885 had had two lyrics published; and to some extent he had formulated an aesthetic theory by reading Matthew Arnold, Herbert Spencer and others. His education at all his schools had been anything but satisfactory; academically he was true to form as a writer. Bernard Shaw sums it up admirably about himself: 'I cannot learn anything that does not interest me. My memory is not indiscriminate: it rejects and selects; and its selections are not academic.'

At the end of it all, Yeats could not spell, wrote in an untidy hand, was poor at languages, and was disconcerted by not having had to wrestle with any form of classical discipline at a university. But he was writing verse, and he knew himself to be a poet—nothing else mattered. Furthermore, he had lived much of his childhood at Sligo, which was to provide that verse with the marrow of Irish folklore, which he used again and again to the end of his life.

Appearance and characteristics

Throughout the poet's life women were undoubtedly attracted by his physical appearance. Men seemed to have been put off by his aloofness, his lack of small talk and his 'unclubbable' qualities. For instance,

J. M. W. Turner. The golden bough. *The Sibyl on the left carries the emblem of immortality, the golden bough. The subject is introduced to literature by Virgil (Aeneid Book VI) but it is possible it is a Celtic myth.*

I cannot find any account of an occasion when he visited a pub except once to drink lemonade in a theatre bar with Sir Herbert Grierson. If you were not prepared to listen but wished to talk, like Monk Gibbon, the writer, you might not get on with him. If you let him talk and encouraged him, though not as a sycophant, you might receive a cornucopia of ideas, beautifully presented in his rich mellow voice with its subtle Irish accent. Were you one of those, like Francis Stuart (Iseult Gonne's husband, see below, pp.117–8) who was not always willing to follow the passionate and energetic presentation of his ideas, then he might have scared you.

Ezra Pound (see below, pp.149–50) as a young man, dreaded having him to stay in a cottage in Sussex, and wrote to his mother in November 1913: 'My stay in Stone Cottage will not be the least profitable. I detest the country. Yeats will amuse me part of the time and bore me to death with psychical research the rest. I regard the visit as a duty to posterity.' But after a month he had changed his tune, for in a letter to William Carlos Williams, the poet, he wrote: 'Yeats is much finer *intime* than seen spasmodically in the midst of the whirl.' This change of opinion may have come about because Yeats had given him 200 dollars—in fact had transferred the money from a literary award he had just won himself.

There are many examples of Yeats helping poets with their verse-writing and in other ways, such as getting money for James Joyce when he was living in poverty in Switzerland. T. S. Eliot, twenty-three years younger than Yeats, spoke warmly of his relationship with him in 'The Poetry of W. B. Yeats', a talk delivered to the Friends of the Irish Academy, at the Abbey Theatre, June 1940:

> People have sometimes spoken of him as arrogant and over-bearing. I never found him so, in his conversations with a younger writer I always felt that he offered terms of equality as to a fellow worker, a practitioner of the same mystery. It was, I think, that, unlike many writers, he cared more for poetry than for his own reputation as a poet or his picture of himself as a poet.

At the poet's birth, the doctor had remarked on his large *os frontis*, usually taken as a sign of intelligence. At the age of ten, when in school at Hammersmith, the poet was, on his own admission, 'delicate and had no muscles'. Katharine Tynan, his first girlfriend, remarked in 1885 on his 'dark face, its touch of vivid colouring, the night-black hair, the eager eyes'. He was then a frail and gentle aesthete, a dreamer of Celtic twilight, having a beard, but by 1893 had shaved it off. Out of doors he used to wear a weighty Inverness cape, once his father's, which gave him a more robust appearance. From 1895 Pádraic Colum remembered his velvet jacket, flowing tie, 'blue-black hair coming over his forehead, his frequent gestures and deliberate utterance'.

Yeats in 1894. Photo by his friend T. W. Rolleston, one of the founders of the Rhymers Club.

By 1904, aged thirty-nine, Yeats was no longer the aesthete of the Pre-Raphaelite type, but the fighter for the Abbey Theatre, Irish National Brotherhood member and a man of action. Augustus John's portrait magnificently catches this change. These months, the poet said, were 'the worst in his life', as he was not able to find time or energy for writing verse. His utter absorption when reading his verse is described by Dr Oliver Gogarty in a letter to George Bell, afterwards Bishop of Chichester. The poet was at one of George Moore's salons, reciting *Deirdre*:

> He forgot himself and his face seemed tremulous as if an image of impalpable fire. His lips are dark cherry red, and his cheeks take colour, and his eyes actually glow black and then the voice sets all vibrating as he sways like a Druid with his whole soul chanting . . .
> I know no more beautiful face than Yeats's when lit with song.

On another occasion, in his *Memoir of W. B. Yeats*, Dr Gogarty as a surgeon, is more anatomical: 'The jaw is clear-cut and firm. The mouth is beautifully modelled. The nose is aquiline with great breadth between the eyes, one of which, the right, is noticeably lower than the other.'

Many others who knew him mention his startling eyes. In point of fact he was very shortsighted. Dorothy Wellesley noticed this towards the end of his life, and deduced its effect on his poetry:

> His small dark eyes turned outwards, appear like those of a lizard and as though at times they were hidden by a film. His perspective is therefore abnormal. Perhaps he cannot see very much out of doors. Certain it is he sees nothing, when we sit together in my walled garden, in the beauty of any flower.

From this she concludes that 'most of the Celtic poets are not concerned with nature at all. Yeats did not himself draw much inspiration from Nature, certainly from no details; only sometimes massed effects, such as a painter sees, influenced his verse.'

As he was also tone-deaf, it was a major disadvantage when he was choosing music for his plays; but he was far from deaf in his acute hearing of intonations in the reading of verse. There are many stories of his own method of composing verse by intoning the lines over and over again until he arrived at a solution that satisfied him. Staying with her grandmother, Lady Gregory, at Coole (see pp.165–9) Anne Gregory used to hear him 'humming away for hours' while he was writing. Dorothy Wellesley's butler was once 'worried', as he said, by 'Mr Yeats a-moaning to hisself'. And I know an inhabitant of Steyning, Sussex, who heard Yeats practising variations of his epitaph, 'Cast a cold eye' when he was walking down the main street of the town in the 1930s.

A vivid description of the poet when he was in his late forties, is

George Russell (nearest), W. B. Yeats and Synge (in the bow), fishing on Coole Lake.

21

given by Mrs Alfred Lyttelton:

> His hair was rather long and it seemed very grand and black, and
> to have a life of its own which he could not always control; it
> swayed when he spoke, but often in a different rhythm from his
> speech, as if it were impatient of its owner's words. Then there
> were his eyes, burning with vehemence, smouldering with a
> deeper emotion than he was expressing, and finally a general
> sense that he did not belong . . . perhaps to the life of the Earth
> itself.

Austin Clarke in *The Yeats We Knew* (ed. MacManus), describes
an incident in the woods of Coole: 'A tall sportsman, wearing an
unusual rain-coat of sky-blue watered silk, and carrying the rods and
fierce tackle of his craft . . . the angler was crossing a side lawn
towards the portico of a Georgian mansion. To my complete astonishment, I saw that it was the poet himself.'
Fishing and swimming were the only sports in which Yeats
indulged. He was 'useless at games' at school in Hammersmith.
As a boy he had shot with a muzzle-loading pistol, but never did
again after hearing a rabbit squealing in pain. Austin Clarke had
noticed his height when he saw him striding across the Coole lawn;
and George Moore (*Ave*, p.212), remarked upon 'a tall black figure
standing at the edge of the lake, wearing a cloak which fell in straight
folds to his knees looking like a giant umbrella forgotten by some
picnic party'. Equally irreverent was Anne Gregory's view of the
poet in her *Me and Nu*. When she was a child at Coole,

> He always seemed to be there, leaning back in his chair at table—
> huge with (in our eyes) an enormous tummy. He wore a signet ring
> with an enormous stone in it on his little finger and Nu [her sister]
> and I used to giggle like mad, and say he expected everyone to kiss
> it, like the Pope. She and I used to copy his habit of running his
> fingers through the great lock of hair that fell forward over his
> forehead, and then hold out our hand with the imaginary ring,
> saying: 'This ring is a holy ring: it has been in touch with my
> holy halo.'

At the age of sixty he was very much the smiling public man, with a
black velvet coat, silver-buckled shoes, a wide black ribbon attached
to tortoiseshell glasses, the large gold ring on his finger—the *grand
seigneur* in his elegance, and putting on weight. Until the end of his
life he continued to dress with distinction. Dorothy Wellesley was
impressed, and describes him thus:

> His clothes perhaps belonged to the most elegant Bohemian sort
> that our generation has seen. He was always immaculately clean,
> always precisely shaved. . . . His suits were of soft corn or brown

tweeds, with bright blue or dark green shirt, and always with handkerchief to match. The grand white-blue hair, which was raven blue in his youth, added much to his personality. (*Letters on Poetry from W. B. Yeats to Dorothy Wellesley*, ed. Kathleen Raine.)

William Force Stead, who has two poems in *The Oxford Book of English Verse*, after he had got to know the poet well when he lived in Oxford in the 1920s, told me he was the only man he had ever met of whose genius he was 'absolutely certain when talking to him'. More important, 'he was', in Augustus John's phrase which he used about Hugh Lane, 'one of those rare ones who, singlehanded, are able to enrich and dignify an entire nation'.

2   The History of Ireland as it concerned the Poet

This chapter is not a political or social history of Ireland, but a background to the Irish contribution to the civilization of Europe as it affected both Yeats's writing and his life: therefore invasions and battles, reigns and laws are important only so far as they become a part of the tradition he made for himself—his heroic mythical figures, his ancestors and his philosophy, all of which make up the core of his work. For Irish readers, it may not be sufficiently nationalist in concept, for English it may be patriotic and sentimental. But the answer lies in the significance of the event for Yeats, who as an Anglo-Irishman (although he did not use the term) was constantly tugged by his love-hate for Ireland, seeing Irish history and what was going on around him (now itself history) from two perspectives: inspired by its idealism but maddened by its politics.

> Out of Ireland have we come.
> Great hatred, little room,
> Maimed us at the start.
> I carry from my mother's womb
> A fanatic heart.
>
> *Remorse for Intemperate Speech*, CP, p.287

It is as trite to repeat how little the English know of either the Gaelic epic legends or of the events of Irish history, as it is necessary to emphasize how vital both these are to an understanding of the nucleus of Yeats's thought.

Tales of gods and heroes

Gaelic Celts invaded Ireland, which they called Eriu (Erin) in about 350 B.C. They found a Bronze Age culture, with hill forts such as Tara, hallowed burial grounds, sacred groves for gods, and one small, superior state, the Túatha de Danaan, among many others. Like the British Celts who conquered England, but came from further north in Europe, they were strong, tall and militant, and used tempered iron rather than bronze weapons. Most of the epic stories belong to the closing days of this prehistoric Iron Age, from the arrival of the Celts to the establishment of Christianity about A.D. 450. One of the features of these Celtic romances is their sense of the Otherworld, of supernatural happenings, even by gods when they have become reduced to the level of the sidhe (fairies) or hobgoblins. Yeats was lucky to be born into a culture so based, in which traditional memory still lived, and he took full advantage of it. 'The Unappeasable Host' from *The Wind among the Reeds* (1899), CP, p.65, shows this:

The Danaan children laugh, in cradles of wrought gold,
And clap their hands together, and half close their eyes,
For they will ride the North when the ger-eagle flies,
With heavy whitening wings, and a heart fallen cold:
I kiss my wailing child and press it to my breast,
And hear the narrow graves calling my child and me.
Desolate winds that cry over the wandering sea;
Desolate winds that hover in the flaming West;
Desolate winds that beat the door of Heaven, and beat
The doors of Hell and blow there many a whimpering ghost;
O heart the winds have shaken, the unappeasable host
Is comelier than the candles at Mother Mary's feet.

In this short poem he shows his knowledge of Danaan folklore, and his awareness of early Celtic culture. He knows all the details: the 'unappeasable host', the sidhe, who carry off children or substitute changelings; their disguises as birds or animals, here as a ger-eagle; and their beauty, 'comelier than candles'. Secondly, it is a possibility that the Danaan children indeed slept 'in cradles of wrought gold', for these Celtic people of the La Tène culture made ornaments, like the magnificent gold collar, the bronze dishes and horse trappings (as fine as any in Europe), which today can be seen in the National Museum, Dublin.

Yeats's poetry, with its roots in the great Irish folk tales, cannot be fully appreciated unless these tales are known and loved: Oisin and Finn; Cuchulain and Emer; Deirdre and Naisi; Diarmuid and Grainne. Incomparably the best translations are those of Lady Gregory. Yeats wrote a Preface for her *Cuchulain of Muirthemne* (1902) which we quote at some length for it shows not only the beauty of Yeats's early prose and Lady Gregory's translation, but also how these stories pulled him like a lodestone.

If we do not set Deirdre's lamentations among the greatest lyric poems of the world, I think we may be certain that the wine-press of the poets has been trodden in vain; and yet I think it may be proud Emer, Cuchulain's fitting wife, who will linger longest in the memory. What a pure flame burns in her always, whether she is the newly married wife fighting for precedence, fierce as some beautiful bird, or the confident housewife, who would awaken her husband from his magic sleep with mocking words; or the great queen who would get him out of the tightening net of his doom, by sending him into the Valley of the Dead, with Niamh, his mistress, because he will be more obedient to her; of the woman whom sorrow has sent with Helen and Iseult and Brunnhilda, and Deirdre, to share their immortality in the rosary of the poets.

'And oh! my love!' she said, 'we were often in one another's company, and it was happy for us; for if the world had been searched from the rising of the sun to sunset, the like would never have been found in one place, of the Black Sainglain and the Grey of Macha, and Laeg the chariot-driver, and myself and Cuchulain.'

And after that Emer bade Conall to make a wide, very deep grave for Cuchulain; and she laid herself down beside her gentle comrade, and she put her mouth to his mouth, and she said: 'Love of my life, my friend, my sweetheart, my one choice of the men of the earth, many is the woman, wed or unwed, envied me until today; and now I will not stay living after you.'

The oldest national epic is the *Taín Bó Cualgne*, the *Driving away of the Bull of Cooley*, which tells the story of Maeve, Queen of Connacht and her war with Conchobar, King of Ulster, whose most famous Red Branch hero was Cuchulain. Contemporary with this were many anonymous lyric poets, some pagan and some Christian, whose poems are very beautifully translated by Frank O'Connor in his anthology, *Fountain of Magic*. These poets also tell the great stories: Oisín returning to earth from Tir-na-nÓg (the Land of the Young) to find St Patrick; Grainne singing as her lover Diarmuid sleeps when they are hunted by their enemies; Deirdre, after she has been separated by King Conchobar from Naisi, her lover, remembering her happiness with him. It is from these lyrics that one senses the life of these townless people who fought, hunted, loved, ate and drank, enjoyed the changing seasons and were mildly agricultural. As pagans they never worked out a detailed religion other than mere animism. The heroic stories show areas where there were groups under warrior kings or nobles: Ulaidh (Ulster) in the north; Mumha (Munster) in the south; in Laighin (Leinster) in the east and Connachta (Connacht) in the west. Until about 300 there was no idea of a High King, and no Roman concept of unity, with roads and order; for although Roman influences did cross the sea, no legionary ever landed in Ireland. A semi-feudal set-up, in petty states still called túatha, organized on a family blood basis, was the usual form at this time. One of the first to unite many túatha and to make the sacred hill of Tara the capital of Ireland, was Cormac MacArt, *c.* 300, and there he presided over the Fies, a law-making body, and lead the Fianna, a warrior force. Heroic tales of the Fianna, led by Finn and his son, the poet Oisín, are the core of Gaelic legend known to Yeats.

By about 430 most of the island was Gaelic speaking and showing signs of a more advanced social and hierarchical set-up with specific Irish characteristics. One of these with particular interest for Yeats was the warrior aristocracy which supported poets who were the successors of the bards of the earlier La Tène culture. Between the nobles and the commoners was an influential group whom we might now call lawyers, Latin scholars, historians, clergy and poets. The druids were regarded as seers capable of prophecy and divination, the bards or poets were expected to write poetry and record heroic tales; and there was a Celtic writing called Ogam, based on Latin but used only on burial stones. For information on this mythology see M. Dillon and N. Chadwick, *The Celtic Realms* (Weidenfeld, 1967).

The coming of Christianity

Christianity was brought to Ireland officially by Palladius, sent by the Pope from Rome in 431; but it had come earlier through emigrants, foremost of whom was Bishop Patrick, a romanized British Celt. Much of this period is shrouded in historical mist through which one peers to find tradition associating St Patrick with the church at Armagh. Culturally the coming of Christianity meant a wonderful flowering of Celtic art, and the development of a direct link from this remote island with Mediterranean thought and writing. Great British saints founded hundreds of monasteries in Ireland during the sixth and seventh centuries; the best known, often mentioned in the writings of Lady Gregory, Yeats and James Joyce, are: Enda of Killeany in Aran; Finnian of Clonard; Colum (Columcille) of Derry and Iona; Columba of Terryglass and Iona; Ciaran of Clonmacnois; Kevin of Glendalough; Brendan of Clonfert; and Finnbar of Cork. The tales of these Irish saints and some of their hymns were translated from the Gaelic by Lady Gregory and were then read to Yeats. She tells the 'Breastplate of St Patrick' ('The Deer's Cry') or 'Blessed Cellach's Lament' in splendid poetic prose in her *Book of Saints and Wonders*. St Brigit's hymn is typical of her style, based partly on Gaelic, partly on the Authorized Version of the Bible:

Brigit, excellent woman; sudden flame, may the bright fiery sun bring us to the lasting kingdom.

May Brigit save us beyond troops of demons; may she break before us the battles of every death.

May she do away with the rent sin has put upon us; the blossomed branch; the Mother of Jesus; the very dear young woman greatly looked up to. That I may be safe in every place with my dear saint of Leinster!

These tales of Irish saints are often joined to myths of animals, talking birds, giants or wizards, and human heroes with superhuman characteristics. We read of how St Patrick was told by the Angel to take down the stories of the Fianna from the fighting men, and how St Columcille pleaded for the poets who were driven out of Aedh's kingdom; so the interaction of Christian and pagan is the warp and woof of history. The last great pagan warrior, Oisín (Ossian), was in contact with St Patrick, a meeting between the two worlds movingly related by Yeats in *The Wanderings of Oisin* (1889). In *The Trembling*

27

of the Veil (*AU*), he describes a mystical experience he had when crossing a stream in Coole Park. At that moment, he says, his 'whole imagination was preoccupied with the pagan mythology of ancient Ireland'. At Coole, the birthplace of St Colman, he must have heard the songs of beggars and travelling men, and, like St Columcille, been carried by their imagination 'over the plain in the company of the angels of God'.

At the time of the saints we have mentioned, Irish monasteries became internationally famous, being visited by students from all over Europe. The arts also benefited from their patronage: metalwork flourished, for example, the eighth-century gold Ardagh chalice in the National Museum; High Crosses were carved and, above all, the monks were skilled at illuminated book illustration, as for example in the *Book of Kells*, one of the most beautiful books in the world, now in the library of Trinity College, Dublin.

A Viking raid on Lambay island off Howth, County Dublin, in 795 was the start of a death-knell to much of the best of Irish monasticism and learning, being the first of many such raids for two centuries. The Norsemen were civilized neither by Christianity nor by Roman influences, and except for leaving some traces in Irish art, their warlike and efficient record is black. Unfortunately the Irish seem to have adopted Norse methods by tribal fighting. Not until the tenth century does any one king again emerge as High King at Tara, and that was Brian Boru, who was titled 'Imperator Scottorum' (Emperor of the Irish). This was the zenith of Gaelic Ireland. Despite the Norsemen, unity in language, law, religion and culture had survived, and the Irish were the first nation north of the Alps to produce a national literature. Yeats could neither read nor speak Gaelic, so had to be content with translations; yet it still fired his imagination and provided a mythological basis for his poetry such as no English poet could ever hope for.

Gaelic Ireland in Norman, Tudor and Stuart times

After Brian Boru's death in 1014, quarrels broke out with renewed vigour between the various rulers. Finally one of them, Dermot MacMurrough, King of Leinster, appealed to Henry II of England for help, so laying the way for the Norman conquest under Henry's lieutenant, the Earl of Pembroke, called Strongbow. His expedition was backed by the Pope's blessing, as he would carry religion to a barbarous people. However, Ireland for the next four centuries proved almost impossible to rule, even by the Normans; and weaker kings such as Richard II came to grief there. Another who failed, in Tudor times, was Robert Devereux, Earl of Essex, who was executed on his return to England. Subsequently, a rigorous policy of Protestant Plantations, or colonization, established some form of order, though

28

the burning of Edmund Spenser's castle at Kilcolman during Desmond's Rebellion, was a far from isolated incident. The Plantation policy, giving land confiscated from the native Irish to such as Sir Walter Raleigh, who became the largest landowner in the south, aroused opposition which was put down with much severity.

This policy continued throughout Stuart reigns. In Ulster the Earls of Tyrconnell and Tyrone were restored by James I in 1603, but soon quarrelled with the English and therefore, with more than a hundred chiefs, left Ireland. This 'Flight of the Earls' irreparably weakened Gaelic Ireland, leaving only the language, as Gaelic aristocracy did not long survive. The Plantations continued with renewed strength, 'undertakers' annexing 500,000 acres, including the lands of the earls which were the best. The town of Derry was presented to the City of London, and London Companies (absentees) received grants for business in the county. Many Scottish and English landowners were therefore established in the north; similarly in Munster, an adventurer like the remarkable Richard Boyle (Earl of Cork, 1620) could arrive in the country penniless in 1588 and become a millionaire before he died.

In Charles I's reign Thomas Wentworth, later Earl of Stafford, was Lord Deputy, 1633–40, extracting subsidies and organizing the Irish equivalent of the Court of Star Chamber with efficiency, but in 1641, the year he was executed in England for his illegal actions, there was a rising of Catholics in Ulster, many of the colonists being murdered or fleeing the country. Cromwell thought he was appointed by God to root out the Catholics. He was nearly successful, as by famine, plague and war the population was reduced to about half a million. His memory lives on in the sack of Drogheda in which all the soldiers and civilians, about 3500, were massacred. He wrote: 'It has pleased God to bless our endeavours.' Wexford was similarly dealt with. His final objective—to drive all the native Irish into Connacht —failed through its impractability, before his death in 1658.

The Restoration of the monarchy still meant a Protestant Anglican ascendancy in the country, with a Protestant State Church, only a few Catholics being restored to their lands taken by Cromwellian followers. But the Catholics still had about a third of the freehold land and during Charles II's reign they were protected by royal prerogative from religious persecution. The hopes, therefore, of Catholics stayed with the Stuart monarchy, and rose high on the accession in 1685 of James II, a Catholic. Three years later, after James had quarrelled with the Church and the Tory party in England, and the Whigs had invited William Prince of Orange to England, the Irish still regarded James as their lawful king. Ireland now became a battleground. The Protestant apprentices of Derry closed the gates of the town on the Catholic armies of James and withstood a siege for 105 days. A Patriot parliament was summoned

29

by James in Dublin, which proved to be the last 'Old English' legislative assembly until 1922, and the last in which the Catholic faith was represented. William landed in Ireland and on 1 July the Battle of the Boyne decided the fate of Jacobite Ireland. Yeats's Protestant ancestors were on the winning side:

> A Butler or an Armstrong that withstood
> Beside the brackish waters of the Boyne
> James and his Irish when the Dutchman crossed;
>
> (*CP*, p.113)

Resistance continued in Limerick under Patrick Sarsfield until he was forced to surrender after the Battle of Aughrim (1691), after which all those Catholic soldiers who wished were allowed to serve in France, where Sarsfield died fighting. The 'flight of the wild geese', as it was called, put an end to any Catholic hopes for a solution to their grievances.

The Anglo-Irish of the eighteenth century

At the start of the eighteenth century Protestants dominated the Irish Parliament. Penal laws tied and bound Catholics; they could not buy land or lease it for more than thirty-one years; estates had to be portioned among all sons rather than the eldest unless he were to turn Protestant; higher posts in the government were given to Englishmen; rents were spent in England by countless absentee landlords; and no Catholic could vote or enter Trinity College, the only university.

Jonathan Swift, Protestant Dean of St Patrick's Cathedral, Dublin, from 1713 until his death in 1745, was one of the bitterest critics of English rule. *A Short Character of His Excellency t[he] E[arl] of W[harton], L[ord] L[ieutenant] of I[reland]* in 1711 denounces 'the arbitrary power and oppression . . . whereby the people of Ireland have for some time been distinguished from all Her Majesty's subjects'. It was, in Swift's own words to Stella, 'a damned libellous pamphlet'. Again, in 1724, he took up his pen against a patent which had been granted to a certain William Wood of Wolverhampton to coin over £100,000 worth of halfpennies and farthings, which Swift pointed out in his four pseudonymous *Drapier's Letters* would devalue the coinage and enable Wood to make a possible profit of £40,000. In the fourth of these *Letters* he criticized the whole dependence of Ireland on England. The coinage scheme was dropped and medals were struck in Ireland in Swift's honour. His *Short View of the State of Ireland* (1727) and *Modest Proposal* (1729) further revealed the national tragedy.

Edmund Burke (see below pp.56–8) as M.P. for Bristol tried to get trading equality and religious emancipation for Ireland, but failed: 'Is Ireland united to the crown of Great Britain for no other

30

purpose than that we should counteract the bounty of Providence in her favour?' he asked the citizens of Bristol. Similarly, Berkeley (see below pp.55–6) in *The Querist* (1737) asked questions about the unsatisfactory state of economic and social affairs in the country; but nothing was done because the legislative work of the Irish Parliament was limited by the Parliament at Westminster. Thus did three of Yeats's favourite figures from the eighteenth century protest at the inequalities suffered by the Irish in dealing with England.

Until 1760 Protestant rule was complete, and although there was peace in the country for a hundred years after the Battle of the Boyne, it was far from satisfactory for the majority of the population. Edmund Burke summarized the situation: 'The Protestant ascendancy is nothing more or less than the resolution of one set of people to consider themselves as the sole citizens of the Commonwealth and to keep a dominion over the rest by reducing them to slavery under a military power.'

The finest period in the Protestant ascendancy was during Henry Grattan's Parliament in the last fifteen years of the century. By 1770 Henry Grattan led a group called the Patriot Party which sought a 'free Constitution and freedom of trade' for Ireland. After the American War of Independence this Party managed to obtain a relaxation of trade restrictions and some real independence for the Irish Parliament—the abolition of the severe penal code and the status of citizens for Catholics, as well as a period of economic prosperity. The reform of Parliament was one of Grattan's objectives, but he was always thwarted by the ruling class of landowners, from which he himself came. However, the French Revolution changed the political thinking of Europe, and soon the leaders for reform were to be found outside Parliament.

The chief of these was Wolfe Tone, a young Protestant lawyer who was an admirer of what the French Revolution achieved in getting rid of a corrupt aristocracy. In 1791 he formed the Society of United Irishmen, which included Protestants and Catholics, its objective being to form a national Irish Parliament entirely free from the influences of Great Britain. He managed to obtain further concessions for Catholics, but they were still debarred from Parliament, from the higher positions in the state and from Trinity College. Small concessions were insufficient for the revolutionary Tone who, when in France in 1796, proclaimed himself to be a republican who hated England, and a defender of peasants against ruling tyranny. Conciliatory reforms were suggested at this point by Grattan in Ireland, but defeated in the English Parliament. Had these reforms taken place—full emancipation for Catholics, some increase in the number of voters, and certain rights for peasants with reference to tithes and land taxes by landlords—the 1798 rebellion would not have taken place. The last Parliament of the Kingdom of Ireland began in

January 1798, and an armed insurrection broke out in May; before that Lord Edward FitzGerald, the much-loved commander-in-chief of the United Irishmen, had died of wounds received while resisting arrest. French troops helping Wolfe Tone arrived too late in Killala Bay, County Galway, were defeated in battle and Tone was captured. In his pride he asked to be shot as a soldier, but was sentenced by a court-martial to be hanged and disembowelled as a criminal. 'A fig for disembowelling if they hang me first,' he replied, and eventually avoided that fate by a self-inflicted mortal wound from which he died in prolonged agony.

Yeats inherited

> The pride of people that were
> Bound neither to Cause nor to State,
> Neither to slaves that were spat on,
> Nor to the tyrants that spat,
> The people of Burke and of Grattan
> That gave, though free to refuse—
> Pride, like that of the morn,
> When the headlong light is loose,

(*CP*, p.222)

From then on, William Pitt, the British prime minister, was determined on an Act of Union between the two countries. Grattan opposed it, but his supporters were eliminated by bribes, or offered places and pensions by Pitt's government, and the Bill was carried. Ireland was to have 100 M.P.s in the House of Commons at Westminster, the Churches of England and Ireland were to unite, Catholics were to have equal rights, and there was to be free trade. But Grattan knew that all was not well for Ireland. His final speech was a poetic lament for his life's work: 'Yet I do not give up my country. I see her in a swoon but she is not dead; though in her tomb she lies helpless and motionless, still on her lips is the spirit of life, and on her cheeks the glow of beauty.' Pitt subsequently defaulted on Catholic emancipation, and the Union never in Irish eyes became 'a treaty between two nations'.

One of the outward signs of the prosperous period of Grattan's Parliament is the grace and magnificence of Irish eighteenth-century town architecture, expressed in countless squares, terraces and crescents in Dublin, Limerick and other towns. With fine public buildings, this was excellent town-planning, and Yeats knew it when he lived in Merrion Square, and passed by the Rutland Memorial and through some of the most elegant eighteenth-century streets on his way to the Seanad Éireann in Leinster House. Throughout the country, landlords built elegant Palladian houses, known to their tenants as 'the Big House', surrounded by pleasant gardens and landscapes, often formed by them into a special Irish picturesque style, using the scenery of the many loughs and mountains. In 'Private Thoughts' (*EX*), Yeats remarks that the best landed gentry were 'great architects' and 'travelled everywhere, read the classic authorities and designed buildings that still stir our imagination'. This is an idealized view, for most of the gentry were more interested in country sports; but Yeats was influenced by the modest example of Coole Park (see below pp.165–9) in providing a haven for writers, in the tradition of those friends whom Swift used to visit in the summer months.

The Irish eighteenth century, 'that one Irish century that escaped from darkness and confusion', as Yeats wrote in *Wheels and Butterflies* (1934), provided for him a union of opposites: 'all the delirium of the brave' in the rebel-martyrs who knew that death did not mean failure, and were able to laugh in its presence, combined with the order, grace and splendour of living in the country houses:

> Beloved books that famous hands have bound,
> Old marble heads, old pictures everywhere;
> Great rooms where travelled men and children found
> Content or joy; . . .

With his passionate love of the eighteenth century in Ireland, Yeats is not popular with Irish historians. This is a period for them when Gaelic resistance to the English was at its lowest; when Gaelic bards lamented the disappearance of Gaelic traditions, in ballads which either personified Ireland as Cathleen ni Houlihan or Dark Rosaleen —the beautiful girl deprived of her birthright—or sang of their hopes for a restoration of the Gaelic aristocracy. Yeats's admiration is centred on a few figures, who he thought had the courage to fight against wrongs imposed by England. None of them, as Joseph Hone wrote, was from the landlord class: 'Neither Swift nor Berkeley was born in a great house; Goldsmith came from a country rectory; Burke was the son of a lawyer, Wolfe Tone of a coachmaker; Grattan's father was a Recorder . . . and these men were not only born in Ireland but educated there.'

The most important to Yeats was Jonathan Swift, whose plain and honest speaking seemed to him to be 'Passion ennobled by intensity, by endurance, by wisdom'. In *The Words upon the Windowpane* (1930), his play about Swift's spirit returning to a séance, one of the characters, a Cambridge undergraduate, expresses clearly what Yeats himself thought about the eighteenth century:

> . . . when men of intellect reached the height of their power— the greatest position they ever attained in society and the State, that everything great in Ireland and in our character, in what remains of our architecture, comes from that day: that we have kept its seal longer than England.

33

The fight for freedom, 1800–1923

Dublin, after the signing of the Act of Union, its Parliament gone, ceased to be a flourishing metropolis and became a provincial city. Soon the culture, independence, and prosperity of the period of Grattan's Parliament became a memory. In 1803 there was one more brief and unsuccessful insurrection against English rule, similar to Tone and the United Irishmen, ending in the scaffold for another hero, Robert Emmet. Although his action little affected subsequent history, we mention it as he also was a link in the chain of rebels, and as such for Yeats was important. In fact, Yeats idealized Tone and Emmet as much as he despised Daniel O'Connell, who was to dominate Irish politics in the first half of the nineteenth century. O'Connell was a Catholic landlord from County Kerry, speaking Gaelic yet spurning it, a man who thought nothing of the past, who expressed loyalty to the Crown (once presenting George IV with shamrocks and laurel wreath), who did not believe in force as a method of achieving his ends; a demagogue, able to sway thousands by his oratory yet fundamentally unscrupulous and vulgar, in sharp contrast with Grattan, the dignified eighteenth-century aristocrat. Nevertheless, O'Connell, 'the Liberator', became a national hero from the moment he won the Clare election (1828) and, as a Catholic, demanded emancipation and the repeal of the Union. By this he meant national independence for Ireland, but not national separation from Britain. During his leadership of the Irish party, the Catholic Emancipation Act was at last passed (1829), liberal reforms were made to the franchise, and Poor Relief and Tithe Acts helped the poor. In talking to Americans on his lecture tour in 1904, Yeats made clear his distinction between Emmet and O'Connell:

> I sometimes think that O'Connell was the contrary principle to Emmet. He taught the people to lay aside the pike and the musket, the song and the story, and to do their work now by wheedling and now by bullying. He won certain necessary laws for Ireland. He gave her a few laws, but he did not give her patriots. He was the successful politician, but it was the unsuccessful Emmet who has given her patriots. O'Connell was a great man, but there is too much of his spirit in the practical politics of Ireland.

Yeats was right. It is about the heroism of Tone, Lord Edward and Emmet that ballads are sung, whose portraits hang on cottage walls, and who have become symbols of freedom to the Irish poor for over a hundred years.

In 1842 another nationalist group called the Young Ireland Party survived for a few brief years, among them Thomas Davis and John Mitchel (see below p. 106). At first they worked with O'Connell but it was an uneasy partnership. Soon, however, the appalling crisis of the Great Famine descended on Ireland like the Angel of Death (1845–48). The potato to the Irish peasant was as rice to the Indian—the staple crop. When epidemic blight killed the potato plant, thousands died of starvation. Despite charitable measures on a vast scale, the population fell from over eight million to six and a half, and thousands emigrated to the U.S.A. It was the worst famine known in the history of Europe in peacetime, and it took Ireland years to recover, firstly because emigration increased, and secondly because most of those who died were Gaelic speaking. By the 1850s the population was only five million. O'Connell did not live to see the full disaster, as he died, an invalid on a journey to Rome, in 1847.

Of the three most important and positive movements in Irish nineteenth-century history—Catholic Emancipation, Land Reform and the Irish Literary Renaissance—only the first was before 1850. In that year a Land Act was passed that protected tenants from certain unjust forms of eviction and gave a fairer scale of rents, fixity of tenure and freedom to sell; but there were still many unfair evictions of tenants who were too poor to pay their rents, up to Maud Gonne's time (see below pp.118–20). Also in 1850 the Irish Franchise Act increased the electorate to 160,000 voters, much to the advantage of the Irish Party in Parliament.

The Irish Republican Brotherhood (the Fenians, from Finn's-Fianna) was founded in 1858. As its name implies, it was based on Wolfe Tone's Jacobin ideas, and so was not content with the Home Rule movement (which hoped to achieve its ends through constitutional measures), but claimed complete national independence. One by one the long-established English injustices disappeared. Gladstone, a lifelong friend of Ireland, who came to power in 1869, saw an Act through Parliament by which the Protestant Church of Ireland was disestablished, after which, a few years later, an Act by which fellowships and higher degrees were open to all creeds at Trinity College. Then he decided to tackle the Home Rule question, and in this he had the cooperation of the most able Irish politician of the century, Charles Stewart Parnell, a Protestant squire from County Wicklow—reserved, inscrutable, proud, with an inflexible attachment to the Irish cause. He may be said to have taken up the leadership of the Irish party where O'Connell left it, nevertheless it was more in the tradition of Swift that Yeats saw him. In 1877, as M.P. for Cork City at the age of thirty-one, he was leader of about thirty M.P.s forming the Irish party in the House of Commons. He was determined first, that Irish farmers should own their land, and that the existing landlord-peasant relationship must become a thing of the past; and second, that Home Rule must be achieved as soon as possible.

Gladstone and his Liberal party returned to power in 1880, and a

35

Land Act was passed which reduced Irish rents by about 20 per cent, giving both landlord and tenants a right in the land. When the first Home Rule Bill was introduced to the Commons in 1886 the Tories opposed it and some of Gladstone's party deserted him, forming the Liberal Unionists, so the Bill was thrown out. Only about a fifth of the population of Ireland, mostly landlords, supported the Union, except for Ulster, which became the centre of the Unionist cause to resist Home Rule. At the height of the crisis, crowds of Orangemen burnt an effigy of O'Connell in Belfast during a riot. It soon became evident to politicians that the Plantation of Ulster under James I, with Anglo-Scottish Protestants, was a fact which cannot be over-looked—indeed, it has effected the history of Ireland into our own times.

The partnership between Gladstone, aged eighty-six, and Parnell was now suddenly fractured. Parnell's attachment for the wife of a certain Captain O'Shea became the subject for a divorce in which he was found guilty; and, although Parnell afterwards married her, his supporters faded away on moral grounds—the Pope and Catholic bishops, Gladstone himself, Nonconformists, and a majority of Parnell's own party. In a year's time he had died from the sheer strain and exhaustion of trying to fight his way back to the leadership. At his funeral in Glasnevin cemetery, Dublin, a shooting star was seen by many to fall across the clear sky at the moment that his body was lowered into the grave. Yeats was told about the incident by Maud Gonne who was present.

More than thirty years later Yeats remembers this in 'Parnell's Funeral' (*CP*, p.319), as he contrasts the 'animal' crowd beside the Great Comedian's tomb (O'Connell's) in Glasnevin cemetery, and the falling star, that symbol in its clarity for the pure intellect of Parnell, and his sacrificial death. Yeats goes on to contrast the fact that for the deaths of Emmet and Tone, England was responsible, but Parnell's own countrymen destroyed him.

> Through Jonathan Swift's dark grove he passed, and there
> Plucked bitter wisdom that enriched his blood.

It is Yeats's harshest political poem, as well it might be, for he passionately believed that this solitary proud man was sacrificed by the meanness of priests, politicians and people. His death was not rebirth but destruction. In 1913 he had first written in anger of Parnell's treatment (*CP*, p.123). The lines here are addressed to Lady Gregory:

> A man
> Of your own passionate serving kind who had brought
> In his full hands what, had they only known,
> Had given their children's children loftier thought,

Sweeter emotion, working in their veins
Like gentle blood, has been driven from the place,
And insult heaped upon him for his pains,
And for his open-handedness, disgrace.

Yeats shows a similar reaction when he recounts an interview with a
biographer of Parnell, who reveals the true story, in *The Trembling
of the Veil* Book II *(AU)*. Gladstone retired from politics in 1894; the
Home Rule Bill had failed to get through Parliament two years
previously, having been thrown out by the House of Lords.

The second important movement of the century, which we
mentioned, has a happier sequel. The Land Act (1903) offered a
bonus to landlords who would sell, and enabled tenants to purchase
on easy terms; tenant farmers therefore became yeomen farmers
like their English counterparts. The Act affected Coole Park, where
the Gregorys sold farms to tenants who became owners. Yeats did
not like this dismemberment of the Coole estate and made his views
quite clear in the twelve lines of 'Upon a House shaken by the Land
Agitation' *(CP*, p.106). He evidently did not appreciate the hard life
that those who lived under 'mean roof-trees' had been forced to live
as tenants, paying huge rentals; an ironic attitude for one who was a
guest at Coole, because one of the leaders of the movement which
managed to get landlords and nationalist leaders together, and helped
to make recommendations for the Land Act, was Captain John
Shawe-Taylor, a nephew of Lady Gregory's (see *E&I*, 'John Shawe-
Taylor', and Donald Torchiana, *W. B. Yeats and Georgian Ireland*,
pp.44–57).

The Irish Literary Renaissance *(c.* 1890–1920) was the work
initially of Standish O'Grady, Douglas Hyde, Lady Gregory, George
Russell (AE), and W. B. Yeats. The playwrights Synge and O'Casey
followed, after the founding of the Abbey Theatre. The scholars
who translated the folk tales from Gaelic into English poetry and
prose, and, indirectly, those who wrote their own work in Gaelic,
contributed to the revival, during which the Gaelic language, with
the oldest vernacular literature in Europe, became widely known.

In 1900 the spoken language was dormant, although about half a
million people in the West still spoke it. In passing, it is worth noting
that though the history and folk legends of Scotland are well known
to English readers—Rob Roy, Robert the Bruce, Mary Queen of Scots
and Bonnie Prince Charlie being household names—yet the deeds of
Grainne O'Malley, Hugh O'Neill, Patrick Sarsfield and Robert
Emmet, who are equally valiant Irish heroes, are unknown. Perhaps
Ireland needs a Walter Scott, but certain it is that the English neglect
Irish myths and history, compared with Scottish. In 1900 the Irish
speakers in the West had a large vocabulary, estimated by Douglas
Hyde at more than 5000 words, and some could recite a saga of

37

Cuchulain or of the Fianna when they could not read or write. (From 1922–73, the language was compulsory in Irish schools.) But English in Ireland is filled with Gaelic idiom to its advantage, and it is this tongue that Yeats heard about him as a boy. Pádraic Colum gives two examples which are relevant: in the first he deals with the English question, 'Are you selling a horse today?'

> The speaker of correct English has to move the emphasis from one word to another of the four last according to the information he seeks. For successive positions of the chief stress give four different meanings to the question. The Anglo-Irish idiom, which in this matter follows the locution of Gaelic, has no need of accentuating. Its user would say: (a) 'Is it you who are selling the horse?" or (b) 'Is it the horse you are selling?' or (c) 'Is it today you are selling the horse?'. Where the English purist depends upon stress to bring out his meaning, the Irish idiom employs construction for the same purpose, and much more effectively.

The second example is in reply to the query, 'Does it rain here?' The Irishman says:

> 'It bees raining' or 'It does be raining'. He is attempting to reach an exactitude that is possible in Gaelic; in that language there is a distinct form of the verb 'to be' to indicate habitual, the frequentative tense. The Irishman who has the tradition of Gaelic, even though he may never have heard it spoken, feels the want of a frequentative tense in English, and he attempts to supply it.

This may seem like a digression from Irish history with which this section is dealing; but the history of the Irish Literary movement, and its revival of Gaelic speaking and writing is an integral part of the nationalist spirit, which is about to come to fruition—apart from its influence on Yeats, as has been said, by revealing to him the glories of the Irish myths and sagas.

Despite Maud Gonne's fiery speeches, the Wolfe Tone Centenary celebrations in 1898 passed off without any major incident, and when in the next year the South African War broke out, infinitely more Irishmen served in the Dublin Fusiliers in the British Army than in the Transvaal Brigade, commanded by Major John Mac-Bride against the British. But in that year, Arthur Griffith, a journalist, founded a paper called the *United Irishman* (later Sinn Féin, meaning We Ourselves), and many of the younger men such as Pádraic Pearse (see below, pp.143–8) eventually found that a solution by the Union was not satisfactory and broke away from those such as Griffith who supported the Union. In January 1913 the Third Home Rule Bill was at last passed in the Commons, and although it was again thrown out by the Lords, it was no longer possible, under the recent Parliament Act, for it to be so held up by them for more than a year.

Except for Ulster, under its leader Edward Carson, who vehemently opposed the Bill, the majority of Irishmen accepted it. To strengthen their position, Ulstermen openly drilled and armed themselves, and in October 1913 a National Volunteer Force to oppose this was organized in Dublin, in addition to a smaller Citizen Army under James Connolly (see below, p.113). It looked very like civil war as the two sides continued to arm. But the outbreak of the First World War (August 1914) radically changed the situation; the Home Rule Act could not be put into force until hostilities were over, whenever that would be. For the moment all seemed well as about 100,000 Irishmen voluntarily joined the British forces. However, the opponents of the Union saw their chance, and the Irish Republican Brotherhood prepared the ground for the Rising which broke out in Dublin in Easter Week 1916. The subsequent sentences on the leaders united public opinion on Sinn Féin, and 1916, in Seán O'Casey's words, 'became the Year One in Irish history and Irish life'. That is so, but the first five years must be some of the worst suffered by any people trying to gain their independence, and having gained it to restore order and good government.

Home Rule was gradually pushed out of the picture as Sinn Féin, with de Valera as President, gained more and more M.P.s through by-elections, yet refused to take their seats at Westminster. By the time the war ended, there were more than 100,000 Sinn Féiners in clubs, and the rule of law and order started to break down as Sinn Féin terrorists started to commit atrocities as bad as any which have followed. At the general election in December 1918 Sinn Féin was triumphant and then formed an Assembly of delegates, Dáil Éireann, which declared itself the national government of Saorstát Éireann (the Irish Free State).

Lloyd George then proposed an Amending Act to the Home Rule Act, by which the Six Counties in the north with Protestant majorities should be self-governing, with a Parliament at Stormont. Although it may have pleased Carson, Partition, when it became fact in 1920, did not satisfy Sinn Féin, nor does it seem to have been a satisfactory solution after fifty years. In southern Ireland, Lloyd George endeavoured to bolster up the Royal Irish Constabulary by recruiting a force of ex-soldiers, who came to be known as Black and Tans (on account of the dark green in their uniforms appearing to be black). Their atrocities in answer to those of the I.R.A. make appalling reading, even to a generation which is seeing such things happen again. In the Gort district alone, Lady Gregory reports the Tans dragging young men behind lorries until their bodies were torn to pieces, and the shooting of an innocent widow on a bridge as she sat there. Details of some of these incidents were related by Yeats in his speech in the Oxford Union (see below p.186). In May 1921 the I.R.A. ambushed and killed four friends, who were with the widow of

Major Robert Gregory, as they left a tennis party at Ballinamantane
House on the Coole estate, where the Yeatses had lived in 1918 when
Thoor Ballylee was being repaired.

> Now days are dragon-ridden, the nightmare
> Rides upon sleep; a drunken soldiery
> Can leave the mother, murdered at her door,
> To crawl in her own blood, and go scot-free;
> The night can sweat with terror as before
> We pieced our thoughts into philosophy,
> And planned to bring the world under a rule,
> We are but weasels fighting in a hole.

(CP, p.233)

In June of the same year, a truce was declared when the British
Government decided to negotiate with Sinn Féin, and after a
conference in London a Treaty was signed by which the Irish Free
State was recognized as a Dominion in the Commonwealth. When
Dáil Éireann met in Dublin, it ratified the Treaty, despite opposition
from de Valera, who resigned rather than accept anything but
complete independence from the Crown. Griffith became President
of the Executive Council, a post similar to prime minister. de Valera
and his followers then formed the Republican Party in opposition to
the government and were supported by the I.R.A., who became
known when in uniform as Irregulars. Gradually the situation drifted
into civil war as ambushes, murders and reprisals followed one
another with sickening regularity.

> An affable Irregular,
> A heavily-built Falstaffian man,
> Comes cracking jokes of civil war
> As though to die by gunshot were
> The finest play under the sun.

Then Yeats calls on the honey-bees, those Platonic symbols of wisdom, patience and virtue, to build in the 'empty house of the stare'.
In addition, sectarian hatred flared up in the Six Counties, and murders of Catholics by Protestants and vice versa became everyday
examples of hatred. The material destruction was immense: twenty-
three out of twenty-eight great houses in County Clare alone were
burnt, and the Four Courts, which the Irregulars occupied, was
bombarded. Wantonly, as they left the building, the Irregulars
exploded a land mine which destroyed the Public Records Office
with all the historical records of Ireland for centuries. Amidst this
fighting, the Free State Cabinet, including Kevin O'Higgins (see
below, pp.141–2), continued the government of the country and in
December 1922 the Dáil passed the Free State Constitution Bill,
including the Oath of Allegiance to the Crown. Northern Ireland

exercised her right to contract out. Gradually the Irregulars were captured and their supply of arms ran short, so that eventually on 23 May 1923 de Valera ordered them to cease fire. The drama which had opened with Pearse and Connolly in the Post Office had ended.

The last years, 1923–39

The Constitution of the first Irish Free State Parliament created two Houses: the Lower House of democratically elected members, and the Upper House or Seanad (Senate) of sixty members, half of whom were elected by the Dáil, and half appointed by the President of the Executive Council. Like the House of Lords, it could initiate legislation, except concerning finance, but could not reject legislation already passed by the Lower House. To qualify as a Senator, one had to have 'done honour to the nation by useful public service', or have special qualifications or attainments representing 'important aspects of the nation's life'. As the most distinguished Irish writer, especially with regard to the Irish Literary Renaissance and his passionate support of Irish nationalism in his plays and verse, Yeats certainly qualified, and for six years he served as a Senator. He is chiefly remembered for his work as Chairman of the Committee which dealt with the design of the new coinage, which was outstandingly beautiful, and for his speeches on censorship and divorce, in both of which he expressed liberal views which were years ahead of the times in Ireland. In this public role he revealed an eloquence as a speaker which is reflected in the more oratorical structure and syntax of his later verse. His constant problem was how best to unite the best of what Anglo-Irish Protestant Ireland had stood for with the resurgence of Gaelic Ireland and its deep-rooted culture.

Though the Civil War was over, political assassinations did not cease, the most shocking being the murder of Kevin O'Higgins (see below, p.141) to which 'Blood and the Moon' (*CP*, p.267) and 'Death' (*CP*, p.264), refer. (Even O'Higgins's father, a goodnatured country doctor, was murdered at his door by Republicans.) During the 1930s, Yeats kept clear of politics except for his brief flirtation with Eoin O'Duffy and his Blueshirt fascists (see below, pp.139–40). Basically Yeats hoped for a political system which would produce leaders who were honest, courageous, farsighted and statesmanlike, and he found it hard to find these in the Ireland of his later years. He sums up what he wanted in *On the Boiler* (p.13):

> I was six years in the Irish Senate; I am not ignorant of politics elsewhere, and on other grounds I have some right to speak. I say to those that shall rule here: If ever Ireland again seems molten wax, reverse the process of revolution. Do not try to pour Ireland into any political system. Think first how many able men with

41

public minds the country has, how many it can hope to have in the near future, and mould your system upon those men. It does not matter how you get them, but get them. Republics, Kingdoms, Soviets, Corporate States, Parliaments, are trash, as Hugo said of something else 'not worth one blade of grass that God gives for the nest of the linnet'. These men, whether six or six thousand, are the core of Ireland, are Ireland itself.

Not until 1948, the year that Yeats's body was brought back to Ireland, did the 'Twenty-six Counties' secede from the British Commonwealth and become the sovereign republic of Ireland (Eíre). But the end of partition still remains a dream. Yeats's ghost may well say;

> One man, one man alone
> In that outlandish gear,
> One solitary man
> Of all that rambled there
> Had turned his stately head.
> 'That is a long way off,
> And time runs on', he said,
> 'And the night grows rough.'

3 The Poet's Reading

It is increasingly the habit of modern Yeatsian scholars to deduce, from an investigation of Yeats's reading, the source of his imagery. Thus many of his greatest poems become like a secret code which when cracked has a way of breaking open the poems into fragments also. Yeats makes it clear that *A Vision*, which is based on much of his philosophical reading, is not written to enable the ordinary reader to 'understand' his poetry better, but was 'intended . . . for my school-mates only'. He writes elsewhere

> I have always come to this certainty: what moves natural men in the arts is what moves them in life, and that is, intensity of personal life, intonations that show them, in a book or a play, the strength, the essential moment of a man who would be exciting in the market or at the dispensary door.

Although he may have found much in the philosophy of Vico, Berkeley or Nietzsche which became the source of the main stream of his ideas, it is the emotional effect of the poem on his readers which matters. His many philosophical readings, from which he takes these ideas with which he feels in sympathy, lead to the ultimate truth of the poem. This is admirably summed up by Professor Stock, in *W. B. Yeats: His Poetry and Thought*:

> A poem is not great because of the beliefs it expounds, but when it convinces us of its greatness we know it cannot have been made from false or trivial thoughts. The images in his poems had to impress by their poetic rightness. What they symbolised was of no importance to the reader till their own power carried it home to him.

This chapter skims the surface of his literary and philosophic studies, which were extensive: Theosophy and occult works; Plato and the Neoplatonists; St Thomas Aquinas; the Hindu *Upanishads*; the *Kabbalah*; Irish myth and legend; Dante, Shakespeare, Ben Jonson, Donne, Castiglione, Vico, Swift, Berkeley, Burke, Blake, Shelley, Kant and Neitzsche are but some of the fields in which he read widely. Yet I should emphasize that his poetry is illuminated by nothing so much as a reading, in conjunction with his life story, of his critical prose, autobiographical works and senate speeches.

Occult and magic

A Theosophical or Hermetic Society was founded in New York in

Altar symbol of post-lapsarian world from ritual of the Golden Dawn which Yeats entered in 1890. The woman clothed with the sun dominates the whole, while images of divine wrath attack Fallen Man.

1875, and ten years afterwards a London headquarters also was opened by the founder, a Russian lady, Helen Petrovna Blavatsky (1831–91). Theosophy (from *theos*: god, and *sophia*: wisdom), originated in India, and was the study of the divine essence by mystical revelations from Mahatmas in India and gurus in Tibet. Madame Blavatsky, on her worldwide travels, had attached herself to one such Master, learning some of the secret doctrines which she then wished to make available to mankind. The aims of her Society were, to found a universal brotherhood, irrespective of race, creed, colour, caste etc; to study comparative religion, philosophy and science from sacred books; and to investigate certain unexplained laws of nature (psychic phenomena) and latent powers in man, such as the spiritual body taking control of the physical body, which she had witnessed in India. The goal was Nirvana, in which the Lower Self is dead. These ideas are set out in her book *Isis Unveiled* (1877), which Yeats read. In acknowledging Man as a spiritual being, theosophy had much in common with the 'middle way' of Buddhism, and the Kabbalah, and with the mystic tradition of the Upanishads and Yoga systems of Hindu religion.

In 1885 Yeats helped to found a Dublin Hermetic Society to study oriental religions and theosophy, and he read books by A. P. Sinnett, a fellow-Irishman, entitled *The Occult World* and *Esoteric Buddhism*, as well as meeting Mohini Chatterjee, a Brahmin, to whom he was much attracted. Nearly forty years later, in 'Mohini Chatterjee' (*CP*, p.279), he remembers meeting this Master and repeats the declaration of faith he then heard:

> I have been a king,
> I have been a slave,
> Nor is there anything,
> Fool, rascal, knave,
> That I have not been,

thus establishing his belief in reincarnation, which he was later to find in the Neoplatonists and never to abandon. In the splendid second verse of the poem, he expresses his own belief, not found in either oriental philosophy or Neoplatonism, that God had contrived reincarnation so that all unsatisfied ones may live happily in another life. (F. A. C. Wilson deals with this poem in *Yeats's Iconography*, pp.283–90.) Yeats joined the Blavatsky Lodge of the Theosophical Society in 1887, and arising from contact with this group was his initiation into another Rosicrucian occult society, the Hermetic Order of the Golden Dawn, with its leader, MacGregor Mathers (see below, pp. 137–8) who controlled the London temple. (Rosicrucian societies had been founded in Germany by a certain Father Christian Rosenkreutz.) There were ten initiation rites centred on the Sephirotic Tree of Life which one climbed by means of a series of spiritual deaths and rebirths, to reach, ultimately, union with God.

Mathers's interests were twofold: in the practice of attaining psychic phenomena or visions as a result of meditation on certain chosen symbols, and, secondly, in the following out of ancient magical rituals which he had discovered. Yeats discusses this:

> I am confident from internal evidence that the rituals, as I knew them, were in substance ancient though never so in language unless some ancient text was incorporated. There was little that I thought obvious or melodramatic, and it was precisely in this little, I am told, that they resembled Masonic rituals, but much that I thought beautiful and profound. I do not know what I would think if I were to hear them now for the first time, for I cannot judge what moved me in my youth. (AU, p.576).

Maud Gonne, who was also a member briefly, thought the ceremonies definitely smacked of Free Masonry, and as she regarded this as a product of the hated British Empire, she resigned.

Of equal interest to Yeats were the visions of trancelike states which arose from the examination of symbols, and which so stimulated his imagination. In 'Ideas of Good and Evil. Magic' (E & I, p.50) he explains this: 'The symbols are of all kinds, for everything in heaven or earth has its associations, momentous or trivial, in the Great Memory.' Here we have Yeats mentioning his belief in *Anima Mundi* (see below, pp. 49–50). On other occasions when in a group, the visions which sometimes appeared might have been telepathically transmitted by the strongest member of the group. In his experiments at Sligo with George Pollexfen, he had remarkable results.

Mathers's methods are described in *The Trembling of the Veil, Four Years, 1887–91 (AU)*:

> He gave me a cardboard symbol and I closed my eyes. Sight came slowly, there was not that sudden miracle as if darkness had been cut with a knife, for that miracle is mostly a woman's privilege, but there rose before me mental images that I could not control: a desert and a black Titan raising himself up by his two hands from the middle of a heap of ancient ruins. Mathers explained that I had seen a being of the order of Salamanders because he had shown me their symbol, but it was not necessary even to show the symbol, it would have been sufficient that he imagined it.

The occult symbols would have included the Rose, the Cross, the Sun, the Moon, the Tree, the Water and the Bird. Poems in which these symbols and others occur are 'The Two Trees' (CP, p.54) where one finds the Kabbalistic Tree of Life and the Tree of Knowledge; 'To Some I have Talked with by the Fire' (CP, p.56) with its reference to the Ineffable Name of Jehovah, which in the four Hebrew letters can be anagrammatized countless times; and 'The Poet pleads with the Elemental Powers' (*CP*, p.80) where the Seven Lights are the seven planets.

Although Yeats was admitted to the inner conclave, the Esoteric section of the Theosophical Society, his sense of fun did not desert him: 'A sad accident happened yesterday at Madame Blavatsky's lately. A big materialist sat on the astral double of a poor young Indian. It was sitting on the sofa and he was too material to be able to see it. Certainly a sad accident.' Soon, however, the internal quarrels of the Society were too much for him: 'The Society is like "the happy family" that used to be exhibited round Charing Cross Station—a cat in a cage full of canaries.' Even after he had shaved off his beard (a modest one), and Madame Blavatsky had predicted a severe illness through loss of mesmeric force which collects in a beard, he still continued to attend meetings for a few months. But an article in *The Weekly Review* brought matters to a head: he had criticized the Society and he refused to promise never to criticize it again. He was a member of the Blavatsky Lodge for only three years, but he progressed from the lowest to the highest grade of the Order of the Golden Dawn, becoming Adeptus Exemptus in 1916 after twenty-five years of involvement.

It is easy to laugh at or be shocked by Yeats's membership of these societies, as were his friends John O'Leary and George Russell, who thought he was wasting his time when he should have been writing. Yet one can now see how vital to Yeats was this searching for a non-materialist world, and the imagery, even though artificially inspired by conscious pictorial symbols, which was fuel to his poetic imagination. It is the start of Yeats's lifelong search for symbols and thought forms, after having been brought up by an agnostic father in a world whose poverty of spiritual symbols derived from its sacrifice of the spirit before the claims of the intellect. Yeats feared this separation of spirit and matter in the modern world, and used the Rose as a symbol of harmony which he came to call a 'unity of being', though this was not its only symbolism. His gratitude to these early theosophists and clairvoyants is shown in his subsequent dedication of *A Vision* in its first private edition (1925), to Mrs MacGregor Mathers herself, one of the few survivors from these times.

Plato and Neoplatonists

Lionel Johnson (see below, pp.130–2) thought Yeats an 'unlettered lad' and told him he should read Plato; in the same way, Madame Blavatsky had recommended the Neoplatonist philosophers to him. The poet followed this advice, and by selective reading he gradually built up his own philosophic beliefs. Central to these was Plato's principle (from the *Meno* and the *Phaedo*) of the immortality of the soul, which confirmed what Yeats already thought concerning a personal immortality. Put shortly, Plato thought the soul had many lives; when born into this world it had returned from another to inhabit the body as a pilot does a boat. Or, to choose another image from Plato: 'the body is a garment with which the soul is invested'. But it is not always happy in its relationship with the body, which is at the lowest end of the scale. 'Supernatural Songs' v (*CP*, p.330), reflects this:

> Thought is a garment and the soul's a bride
> That cannot in that trash and tinsel hide:

Death is but a separation of the soul from the body. In these other regions through which the soul has been passing it 'recollects' knowledge which, so to speak, is stored there. In the *Meno*, Plato writes: 'Since the soul is immortal and has been born many times and has seen the things of this world and of Hades and all things, there is nothing which she has not learned. So that it is no wonder that she should be able to recollect virtue and all other things, seeing that she has learned them previously.' This Anamnesis (Recollection) is therefore a calling to mind by the soul of its previous state (this is discussed in the opening of the *Phaedrus*) and shows the basis for a belief in incarnation which Yeats had also found in his oriental occult studies. If knowledge is a recollection, the soul before our birth must have been acquainted with it in that state or region where it beheld 'ideas' or 'forms' as Plato calls them, or as we should now say, the archetypes of *Anima Mundi*, the great storehouse of Knowledge.

The Greek Neoplatonist philosophers Plotinus (*c.*200–270) and Porphyry (*c.*223–304) combine much from Platonic philosophy with the mysticism of the East and even some of the beliefs of Judaism: a heady brew, examined by Berkeley in his discourse in *Siris* on 'The Aether or pure invisible Fire', and imbibed by such English poets as Milton, Blake, Coleridge, Shelley and Yeats, for whom a transition from philosophy to mysticism was not difficult. F. A. C. Wilson, in *W. B. Yeats and Tradition* (p.199) makes this very clear:

> The symbolic system of Neoplatonism was fixed and one might even say rigid: the sea, for example, symbolised always 'the waters of emotion and passion', or more simply life; man was consistently thought of as the beggar, dressed in the rags of mortality; the tomb, the forest and the cave were all symbols of the material world; after death, the soul, often accompanied by a mystic escort of dolphins, crossed the sea to heaven, the Isles of the Blessed. Yeats knew this system of symbolism from several sources: from Madame Blavatsky, in his formative years; then from Taylor's translation of the commentators on Plato, and especially from Porphyry's essay on 'The Cave of the Nymphs'; also from Plato himself, Plotinus . . . and the other Platonic philosophers he had read. He took it over

into his verse in the confidence that it would prevent his own symbolism from being arbitrary or unintelligible; it was traditional, for it had persisted throughout the middle ages, where it influenced among others, Dante, and, later, Spenser; and, as the symbolism of a religious system which he himself was largely able to accept, it is clear that he thought of it as profound. In using it, again, he had precedent in the work of two English poets he particularly admired: Blake . . . and . . . Shelley.

The history of myth shows certain recurrent symbols, deep in human psychology and religion, which become a reservoir of thought, fed by *Anima Mundi*, the Great Memory, yet another name for the collective unconscious of Jung. In this region all mythologies are one, expressed through symbols which speak to the unconscious and on which we can all draw. For a poet such as Yeats the Great Memory was reality; not the reality of science or materialistic philosophy which dominates the arts in our own age, but the reality which through myth restores the fullness of imaginative life and gives to poetry an absolute truth. This may be modified by individual genius, but it is never abandoned. Milton is expressing this view of tradition when he writes in 'Il Penseroso':

> Or let my Lamp at midnight hour,
> Be seen in som high lonely Towr,
> Where I may oft out-watch the *Bear*,
> With thrice great *Hermes*, or unsphear
> The spirit of *Plato* to unfold
> What Worlds, or what vast Regions hold
> The immortal mind that hath forsook
> Her mansion in this fleshly nook:

It is important therefore to know the traditional language of symbols used by Plato and by later Neoplatonists, for these symbols are, as Jung says in *Psychology and Alchemy*, 'all variants of certain central types and these occur universally. They are the primordial images from which the religions each draw their universal truth.'

In Plato and the Neoplatonists, soul is reality and form; body is a cloudy vapour with no entity or form. 'What's water but the generated soul?' The soul descends into the body because of some imperfection, and thereby loses its purity through contact with the body or external matter, which is evil. Therefore the soul's descent is a death, so from Heraclitus, B.C. 513, we have: 'We live their [the souls'] death, and we die their life', the body being the sepulchre of the soul.

'The Delphic Oracle upon Plotinus' (*CP*, p.306) is a paraphrase of a passage from Plotinus which Yeats read in the translation of Thomas Taylor, the friend of Blake:

Where streams ambrosial in immortal course
Irriguous flow, from Deity their source.
No dark'ning clouds those happy skies assail,
And the calm aether knows no stormy gale.
Supremely blest thy lofty soul abides
Where Minos and his brother judge presides;
Just Aeacus, and Plato the divine,
And fair Pythag'ras there exalted shone
With other souls who form the general choir,
Of love immortal, and of pure desire.

How much better is Yeats's short, witty, yet serious poem! The
Oracle, 'the last great oracle of Delphi', speaks, showing us Plotinus
struggling to swim in the sea of life, having discarded his mortal rags.
But as he has lived as a saint, and on more than one occasion has
attained to a mystical state of ecstasy by the elevation of his soul to
God, he needs no expiation as impure souls do on arrival at the Isles
of the Blessed. 'Bland Rhadamanthus' (a typical sonority of Yeats),
the son of Zeus and Europa, and, as one of the judges of immortal
souls, the prototype of wisdom and virtue, beckons him, so all is well.

According to Plotinus, the three types of men who have visionary
experience and who provide the welcome on landing at the Isles of the
Blessed, are philosophers, lovers and musicians. Plato is here the
philosopher, and Pythagoras the conductor of the heavenly choir of
love. He had been in life the perfector of the Doric scale and thereby
the establishment of certain musical intervals according to the number
of their vibrations, scientifically worked out. But, more important,
'number' and 'measure' had for him an ideal significance in which the
laws of harmony were the laws of nature, the seven notes of the scale
being related to the seven planets in the music of the spheres.

'News for the Delphic Oracle' (CP, p.378) is admirably dealt with
by F. A. C. Wilson, W. B. Yeats and Tradition, pp.216–23, and this
should be read in conjunction with Kathleen Raine, Blake and Tradition, vol. I, part II.3. 'The Sea of Time and Space' in which she discusses Blake's drawing illustrating the theme of Porphyry's essay,
'The Cave of the Nymphs', which was well known to Yeats. Some
critics would have us believe that these poems of Yeats are frivolous,
but Dr Wilson rightly asserts that although there is levity in 'News
for the Delphic Oracle', it is fundamentally a poem showing belief in
the whole Platonic heaven. The choir of love and Pythagoras appear
in both poems, but in the second the mythology is a mixture of
Ancient Greek and Celtic—the Isles of the Blessed and Tir-na-n'Og.
This mixture is equally evident in 'The Statues' (CP, p.375), in which
Pythagoras and Cuchulain 'stalk' through Athens and Dublin
respectively.

Plotinus's six 'Enneads', as translated by Porphyry, revealed Man as an imaginative and remembering soul, in touch with Anima Mundi and with the Divine Mind; not through discursive, logical reasoning but through intuitive thought. The approach of these Neoplatonists is therefore more mystical than that of Plato himself, rating as they do, matter at the lowest level, and spirit (*nous*) as the divine and highest. This is where Yeats found common ground with the religions of the East.

A knowledge of Platonic symbols such as the spindle or the honey bees, as well as such a story as that of the Cave in the Myth of Er, helps to elucidate such passages as the 'honey of generation' in verse five of 'Among School Children' (*CP*, p.244), and the honey bees of 'The Stare's Nest by my Window' (*CP*, p.230). But it should also be noted how many times Yeats declares his ultimate faith in man himself. See 'The Tower'. III CP, p.222.

Giambattista Vico, 1668–1744

Before 1924 Yeats had read little philosophy, but in that year he attended lectures in London on Benedetto Croce's *Aesthetic*, also reading and annotating Croce's *The Philosophy of Giambattista Vico*, translated by R. G. Collingwood. When Yeats was in Italy the next year, Mrs Yeats summarized some of the passages from other Italian philosophers, as he could not read Italian. One of his discoveries, as a result of the London lectures, was Vico, a Neapolitan jurist and philosopher-cum-historiographer (one who deals with the ways of writing history through the ages). Until the age of forty, Vico had had a contempt for history, having been under the influence of Descartes (1596–1650) who was famous for his mathematically inclined deductions, and in particular for his central statement, the only proposition in which he thought the truth could not be doubted, and therefore that he existed: *Cogito, ergo sum*. But gradually Vico found much of Descartes's thinking to be alien, in particular that the body was a machine united to the soul; and that mind or spirit is pure consciousness and matter its extension. Vico thus freed himself from the shackles of Descartes's intellectualism and mathematical thinking, by starting to work out from a study of the classical writers his philosophy of history, which culminated in his *Scienza Nuova* (New Science), 1725. Of particular interest to Yeats was Vico's premise, a revolutionary one at the time, that myths and traditions are historical, even though they need not refer to real men; that they are a form of Truth for primitive men, from whom, after the senses and feelings comes that primary working of the mind, the imagination, which, allied to Art, he calls poetry. It is easy to understand how Yeats would have joined this to William Blake's belief in the imagination being born of the passions and being the language of the spiritual kingdom, to which primitive men and children both belong. Previous philosophers had considered the primitive state of nature as savage and brutal, so Vico strikes out a new route with regard to primitive man which Rousseau was to follow later, though he did not go as far as Vico in thinking primitive man was 'a poet speaking in poetic characters'. William Blake certainly saw children in these terms.

However, more emphasis seems to be laid by writers about Yeats on Vico's cyclical view of movements in both religious and political history. Religions, thought Vico, begin with unity, go on to heresy, then die with atheism before the cycle recurs (he was always a Catholic). States begin with monarchy, go on to enfeebled monarchy or democracy, then after chaos, return to monarchy; the cycle being interdependent and concentric with the religious cycle. Civilizations start with Gods, go on to Heroes, poetic creatures, during which state there is aristocratic government, then descend to men, during which time religion becomes mere morality, and politics undesirable equality which he calls the 'alphabetical age'. After which barbarism, then a return to unified monarchy. Above all, it is Man who fashions his own destiny, or makes his history in these cycles.

> Whatever flames upon the night,
> Man's own resinous heart has fed.

This removes from Vico's cyclical theory the depressing determinist philosophy from which Yeats was always trying to escape.

In Vico he found a number of important views which he already held or had partly thought out, as well as a statement of a cyclical view of history, to be used later by historians contemporary with Yeats such as Toynbee and Spengler. In the opposition of the imagination, the 'first emanation of divinity' to the intellect, Yeats of course sided with William Blake in his belief in the former. In the importance of Myth and tradition, Yeats not only found echoes of *Anima Mundi* of Plato, but also in the work of the translators from the Gaelic which provides the heart of so much of his own work. In the virtues of a benevolent aristocracy as opposed to the chaos of democracy, which he had suffered in the Civil War in Ireland, he felt sympathetic. 'The Seven Sages' (*CP*, p.271) shows Whiggery in Yeats's sense, to mean liberal, intellectual and possibly scientific thinking, and from which, in somewhat flat verse, he absolves his beloved eighteenth-century figures from holding. Elsewhere he compares certain works of Swift's with Vico's thought (*Wheels and Butterflies*, *EX*, pp.353-4).

> Whether they knew it or not,
> Goldsmith and Burke, Swift and the Bishop of Cloyne
> All hated Whiggery; but what is Whiggery?
> A levelling, rancorous, rational sort of mind
> That never looked out of the eye of a saint
> Or out of drunkard's eye.

Above all, Vico's influence shows in the cyclical view of history as worked out in *A Vision*, with particular reference to certain human types, and which covers all life:

> The Primum Mobile that fashioned us
> Has made the very owls in circles move.
>
> *CP*, p.229.

In *On the Boiler* (1938) Yeats sums up what Vico meant to him by placing him as 'the first modern philosopher to discover in his own mind, and in the European past, all human destiny'. Vico's views which are briefly summarized above, constantly recur in Yeats's late verse, and are an integral part of a consistent pattern in the poet's thought with relation to Man and Eternity.

George Berkeley, 1685–1753

> I declare this tower is my symbol; I declare
> This winding, gyring, spiring treadmill of a stair is my
> ancestral stair;
> That Goldsmith and the Dean, Berkeley and Burke have
> travelled there.
>
> . . .
>
> And God-appointed Berkeley that proved all things a dream,
> That this pragmatical, preposterous pig of a world, its
> farrow that so solid seem,
> Must vanish on the instant if the mind but change its theme;
>
> 'Blood and the Moon', *CP*, p.268.

Thus does Yeats place Berkeley on his 'ancestral stair' with Goldsmith, Swift and Burke. The second of the two stanzas above refers to the basic theme of Berkeley's philosophy as Yeats saw it—that spirit or mind is the sole reality of physical things: in Berkeley's words *esse est percipi*, the existence of objects consists in their being perceived in the mind. This was in direct opposition to the utilitarian philosophy of Locke, who thought there was 'nothing in mind that has not come from sense'. Berkeley therefore considered himself an 'immaterialist' in his denying that 'matter' and the external reality of space existed.

His philosophy appealed to Yeats on many grounds. He was born and educated in Ireland, and Yeats noticed in his *Commonplace Book* the words with reference to a refutation of Locke's philosophy which

Rembrandt van Rijn, A Philosopher in Meditation *(1633), showing the traditional, 'winding, gyring, spiring treadmill of a stair.'*

55

reflected the English philosophical thought of the time. 'We Irishmen think otherwise', namely not in abstractions. In Berkeley's *A Theory of Vision* (1733), he states there is an 'omnipresent eternal mind, which knows and comprehends all things', and which communicates in mental perceptions to human minds. Nothing therefore exists outside the mind of God. This may be thought to be a difficult philosophical hurdle for Yeats to surmount, yet he leapt over it happily, by saying, in his essay on Berkeley in *E & I*, that this was 'Not the God of Protestant theology, but a God that leaves room for human pride'. Yet could Yeats really agree with Berkeley's bringing in God to help when all else in the worldly system had failed? Did he not believe that man fashioned his own destiny in so far as the gyres would let him? Fundamentally, Yeats connects Berkeley with the Neoplatonists in their view of reality, and describes, in the same essay, Berkeley's *Three Dialogues between Hylas and Philonous in opposition to Sceptics and Atheists* (1713) as 'the only philosophical arguments since Plotinus that are works of art, being so well-bred, so sensible'.

Whether it was Berkeley the 'fierce young man' or as 'the good bishop' of Cloyne, his prose has a tightness and lucidity, avoiding abstractions in the best eighteenth-century manner. Berkeley himself, whether as organizer of a plan for a college in Bermuda, or as Bishop of Cloyne, had a versatility in the Renaissance tradition of *uomo universale* (universal man) writing on such diverse subjects as Irish social evils (*The Querist*), and mathematics, and the American Indian cure by tarwater, and what would now be called the Psychology of Vision. Yeats responded to this Protestant graduate of Trinity College in his opposition to the physical science of Locke and Descartes who 'took away the world (dreams) and gave us excrement instead'.

The *Irish Times* of 18 February 1933 reports Yeats as saying in a lecture to the Royal Dublin Society: 'Ireland has produced three world figures . . . George Berkeley, a philosopher—according to Bergson, the creator of modern philosophy . . . Jonathan Swift, the first great modern mind to deny the value of life . . . Edmund Burke, who rolled back the anarchy of the French Revolution, and perhaps saved Europe.'

Edmund Burke, 1729–97

Among his eighteenth-century literary and philosophic ancestors Yeats placed Burke. As we have said (see above, pp.30–1), Burke's mother and his Irish friends were Catholics, and it is very probable that the reason for his father turning Protestant was to enable him to take his law exams, which he was not able to do as a Catholic. His family were certainly not descended from English settlers, but from an older stock of 'native' Irish, therefore Yeats was mistaken in thinking of him as like Swift, Berkeley or Goldsmith—in the Protestant Anglo-Irish tradition.

His influence on Yeats comes late, 'The Tower' III (1927), 'Blood and the Moon' II (1928), and 'The Seven Sages' (1932) being the only references to him by name. Basically Yeats sympathized with Burke's view that man's political duties result from tradition and inheritance rather than from rational thought, and particularly not from abstract thought concerned with liberty. 'The only liberty I mean is connected with order', he wrote in *An Appeal from the New Whigs to the Old Whigs* (1791), a book, so Mrs Yeats told Professor Torchiana (see his *W. B. Yeats and Georgian Ireland*, p.196) which might be called Yeats's political bible. 'Men come (as young people) into a community with the social state of the parents, endowed with all the benefits, loaded with all the duties of their situation. . . . Our country is not a thing of mere physical locality. It consists in great measure, in the ancient order into which we are born . . .'

Burke opposed the French Jacobin revolutionaries' ideals and practices as they destroyed the social order he valued so highly; and he even thought they should be counteracted by war if necessary, (see his *Reflections on the Revolution in France*, 1790). This idea is mirrored in much of Yeats's thought in *Last Poems*, filled as it is with admiration for fighting and violence. Having suffered the turmoil of Ireland in the 1920s Yeats longed for politicians of the statesmanlike calibre of Kevin O'Higgins (see below, p.141), but instead he saw lesser men, with qualities similar to those Burke attributes to Pitt's ministry, which tried to negotiate with the Jacobins (*Letters on the Proposals for Peace with the Regicide Directory of France* (1796): 'In truth, the tribe of vulgar politicians are the lowest of our species. There is no trade so vile and mechanical as government in their hands. Virtue is not their habit.' Moreover, Burke wrote elsewhere, men of wisdom were needed (as Yeats constantly stressed when a Senator):

> None, except those who are profoundly studied can comprehend an elaborate contrivance of a fabric fitted to unite private and public liberty, with public force, with order, with peace, with justice, and, above all, with the institutions formed for bestowing permanence and stability, through ages, upon the invaluable whole.

Burke's rhetoric, much like Grattan's, was regarded by Yeats as having Irish rather than English qualities—eloquent, passionate yet noble. His speeches on the question of the American colonies, published in 1769 and 1770, and the speech which opened the trial at the impeachment of Warren Hastings, are classics of English oratory, having a perfect fusion of feeling and thought into a poetic whole on which they may be judged as literature.

'And haughtier-headed Burke that proved the State a tree' (*CP*, p.268) refers to Burke's often repeated statement that the state was an oak tree, which, as Yeats said to the Irish Literary Society in November 1925, was 'no mechanism to be pulled in pieces and put up again, but an oak tree that had grown through centuries'. The adjective 'haughtier-headed' is used by Yeats as he remembers the set of Burke's head in his statue outside Trinity College, where he stands, hand on hip, looking boldly forward, very different in stance to the adjacent statue of Goldsmith, which portrays him 'sipping' a book, head bowed.

As in his reading of Nietzsche, Yeats picked from Burke the philosophic ideas with which he found himself in sympathy, and it is easy to understand Burke's appeal for the poet when he discusses his union of discipline and self-assertion, which might well be Yeats's unity of being. Also, Burke's acute awareness of man's intuitions, added to his allowing human nature a right to irrationality and complexity, the very opposite of a Lockeian rationality, enables Yeats to base many of his aspirations and political ideas on his beloved Burke's 'great melody'.

William Blake, 1757–1827

> Grant me an old men's frenzy,
> Myself must I remake
> Till I am Timon or Lear
> Or that William Blake
> Who beat upon the wall
> Till Truth obeyed his call;
>
> A mind the Michael Angelo knew
> That can pierce the clouds
> Or inspired by frenzy
> Shake the dead in their shrouds;
> Forgotten else by mankind,
> An old man's eagle mind.

Thus, in these last two stanzas of 'An Acre of Grass' (*CP*, p.346) does Yeats as an old man return to William Blake. When he was sixteen years old, his father lent him a copy of Blake, then he had edited his works with Edwin Ellis (see below, p.115) and now, forty years on, Blake's influence is still pre-eminent. The operative word in the stanzas above is 'frenzy', that passion which is stronger than reason, that can 'pierce the clouds' and was supremely possessed by King Lear, Timon of Athens and William Blake in their old age. Professor Torchiana, *W. B. Yeats and Georgian Ireland*, p.244, points out an explicatory prose passage from a talk given by Yeats on the BBC, 11 October 1936, referring to the growth of naturalism or realism in literature since the seventeenth century, and how we have been overwhelmed by a mechanistic philosophy (Locke and Newton), as well as by an art which merely mirrors nature rather than transforms man's aspirations. This state of affairs, said Yeats, 'lasted to our own day with the exception of a brief period between Smart's *Song of David* (1763) and the death of Byron (1824), wherein imprisoned man beat upon the door'. In that period Blake had lived, seeing human nature as discovering itself in art and being transformed by it—a very different view from his eighteenth century contemporaries. For Blake, poetry and the other arts were not just a mirror to life, but the chief lens of spiritual consciousness.

In believing that the imagination was the 'first emanation of divinity', and that the arts which were the language of imaginative knowledge, were the greatest of divine revelations, Blake showed the traditional nature of his spiritual knowledge, tradition being by that 'golden chain' with the past by which imaginative experience was handed down in the language of myth and symbol. With amazing eclecticism he was able to include in his idea Neoplatonists, alchemists and Christian philosophers. In 'All Religions are One' he writes:

> Principle 5th. The Religions of all Nations are derived from each Nation's different reception of the Poetic Genius, which is every where call'd the Spirit of Prophecy.
>
> Principle 7th. As all men are alike (tho' infinitely various), So all Religions and, as all similars, have one source.

The true Man is the source, he being the Poetic Genius. Yeats would have had no difficulty in believing this and in finding similarities between the philosophical ideas of Berkeley and Blake, for the basis of their worlds was the same, namely, we may doubt the reality of a material object, but we cannot doubt we hear, feel and see. Compare Blake in *A Vision of the Last Judgment* (1810): 'Mental Things are alone Real; what is call'd Corporeal, Nobody Knows of its Dwelling Place: it is in Fallacy, & its Existence an Imposture. Where is the Existence but of Mind or Thought?' with Berkeley in the *Principles of Human Knowledge* (1710) 'It is an opinion strangely prevailing amongst men, that houses, mountains, rivers, and in a word all sensible objects have an existence natural and real, distinct from their being perceived by the understanding.'

Accepting these views, Yeats found his sole reality in the imagination, which he discusses in 'William Blake and the Imagination' *E & I*, p.111: 'In his [Blake's] time educated people believed that they amused themselves with books of the imagination, but that they "made their souls" by listening to sermons and by doing or not doing certain things. . . . In our time we "make our souls" out of some one of the great poets of ancient times.' Thus for Blake and Yeats, 'the marriage of art with symbol' (referring to vision and not allegory) is first a revelation, and second an amusement.

59

William Blake, The Ancient of Days: *colour print. 1794.*

in his hand
He took the golden compasses, prepar'd
In God's Eternal store, to circumscribe
This Universe, and all created things:

Milton, Paradise Lost. *VII.224-7*

Yeats also found in Blake's writing his idea of paired opposites—soul, and self, body and soul, love and death, chance and choice, 'subjective' and 'objective', conflicting yet establishing a unity in a man's life and in history. A passage from 'The Marriage of Heaven and Hell' states: 'Without Contraries is no Progression. Attraction and Repulsion, Reason and Energy, Love and Hate, are necessary to Human existence' (*The Complete Writings of William Blake*, ed. Keynes, p.149).

Concerning such antinomies (as Kant calls them) Yeats writes epigrammatically in 'Those Images' (*CP*, p.367):

> Seek those images
> That constitute the wild,
> The lion and the virgin,
> The harlot and the child.

As T. R. Henn points out (*The Lonely Tower*, p.39) this is both Blakean in rhythm and influenced by an illustration in Blake's 'Marriage of Heaven and Hell'. Yeats knew all Blake's visionary drawings well, 'The Ancient of Days' hung in his rooms for many years, and he places him, before 'confusion fell upon our thought', with other visionary artists who were in touch with reality, Samuel Palmer and Edward Calvert being especially influenced when young by Blake:

> Calvert and Wilson, Blake and Claude
> Prepared a rest for the people of God.

In the period between writing 'Sailing to Byzantium' and 'Byzantium', Yeats was very ill, and after he recovered he turned again to Blake, quoting particularly a letter of Blake's written in the year of his death to his friend George Cumberland, junior: 'I have been very near the Gates of Death, & have returned very weak, & an Old Man feeble & tottering, but not in Spirit & Life, not in The Real Man The Imagination which Liveth for Ever. In that I am stronger & stronger as this Foolish Body decays.' Yeats was immensely moved by this letter, describing it as 'the most beautiful of all letters'. Obviously he found a physical parallel between his own life and Blake's, as also he had always found a likeness in Blake's thought. He saw him as the champion of the soul, fighting the mechanistic, abstract thought of Locke and Newton,

> Beating upon the wall
> Till Truth obeyed his call.

Friedrich Nietzsche, 1844–1900

In 1902 John Quinn (see below, p.150) lent Yeats a book of selections from the works of the German philosopher Nietzsche. After reading the book, Yeats wrote to his father of his admiration for

Nietzsche's philosophy, concerning which John B. Yeats, some years later, remarked with his customary great humanity: 'The sort of men whom Nietzsche's theory fits are only great men of a sort, a sort of Yahoo great men. The struggle is how to get rid of them, they belong to the clumsy and brutal side of things.' He could not have expressed himself in stronger terms, for the Yahoos of Gulliver's final voyage are the epitome of Swift's ultimate disgust with and contempt for humanity—physically repulsive, and 'the most unteachable of all Brutes'. Again, in 1909, Yeats's father, writing from New York, sums up the heart of the matter by saying that W. B.'s talent was benign' whereas Nietzsche's was 'malign'. He was right: Nietzsche had a violent 'objective' irreligious mind; Yeats was tolerant, 'subjective' and religious in the broadest sense.

What were the views which appealed to son but disgusted father? In *The Birth of Tragedy*, Nietzsche sees the essence of Greek art as not in calm, but in tension between Dionysiac forces of cruelty and frenzy, and the beauty, light and rational energy of Apollo. In this violent conflict we have the two movements of the soul, with its accompanying antinomies and paradoxes, so like much in Yeats's own thought. Nietzsche also admired Greek art for its aristocratic qualities, which stirred a sympathetic string in Yeats's philosophic instrument. Nietzsche's admiration for the Greeks was accompanied by a contempt for Christianity (although he respected Jesus Christ), for its weakness and gentleness, and he believed that its morals were fundamentally wrong. For example, loving one's neighbour was merely a Jewish trick to get the strong to submit to the weak. Christianity was born of weakness—'sided with all that is weak and base, with all failure'— therefore he saw it as the enemy of reason, honesty, sex, power, joy and freedom.

These qualities were to be developed by humanity whom Nietzsche called on, in *Thus Spake Zarathustra* (1883–5), to create *der Übermensch*, the Superman, full of daring, initiative, masterfulness, and freed from guilt, repression and introversion. This 'exuberant, vigorous and world-affirming man' was never far from Yeats, whose imagination repeatedly dwelt on Cuchulain. Fierce heroic action is thus glorified by 'that strong enchanter', as Yeats called Nietzsche, and he is put in *VIS* in Phase Twelve, the phase of the hero, where we see him in 'The Phases of the Moon' (*CP*, p.183), the only reference to him in Yeats's verse:

> Eleven pass, and then
> Athene takes Achilles by the hair,
> Hector is in the dust, Nietzsche is born,
> Because the hero's crescent is the twelfth.
> And yet, twice born, twice buried, grow he must,
> Before the full moon, helpless as a worm.

As we say (below, p.69) when discussing *VIS*, which really 'explains' this poem, in the twenty-eight types of human personality, phase one is infancy and phase fifteen maturity; likewise there are twenty-eight phases of the soul in incarnations, phase fifteen being the full moon of complete beauty, subjectivity at its height.

T. R. Henn (*The Lonely Tower*, p.179n) points out the repetition of the reference to Athene leading Achilles to heroic action, mentioned by Homer in the *Iliad*, which Yeats uses in words spoken by the Greek in *The Resurrection* (1931): 'When the goddess came to Achilles in the battle she did not interfere with his soul, she took him by his yellow hair.'

Thus does the Greek in this play exemplify the opposite of the 'self-surrender and self-abasement' of the followers of Dionysus, and then he goes on to enlarge on his theory: 'The man who lives heroically gives them (the gods) the only earthly body they covet. He, as it were, copies their gestures and their acts.' Here we have the deification of the Hero as if it were the very moment described by Vico, when Gods hand over to Heroes in the cycle of history. In fact, Nietzsche's ancestors were Empedocles and Heraclitus, with a view of history as an endless recurring flux, and an image of eternity as a circle. It is a depressing philosophy in its view of the world as ungoverned by a purpose, being but an eternal, senseless play, and we find ourselves in the orbit of Samuel Beckett, rather than of Yeats, who saw joy in man's will to perfect himself.

The horror with which J. B. Yeats reacted to Nietzsche's philosophic ideas—'aristocratic' illusions, sacerdotalism, and the ferocious absurdity of the Superman—has been carried on with renewed intensity since some of Nietzsche's doctrines were unscrupulously borrowed by Hitler to bolster the Nazi regime. Nevertheless, much of the revulsion today for Nietzsche stems from ignorance of his works (which in Yeats's time had not been translated into English), rather like the reaction of Renaissance Englishmen to Machiavelli's *Il Principe*. Hitler indeed glorified the superman, the 'blond German beast' ('yellow hair'?); but Nietzsche was not antisemitic, though he disliked Jewish interpretations of Christianity, nor did he think the Germans a superior race—far from it, for he wholly despised his contemporary fellow-countrymen, and their culture.

Yeats's father once told W. B. that he was a poet and not a philosopher, and here again he was right; yet one must not ignore the philosophic ideas which Yeats tried to make systematic and which are the scaffolding of his poems. He would pick from each philosopher what suited him, and sometimes he would find in such disparate writers as Burke and Nietzsche, a common idea: 'send war in our time' in certain circumstances would have been approved of by both. Over all, Yeats was consistent (as this chapter tries to show), but like Nietzsche he was maddeningly unsystematic in working it out, despite

63

the apparent categorization in *VIS*. Contradictions and paradoxes of a superficial nature did not worry either Yeats or Nietzsche, and sometimes it must be admitted, Yeats made deductions which really will not bear examination, such as when he wrote to Lady Gregory: 'Nietzsche completes Blake and has the same roots.' On no occasion does Nietzsche think of Christ as Blake does, and their attitudes to Him are basic to their philosophy. For further reading see Zwerdling, *Yeats and the Heroic Ideal* (1965) and Engelberg, *The Vast Design* (1964).

4 A Vision

A discussion of this work is an essential summary of Yeats's philosophic reading and thought; but the account given here is limited to some of those ideas expressed which elucidate his poetry, otherwise it would be considerably longer and more complicated. In his introduction to *The Resurrection* (Ex, p.392) Yeats wrote: 'For years I have been occupied with a certain myth that was itself a reply to a myth. I do not mean a fiction, but one of those statements our nature is compelled to make and employ as a truth though there cannot be sufficient evidence.' He refers in this passage to his work on *VIS*, published first in 1925, then in a new and revised version in 1929, after he had read many of the philosophic works already mentioned in chapter 3 above, then in a final version in 1937.

Mrs Yeats was a spiritualist medium and very soon after her marriage she started to communicate to her husband, in automatic writing, much of the matter and imagery which he used in the first version of *VIS*. In Yeats's statement quoted above, it is essential to note that it is as a myth that he wishes *VIS* to be considered; not as an historical fact, whether true or false, nor as a piece of metaphysics to be reasoned out; but as a document speaking the language of myth through imagery by which he gives us values true for himself. This was and is a stumbling block for many people in the understanding of the work. Much of the matter for *VIS* was initially provided by Mrs Yeats's trances, but later, as he worked out his System, he gained a store of mythological symbols on which he could draw from many traditional cultures: for example, swan, sword, spear, arrow, lion, serpent, eagle, apart from the whole mythical background of the work. These symbols are never extrinsic trimming for Yeats, but the inwrought core of his experience through his own imagination. It is through the spirals and cyclic patterns of history, in which he believed, that he is able to connect, for example, the burning of Troy for Helen with Deirdre, the burning of Emain and the death of Usna's children; or can identify the swan of Leda with the nine-and-fifty swans at Coole.

It seems strange, therefore, that *VIS* has been so much misunderstood. I. A. Richards, *Science and Poetry*, (1926) wrote:

Now, he [Yeats] turns to a world of symbolic phantasmagoria about which he is desperately uncertain. He is uncertain because he has adopted as a technique of inspiration, the use of trance, of dissociated phases of consciousness and the revelations given in those dissociated states are insufficiently connected with normal

*Mrs W. B. Yeats 1895–1968. 'Red-brown hair and a high colour which
she sets off by wearing dark green in her clothes and earrings'.
W. B. Y. to his father. 1917.*

experience . . . Mr Yeats takes certain feelings of conviction attached to certain visions as evidences for the thoughts which he supposes his visions to symbolise.

According to this, Mrs Yeats's clairvoyance, Yeats's occultism, spiritualism and his theory of gyres and lunar phases in *VIS* are just a convenient machinery for systemizing his whole philosophy, and therefore external to the central core. This is not so: it is the vital nucleus because it embodies his basic beliefs, and without beliefs no poet like Yeats can feed his own 'resinous heart', his imagination. It never stems from an external consciousness; and as the presumptions of the material world meant nothing to Yeats's imagination, so he found (as we have said previously) the sources of his imagery in *Anima Mundi*, the collective unconscious of myth, on which, of course, he was by no means the first poet to draw.

VIS is clearly divided into three parts: the first outlining a cyclical view of history, the second, a view of human psychology, and the third, a description of the soul's migrations after death.

The first, the theory of history, is the easiest to understand, for the idea of the history of civilization, and also of man's incarnations as a microcosmic being in 2000 year cycles comes from certain Eastern religions, from Plato, the Neoplatonists and Vico, among others whom Yeats had read. He divides the growth, maturity and decline of a civilization into twenty-eight phases—the twenty-eight phases of the lunar month—and this can also be applied to the incarnations of the soul. In this cycle, maturity, or the zenith, is therefore at the full moon of phase fifteen, the decline lasting from phases sixteen to twenty-eight, which is the dark of the moon. History therefore turns on the Great Wheel which Yeats thinks of as three-dimensional, and refers to as gyres (the 'g' is hard). These also are applicable to history and to the incarnations of the soul. The gyres are, as it were, conical spirals of history to which and through which events and man move. The idea is as old as Heraclitus and Plato. The illustration on p.68 shows the gyres as two cones expanding and contracting as they whirl. They are, therefore, space-time symbols gyrating as if any one point moved from one place in an axis, tracing widening gyres as it does so, until it reaches the circumference of the sphere. Simultaneously another point is gyring its way from the opposite end of the sphere as if unwinding the thread. Then occurs a complication: in the double triangle, formed and interlaced by these points going in opposite directions, moves a perne or spool, also unwinding the thread spirally. (The word 'perne' may indeed be unfamiliar as it is an Irish word not to be found in the *Shorter Oxford Dictionary*.) This internal whirling, like a tornado funnel, eventually reaches a catastrophic climax at which it breaks up.

67

THE GYRE & ITS IMAGES

The cones are traced by the revolving spindle which carries the threads. As the gyre disintegrates a new cone starts in a reverse direction. The spiral is associated with the winding stair

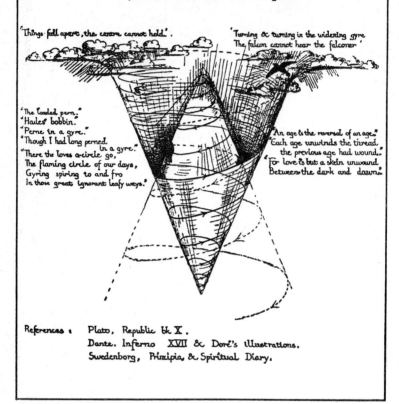

'Things fall apart, the centre cannot hold.'.

'Turning & turning in the widening gyre
The falcon cannot hear the falconer'

'The loaded pern.'
'Haile's bobbin.'
'Perne in a gyre.'
'Though I had long perned
     in a gyre.'
'There the loves a-circle go,
The flaming circle of our days,
Gyring spiring to and fro
In those great ignorant leafy ways.'

'An age is the reversal of an age.'
'Each age unwinds the thread
   the previous age had wound.'
'For love is but a skein unwound
Between the dark and dawn.'

References :   Plato, Republic bk X.
                Dante, Inferno XVII & Doré's Illustrations.
                Swedenborg, Principia, & Spiritual Diary.

A Vision.

Turning and turning in the widening gyre
The falcon cannot hear the falconer;
Things fall apart, the centre cannot hold;
Mere anarchy is loosed upon the world.

Thus the Great Wheel or the gyres are based on the Heraclitean principle of conflict, as the cones, whirl and interpenetrate, as Heraclitus said 'living the other's death, dying the other's life', the one expanding as the other contracts; a conflict of opposites throughout: subjective and objective; natural and supernatural; love and hate; war and peace. The phases of the moon and the gyres are exactly summed up in Michael Robartes's reply to Owen Aherne in 'The Phases of the Moon' (*CP*, pp.184–5).

Twenty-and-eight the phases of the moon,
The full and the moon's dark and all the crescents,
Twenty-and-eight, and yet but six-and-twenty
The cradles that a man must needs be rocked in:
For there's no human life at the full or the dark.
From the first crescent to the half, the dream
But summons to adventure and the man
Is always happy like a bird or a beast;
But while the moon is rounding towards the full
He follows whatever whim's most difficult
Among whims not impossible, and though scarred,
As with the cat-o'-nine-tails of the mind,
His body moulded from within his body
Grows comelier. Eleven pass, and then
Athena takes Achilles by the hair,
Hector is in the dust, Nietzsche is born,
Because the hero's crescent is the twelfth.
And yet, twice born, twice buried, grow he must,
Before the full moon, helpless as a worm.
The thirteenth moon but sets the soul at war
In its own being, and when that war's begun
There is no muscle in the arm; and after,
Under the frenzy of the fourteenth moon,
The soul begins to tremble into stillness,
To die into the labyrinth of itself!

Phase 15 is symbolized by what Yeats calls pure 'subjectivity'; objectivity at its height is therefore at phase twenty-eight. It is salient to understand what Yeats means by these terms—'subjective' and 'objective'. According to a dictionary definition, 'objective' deals with 'the treating of outward things and events rather than inward thought; the converse, 'subjective' is therefore the consciousness of self, and in Jungian philosophy the terms are used in this way. From this it is not difficult to follow how Yeats categorized orthodox Christianity as an objective religion, for it largely relies on salvation imposed externally from a salvation-god, whereas the religions of the East, and in particular India, have a subjective faith in which the self, always aware that God is within one, is exalted. The former tends to worship God by self-denial, self-abasement and mortification; the latter, by a joyful unification with God within oneself. This is briefly expressed by the second verse of the short poem in 'Supernatural Songs' VI, 'He and She' (*CP*, p.331), and can be further understood by examining the rest of that poem:

> She sings as the moon sings:
> 'I am I, am I;
> The greater grows my light
> The further that I fly'.
> All creations shivers
> With that sweet cry.

The two views are clearly exemplified by the different philosophies of T. S. Eliot and Yeats, the former seeking Truth through the *objective*, the Christian (or 'primary' as Yeats calls it in *VIS*), accepting his human inadequacy as a Christian and the necessity for self-denial; Yeats himself claiming a 'subjective' ('antithetical') personality, trying, as he said 'to embody truth' through self-sufficiency. William Blake saw all religions as one, so perhaps the contradictions in Eliot's Christian views and Yeats's Neoplatonism, both of which were accepted by Blake, may make it seem less strange.

Much is clarified on this point if one considers the passage in part 2, of *Little Gidding* Eliot's fourth *Quartet* in which the poet describes his meeting, in the deserted street after the air-raid, with the 'familiar compound ghost', in whose voice he recognizes his own, 'assuming a double part'. The opinions expressed are more those of Yeats than of any other poet, and the understanding shown by Eliot of Yeats's philosophic concepts is very remarkable. It has been pointed out that 'speech impelled us to purify the dialect of the tribe' is from Mallarmé's sonnet—'Donner un sens plus pur aux mots de la tribu'. This sonnet, entitled 'Le Tombeau d'Edgar Poe' is a tribute to all poets, as well as specifically to Edgar Allan Poe, who have, like the angel of long ago in this poem, given a purer meaning to the words of the tribe. Mallarmé, of all poets in France at that time, gave dignity to the language, and as a Symbolist was a vital influence on Yeats and Eliot. Both these poets, with symbols taken from tradition, such, for example as the Rose, speak to the mind through the senses rather than the reasoning faculties in a language

> Too strange to each other for misunderstanding,
> In concord at this intersection time,
> Of meeting nowhere, no before and after,

In concord, with no misunderstanding, because both Yeats and Eliot had read Heraclitus whose thoughts are reflected in this conversation. Images from Heraclitus appear throughout *Four Quartets* and in Yeats's verse. The dance, for example, as the image of life; to be sensed and apprehended rather than known: a momentary incarnation. Compare

> O body swayed to music. O brightening glance,
> How can we know the dancer from the dance?

ending 'Among School Children', with 'at the still point, there the dance is' from Burnt Norton', v. However, these two passages outline the essential difference in the two poets' interpretation of Heraclitus. In Yeats there is no still point in the whirling gyres, but only conflict. The condition of Fire, the chief element of Heraclitus, dominates both *Little Gidding* and the 'Byzantium' poems; the 'refining fire' of the Eliot poem, and the fire in which the sages stand in 'Sailing to Byzantium', and the constant image of joy when used with the dance in 'Byzantium'.

> Where blood-begotten spirits come
> And all complexities of fury leave,
> Dying into a dance,
> An agony of trance,
> An agony of flame that cannot singe a sleeve.

Yet fundamentally Eliot's objective (primary) Christianity is looking outwards for spiritual guidance: a form of mysticism which must be approached through deprivation and leading to an ultimate avoidance of sin, which is 'behovely' (necessary); whereas Yeats accepts every part of existence, by looking inwards to form a unity of being by a faith in self. Of the two poets, Yeats is more in keeping with the psychological and religious writers of modern times, who see the materialist age and war as manifestations of our inner conflicts.

To have introduced Yeats (whom I believe the 'compound ghost' to be) is very remarkable. Only in 1933, Eliot in a lecture, now published in *After Strange Gods*, had written:

> Mr Yeats's 'supernatural world' was the wrong supernatural world. It was not a world of spiritual significance, not a world of real Good and Evil, of holiness or sin, but a highly sophisticated lower mythology summoned, like a physician, to supply the fading pulse of poetry with some transient stimulant so that the dying patient may utter his last words.

After this censorial, orthodox Christian judgment of Yeats's supernatural world a complete volte-face occurs. In his memorial address Eliot describes Yeats as 'the greatest poet of our time— certainly the greatest in this language, and so far as I can judge, in any language'. Two circumstances are of much significance. Firstly, Eliot and Yeats met and talked on a number of occasions when Yeats was in England between 1934 and his death in 1939; and secondly, Eliot saw a performance of Yeats's last play, *Purgatory* in August 1938. Apart from an immense admiration for the brevity and tautness of Yeats's verse line in this short play, he was much moved by the theme (a supernatural one). An Old Man sees his mother's ghost as she returns annually from Purgatory to re-enact what she regards as a transgression—the begetting of a child by a drunken and worthless groom. The Old Man tries to save her by breaking the links of consequence which fall on succeeding generations. To ensure this he stabs to death his own son. But there is no hint that his violent action does help his mother's spirit; and in the final lines of the play we see that it is to God he turns:

> O God,
> Release my mother's soul from its dream!
> Mankind can do no more. Appease
> The misery of the living and the remorse of the dead.

The dead of *VIS* are each in the appropriate circle of their particular purgatory, but in this last play Yeats has gone a step further, which leaves him overlooking a deeper abyss than any he tackled in *VIS*.

In the second section of *VIS*, men are classified by the amount of subjective and objective qualities they possess; but, as 'The Phases of the Moon' quoted above makes clear, with regard to Man there are only twenty-six phases, rather than twenty-eight, as phase one and phase fifteen, complete objectivity and complete subjectivity, are never possible. A further detail in this section is Yeats's division of the soul into what he terms Four Faculties, two pairs of contraries: termed Will and Mask; Creative mind and the Body of Fate. These Four Faculties are gyres superimposed on the existing gyres, so making Yeats's ultimate philosophy not fatalist or determinist as it might at first appear to be.

> And I declare my faith:
> I mock Plotinus thought
> And cry in Plato's teeth,
> Death and life were not
> Till man made up the whole,
> Made lock, stock and barrel
> Out of his bitter soul.

Mechanical predestination will not suffice for Yeats, and in his detailed description of the Four Faculties he shows they are escape routes that Man can choose in order to avoid it. For example, there is a False Mask and a True Mask, a True Creative Mind and a False Creative Mind from which Man can make a judgment. And the Body of Fate embraces such happenings as changes in the human body like old age, and includes details from his environment. Ellmann points out in his brilliant analysis of *VIS* (*Yeats: the Man and the Masks*) that quaternaries such as the Four Faculties have often appeared before, with variations according to their time and place: the Four Zoas of Blake, the four humours of medicine in the Middle Ages, the four elements of Magic, etc. By means of the Four Faculties, an act of choice is possible, although the soul is undoubtedly committed to a cycle of lives. The paradox of the soul being free, yet not free, of living in time and out of it has to be accepted in Yeats and Eliot, and, ironically, will become clarified by an examination of their poetry, in which it is itself the very heart.

In two of the poems analysed in the critical section below, the so-called Platonic Great Year (*Magnus Annus*) is referred to. This time scheme derived from the belief in Plato's time that the planets would eventually return to their starting points in the heavens, taking time to achieve this which varied by some thousands of years. Yeats took 26,000 as an average figure, and this in itself is broken up by twelve cycles, corresponding to twelve lunar months of two thousand years each in the gyres. Thus a first era is from 2000 B.C. to A.D. 1, Greek civilization in its turn having driven out an earlier one. 'Leda and the Swan' is a first annunciation. The second era is Galilean turbulence, Jews, Christianity to modern times, with the gyre widening until modern times when 'things have fallen apart'.

In the third section of *VIS*, which deals with life after death, the soul goes through reliving its earthly life, gradually reaching a blessed state, after many incarnations. Man's soul in eternity is his Daimon or Daemon, a name employed and accepted in the religious hierarchy for many centuries, from Plato on. It may be advisable to point out that the daemon, or intermediary between Man and the Divine Being should not be confused with demon, the malignant spirit of Judaic and Christian theology. Again, from Heraclitus, we can see Yeats's interpretation of Heraclitus's phrase, 'we live their death and we die their life', referring to the never-ending circle of souls descending to death and rebirth; the core of Plato's myth of the Cave of the Nymphs. For Yeats an important addition in this section is his belief that it is possible for the souls of the dead to communicate, through *Anima Mundi*, with writers and artists. In an earlier essay, Yeats describes how he came to believe this: 'In sleep or waking came images which one was to discover presently in some book one had never read . . . I came to believe in a great memory passing on from generation to generation.'

Various literary critics have described *VIS* in abusive terms: 'a philosophic jungle'; 'enormous cranky, pseudo-philosophy'; 'home-made, gimcrack', yet Yeats's verse cannot be fully appreciated without an understanding of how by myth he was searching for a unity.

Only by a pattern of creative order can the disorder the modern world imposes on us be combated; and, as Eliot wrote of James Joyce's *Ulysses*, there is no better way of achieving this than through mythological discourse, which by tradition veils its subtleties. As in Plato, the soul and its incarnations is the starting point, and however difficult the discrepancies and contradictions of the path taken in *VIS* may seem, it is ultimately the summation of Yeats's philosophic thought, and therefore vital to a full understanding of how his poetry was nourished.

Part Two

Critical Survey

Introduction

Of the fourteen books of poems now bound into *CP*, *Last Poems* is the longest, equalling the first three books published. But comparisons of this sort are not always valid. For example, the shortest set, *A Woman Young and Old* would have been included by Yeats in *The Tower* rather than in *The Winding Stair*, but that a rich New Yorker, the owner of a private printing press, offered him £400 for the poems, a sum which Yeats needed to pay the expenses of his illness abroad. This is one exception to the usual chronological order of publication of the books.

But the poems themselves are not chronologically placed. Yeats was most careful to organize the placing of poems for publication so that one illuminated another. Therefore much light can be thrown on a poem by examination of adjacent poems—indeed, it is essential to do this. However, this must not apply to *Last Poems*, for these in *CP* are not in the order which Yeats wished them. Curtis Bradford (*Modern Language Notes*, June 1961) has printed the correct order for these poems from a list in Yeats's own MS, and 'Under Ben Bulben' comes first, not last.

The choice of poems for this critical survey may seem arbitrary, but it is governed by two factors. Firstly, many of the poems related to his friends are included in the first two sections of Part 3 below. Secondly, the better known poems have been often analysed by critics; it is a rash man who thinks he can add much of importance to the vast body of writing on the Byzantium poems. Some of the lesser known, but important, poems have been included, one of the objects of the choices here being to show Yeats's development as a poet: not just his abandonment of 'old mythologies' after 'A Coat' at the end of *Responsibilities*, but his incredible blossoming when he was over sixty years of age. Unlike Wordsworth, whose poetry withered and died when he was forty, Yeats, as AE said, had 'a habit of continued intellectual adventure'. He was working on 'The Black Tower' within a few days of his death.

The following brief chart will show where the poems in this critical survey fit into his life, and thereby help to show his development as a poet with relation to his life.

DATE	AGE	PERIOD	EVENTS AND INFLUENCES
1883–1901	18–36	London and Dublin	Mainly lyrical and narrative verse; Celtic and Romantic influences. Editing of Blake.
'To the Rose upon the Rood of Time'			

76

The Tower. *Cover design by T. Sturge Moore.*

Pre-Raphaelitism. Maud
Gonne. Paris. The Occult.

1901–1909	36–45	Period of the theatre	Organisation and management of the Abbey Theatre with Lady Gregory and Synge. 'Playboy' Riots, 1907. Coole Park.

'The Players ask for a Blessing'

1909–1914	45–50	'The Dark Period' Frustration and Disillusion. 'The Study of Hatred'. Beginning of a new style	Death of Synge, 1909. Troubles over Censorship. Unpopularity in Dublin. 'The Municipal Gallery' and the Lane Pictures. Meeting with Ezra Pound. 'The Green Helmet'.

'The Fascination of What's Difficult'

1914–1916	50–51	First World War	The Volunteer Armies; Ulster; the Home Rule Bill. 'Responsibilities'.
1916	51	The Easter Rising	Turning point in Irish History, and in Yeats's life. 'A terrible beauty is born'.
1917–1918	52–54	Marriage to Miss Hyde-Lees	Death of Robert Gregory. 'The Wild Swans at Coole'.

'An Irish Airman Foresees his Death'

1918–1923	53–58	'The Troubles' 'Meditations in Time of Civil War'	Guerrilla warfare against the British. The Treaty of 1921 Civil War.
1923–1928	58–63	'The Great Period': *The Tower* and *The Winding Stair*. 'Byzantium'. 'A Vision'.	Comparative peace: Yeats a Senator. Wide reading, especially at Oxford. Travels in Italy and U.S.A.

'Two Songs from a Play'
'Leda and the Swan'

1928–1934	63–69	'The Ending of a Gyre'	Fascism. 'The blood-dimmed tide is loosed'. Death of Lady Gregory: end of Coole.

'Speech after Long Silence'
'Her Vision in the Wood'
78

1934–   69–74   *Last Poems*   Politics. Ill-health and fame.
1939   'The One against the Many'.
'The Three Bushes'
'Under Ben Bulben'

To the Rose upon the Rood of Time

Red Rose, proud Rose, sad Rose of all my days!
Come near me, while I sing the ancient ways:
Cuchulain battling with the bitter tide;
The Druid, grey, wood-nurtured, quiet-eyed,
Who cast round Fergus dreams, and ruin untold;
And thine own sadness, whereof stars, grown old
In dancing silver-sandalled on the sea,
Sing in their high and lonely melody.
Come near, that no more blinded by man's fate,
I find under the boughs of love and hate,
In all poor foolish things that live a day,
Eternal beauty wandering on her way.

Come near, come near, come near—Ah, leave me still
A little space for the rose-breath to fill!
Lest I no more hear common things that crave;
The weak worm hiding down in its small cave,
The field-mouse running by me in the grass,
And heavy mortal hopes that toil and pass;
But seek alone to hear the strange things said
By God to the bright hearts of those long dead,
And learn to chaunt a tongue men do not know.
Come near; I would, before my time to go,
Sing of old Eire and the ancient ways:
Red Rose, proud Rose, sad Rose of all my days.

The Rose (1893)

This poem must have been written about 1891 at a time when
Yeats was working on an edition of William Blake. Gaelic legend has
provided the mythological background, the occult mysticism has
given him a symbol (the four-petalled rose and the cross) which he
hopes will be universal and speak to all mankind. Cuchulain's death,
and Fergus accepting the druid's bag of dreams are easily understood.
But the symbol of the Rose is not so simple. Professor Jeffares (*W. B.
Yeats: The Poems*, p.4) thinks the Rose is 'eternal beauty. And it also
symbolized Maud Gonne's beauty and again through her Ireland.'
Although symbols have a way of slipping and sliding, it is unlikely
Yeats wanted Maud Gonne near him while he sang of Old Eire. A

much more likely explanation is provided by Professor Ellmann (*Yeats: The Man and the Masks*, p.140), who points out Yeats's indecisions at this period, and prints a later version of the poem, which is preferable to that in *CP*. Yeats wants the Rose near him, then changes his mind, asks for a 'little space' and finally again wants it near.

> Come near, come near, come near—Ah, leave me still
> A little space for the rose-breath to fill.

In fact, says Professor Ellmann, Yeats wishes for romantic dreams symbolized by the Rose, yet does not like missing the common things of life. Yeats himself (*The Trembling of the Veil* III, *AU*, p.254) later describes the symbol as 'Intellectual Beauty'; he is here using the term 'intellectual' with the same meaning as in 'monuments of unageing intellect', which would include the imagination. It is worth noting that Yeats was shortsighted and therefore often missed the common details of nature, and throughout his poetry there is no comparable observation to Keats's

> The coming musk-rose, full of dewy wine,
> The murmurous haunt of flies on summer eves.

If Yeats is using the symbol of the Rose for dreams or the creative imagination, then he is asking in this poem for what he in fact achieved as a poet by the time of *The Tower* (1926)

> Never had I more
> Excited, passionate, fantastical
> Imagination.

And it is undoubtedly William Blake who in both poems is the background to the thought and symbols. In 1891 Yeats had not met the French Symbolists, nor had Symons written his book on symbolism, therefore it is from Blake and Shelley, and his occult reading that Yeats finds this and other such symbols as tree, water, sun and moon. It is easy to be worried by variants in such a symbol as the Rose, which he frequently uses. In 'The Rose of the World' (in which Maud Gonne is pictured incongruously lingering by Christ's throne) the Rose is intellectual beauty; in 'The Rose of Peace' it is earthly love; in 'The Rose of Battle' the theme is soul versus body; and, later, in 'The Secret Rose' it is the sacredness of passion, associated closely with Maud Gonne. Later still, in 'The Rose Tree' it is Ireland.

Like many of his early poems, 'The Rose upon the Rood of Time', seems overladen with adjectives, many of which in other poems he removed in subsequent revisions. There is perhaps a certain regularity in some of the end-stopped lines of the heroic couplets; yet despite William Morris's influence there is more than a hint of the very individual internal rhythms in the iambic pattern, which Yeats was soon to develop further in his verse. He would have read this poem aloud rather slowly, giving full weight to the many spondees, thereby achieving its mood of sad, wistful other-worldliness. The poem reflects the spirit of the Pre-Raphaelites, especially of Rossetti in describing Beauty 'wandering' in her dreamy indecision. It is a marvellous poem of its period, memorable for the monosyllabic line which begins and ends it; and prophetic of the poet's determination to 'sing of old Eire and the ancient ways'.

The Players ask for a Blessing on the Psalteries and on Themselves

Three Voices (*together*). Hurry to bless the hands that play,
The mouths that speak, the notes and strings,
O masters of the glittering town!
Though drunken with the flags that sway
Over the ramparts and the towers,
And with the waving of your wings.

First Voice Maybe they linger by the way.
One gathers up his purple gown;
One leans and mutters by the wall—
He dreads the weight of mortal hours.

Second Voice O no, O no! they hurry down
Like plovers that have heard the call.

Third Voice O kinsmen of the Three in One,
O kinsmen, bless the hands that play.
The notes they waken shall live on
When all this heavy history's done;
Our hands, our hands must ebb away.

Three Voices (*together*). The proud and careless notes live on,
But bless our hands that ebb away.

In the Seven Woods, 1904

This is one of the poems from *In the Seven Woods* which shows Yeats's interests widening. It was written for recitation by the Abbey Players, and the musicians were Arnold Dolmetsch and his group who had made a type of psaltery for Florence Farr, Yeats's actress friend (see below pp.115–6).

It is a simple invocation to the angels to come down to bless the hands and mouths of the musicians who play and speak or 'cantillate'; the emphasis being on their hands. Yeats is not so much concerned with singing as with the art of accompanying speech on the psaltery, and music always took second place, being the servant of poetry as he saw it. He once even managed to fit 'The Ballad of Father Gilligan'

(*CP*, p.52), to the tune of 'A Fine Old English Gentleman'! This problem of music stayed with him until his very last years. In 1937 he broadcast on the subject, and, according to Dorothy Wellesley, 'words for music was the passion of his old age'; he was constantly asking friends to find suitable musicians. But with regard to the speaking of verse, whether accompanied by an instrument or not, no other poet has brought to life such rich, sensitive interpretations. The 'green branch hung with many a bell' (*CP*, p.51) was traditionally held in ancient times by the spell-maker, the reciting bardic poet, and Yeats saw himself in this role:

> And from its murmuring greenness, calm of Faery,
> A Druid kindness, on all hearers fell.

a twofold symbol for keeping alive the speaking of Irish verse, and as a magical instrument in the hands of the poet.

'The Players ask for a Blessing', although very short, shows a number of poetic skills and reveals one philosophic view which Yeats afterwards develops: also the tight rhyme scheme, only six rhymes in twenty lines, the many repetitions of the important words, 'hands' (5), 'notes' (3), 'bless' (3), 'hurry' (2), 'kinsmen' (2), 'ebb away' (2), 'play' (2) and 'O' (5), this last a poetic archaism which he abandons in his late verse, except for ballads or ballad-type poems, whether it is exclamatory or invocatory, both of which it is here. The behaviour of Yeats's angels at this period reveals his wry humour—one 'leans and mutters by the wall' because he dreads having to come back to Man's time; likewise, Michael and Gabriel have the failings of mortals in 'The Happy Townland', the next poem in *CP*. There is also an indication of the poet's very unusual and startling adjectives—angels *drunken* with the flags swaying and the waving of their wings; playing the *shrilly* trumpet, an archaic, poetic but more onamatopaeic version of 'shrill', and 'proud and careless' notes, those two qualities which he later was to associate with aristocratic behaviour. But above all, this poem begins to show the consistency of one of Yeats's longest held views, the immortality of art, which lives on 'When all this heavy history's done'. This is the supremacy of art in 'the artifice of eternity', into which Yeats later asks 'the singing masters of his soul' to gather him, by which time the Three in One and the angels have been replaced.

The Fascination of What's Difficult

The fascination of what's difficult
Has dried the sap out of my veins, and rent
Spontaneous joy and natural content
Out of my heart. There's something ails our colt
That must, as if it had not holy blood
Nor on Olympus leaped from cloud to cloud,
Shiver under the lash, strain, sweat and jolt
As though it dragged road-metal. My curse on plays
That have to be set up in fifty ways,
On the day's war with every knave and dolt,
Theatre business, management of men.
I swear before the dawn comes round again
I'll find the stable and pull out the bolt.

The Green Helmet and Other Poems (1910)

In order to grasp the progression of Yeats's verse it is as well to examine a poem from each period of his writing. *The Green Helmet and Other Poems* (1910), so called because the verse was bound in with his satirical play, *The Green Helmet*, is a short collection of twenty-one poems, none of them longer than about twenty lines. Many of them have Maud Gonne in the background (see below pp.120–4), the majority are bitter and some are disillusioned. He has suffered difficult years dealing with the affairs of the Abbey Theatre, including a lecture tour in the U.S.A., as well as writing plays, and has therefore had little time for more than a few short lyrics. Yet these are significant in showing his emergence from Celtic twilight into the hard light of Irish day. The diction matches the change: no longer overladen with epithets like 'honey-pale', 'lute-thronged' or 'wine-stained'; but apt, few, unexpected and straightforward like 'spontaneous joy', 'natural content' or 'theatre business'. The form of this thirteen-line poem is miraculous: only five rhymes in all, with the brittle monosyllables 'colt', 'dolt', etc., placed with couplets between them, the initial 'difficult' being a half-rhyme. The important syntactical stops in lines four and eight do not occur at the ends of the lines, thereby showing a glimpse of his future rhetorical manner with its counterpointed rhythms. Here

Shiver under the lash, strain, sweat and jolt
As though it dragged road-metal

is very like a Hopkins sprung rhythm.

Ellmann (*Yeats: The Man and the Masks*, p.185) writes of this poem: 'There can be little doubt that Yeats's Pegasus during this period did drag road metal'. Is this really so with regard to this poem? 'Players and painted stage' have taken all his love, but there is a vitality in his curse on producing plays and dealing with stupid people, which firmly ends the poem—those abrupt monosyllables 'pull out the bolt', as he frees his Pegasus. And in using the first person pronoun he further strengthens his intent.

An Irish Airman Foresees his Death

I know that I shall meet my fate
Somewhere among the clouds above;
Those that I fight I do not hate,
Those that I guard I do not love;
My country is Kiltartan Cross,
My countrymen Kiltartan's poor,
No likely end could bring them loss
Or leave them happier than before.
Nor law, nor duty bade me fight,
Nor public men, nor cheering crowds,
A lonely impulse of delight
Drove to this tumult in the clouds;
I balanced all, brought all to mind,
The years to come seemed waste of breath,
A waste of breath the years behind
In balance with this life, this death.

The Wild Swans at Coole (1919)

On 23 January 1918 Major Robert Gregory of the Royal Flying Corps (as the R.A.F. was then called) was shot down when returning to base in Northern Italy. These sixteen lines are not an implicit lament for a personal friend, but the presentation of Robert Gregory, who speaks as a prototype fulfilling everything which Yeats most admired. To start with, Gregory possessed psychic second sight which gave him a premonition of his death—a faculty Yeats believed in and admired. As a reason for fighting he gave no shallow political emotions, neither hating the Germans nor loving the English. This was an astonishing view for First World War times, when most young Englishmen thought it their duty to die for their country. Gregory's roots were specifically in his demesne at Kiltartan, where he realized the poor would not benefit whether the war was lost or won, and he was sufficiently aloof to be uninfluenced by cheering crowds or political demagogues. This solitary detachment could be consummated in the 'tumult of the clouds', the lofty height from which he could view the conflict in its true perspective. He had thought it out, and been struck by the paradox of death in life, which alone could bring him fulfilment. So he made his decision with cold, dispassionate bravery, knowing the consequences.

Despite his love for Kiltartan as his 'country', Gregory had spent much of his youth in England and France, having been educated at Harrow School, Oxford University and the Slade School of Art. His all-roundness at sports is not mentioned in this poem, as in 'In Memory of Major Robert Gregory', the long elegy. But sooner or later, his sporting talents had to be brought to terms with his ability as an artist; by the age of thirty-seven, when he died, his versatility had evidently precluded his becoming a dedicated painter, if either the quality or quantity of his work is any indication. It is doubtful if he ever would have been a successful painter, and this is what Yeats sensed: so the implications of the last four lines of the poem. As in 'Ego Dominus Tuus' and 'A Dialogue of Self and Soul', there is a conflict in the same personality between the subjective vision of the artist and the antiself or objective viewpoint of the sportsman-soldier. This inevitably leads to the paradox of death in life, in the last line of the poem, which Gregory determines to resolve in the only possible way—by heroic death in the clouds: the joy and loneliness of the heron.

It is a magnificent, short poem, showing Yeats's development as a poet in verse absolutely suitable to his living in the Ireland of his day, rather than in any Celtic dream world. A strong statement is secured by the many rhetorical repetitions:

> Those that I fight I do not hate,
> Those that I guard I do not love;
> My country is Kiltartan Cross,
> My countrymen Kiltartan's poor,

which mount until the climax of

> A lonely impulse of delight
> Drove to this tumult in the clouds;

with its sudden trochaic foot on 'Drove' itself urging forward the internal rhythms. The four-footed lines, nearly all end-stopped with tight rhymes, give the poem an inexorable finality, like death itself; and as two-thirds of the words are monosyllabic, this proud simplicity makes it hang in the memory.

Two Songs from a Play

I

I saw a staring virgin stand
Where holy Dionysus died,
And tear the heart out of his side,
And lay the heart upon her hand
And bear that beating heart away;
And then did all the Muses sing
Of Magnus Annus at the spring,
As though God's death were but a play.

Another Troy must rise and set,
Another lineage feed the crow,
Another Argo's painted prow
Drive to a flashier bauble yet.
The Roman Empire stood appalled:
It dropped the reins of peace and war
When that fierce virgin and her Star
Out of the fabulous darkness called.

II

In pity for man's darkening thought
He walked that room and issued thence
In Galilean turbulence;
The Babylonian starlight brought
A fabulous, formless darkness in;
Odour of blood when Christ was slain
Made all Platonic tolerance vain
And vain all Doric discipline.

Everything that man esteems
Endures a moment or a day.
Love's pleasure drives his love away,
The painter's brush consumes his dreams;
The herald's cry, the soldier's tread
Exhaust his glory and his might:
Whatever flames upon the night
Man's own resinous heart has fed.

The Tower (1928)

Yeats's plays and poetry illuminate one another like adjacent mirrors in sunlight. Therefore these two lyrics from *The Tower* are here chosen in the hope that it may lead to a reading of Yeats's short (seventeen minutes only) prose play *The Resurrection* (*CPl*, p.577) in which they are prologue and epilogue; furthermore to show the interconnection between poem and poem, in this case between 'Two

Songs' and 'Leda and the Swan'.

The Resurrection was started by Yeats in 1925 or earlier, a draft being read by the poet to his Dublin literary friends in the drawing room of 82 Merrion Square in that year. Then it was rewritten more than once, receiving its first performance, in Dublin, in 1934. The two lyrics were added after 1929, and they are meditations on the theme of the play, yet will stand on their own when detached.

The play is placed in time just after the Crucifixion: three young men, a Hebrew, a Greek and a Syrian are discussing their religious attitudes and the Christian events they have just witnessed. The scene is set in a house within sight of Calvary, the Apostles being in the next room, while the excited followers of Dionysus, the 'dregs of the population' according to the Greek, pass and repass the window, singing and shouting, coupling in the street, gashing themselves with knives. The climax and end of the play is worth quoting, if only as an answer to those who declare that Yeats's plays are undramatic:

THE GREEK The curtain over there is moving.

THE HEBREW No, it is quite still, and besides there is nothing behind it but a blank wall.

THE GREEK Look, look!

THE HEBREW Yes, it has begun to move. (*During what follows he backs in terror towards the left-hand corner of the stage.*)

THE GREEK There is someone coming through it.

(*The figure of Christ wearing a recognizable but stylistic mask enters through the curtains. The Syrian slowly draws back the curtain that shuts off the inner room where the apostles are. The three young men are towards the left of the stage, the figure of Christ is at the back towards the right.*)

THE GREEK It is the phantom of our master. Why are you afraid? He has been crucified and buried, but only in semblance, and is among us once more (*The Hebrew kneels*). There is nothing here but a phantom, it has no flesh and blood. Because I know the truth I am not afraid. Look, I will touch it. It may be hard under my hand like a statue—I have heard of such things—or my hand may pass through it—but there is no flesh and blood. (*He goes slowly up to the figure and passes his hand over its side.*) The heart of the phantom is beating! (*He screams. The figure of Christ crosses the stage and passes into the inner room.*)

The play is thus set at the moment when one of the 2000-year cycles is ending, that is to say, the end of classical Greece and Rome, and the start of Christianity (see above p.67): the time when the fierce virgin of the Dionysus rites is tearing out the heart of the god Dionysus so that those who taste his blood can live again. And this starts the uncoiling of the spring or gyre of Magnus Annus, the Great Year of Plato, in which 2000-year cycles are repeated again and again. For this reason, the Muses sing 'As though God's death were but a

87

play', that is to say, it will be performed again. So more Troys will fall, and more Jasons and Argonauts will seek a Golden Fleece. (The derivation of these lines is given by Dr Henn in *The Lonely Tower* as Virgil's *Fourth Eclogue*, which Yeats was reading in a translation by Samuel Palmer, the artist, see below p.86. The 'fierce' virgin is synonymous with the Virgin Mary, however strange the epithet may seem when 'sweet' is usually applied to her, for to Yeats the thought of the emergence of Christianity out of the 'fabulous darkness' was violent (see 'Her Vision in the Wood' below). The beginning of each cycle of the Great Year is at the new moon, the *dark* of the moon; the apogee of the cycle is the full moon after which it wanes as the civilization declines. Christianity with its 'odour of blood' rendered vain all 'Platonic tolerance' and 'Doric discipline' of Classical Greece. As Yeats says in *VIS* (p.278), 'The world became Christian, "that fabulous formless darkness" as it seemed to a philosopher of the fourth century, blotted out "every beautiful thing"'. And as the roots of Christianity were in Syria, the 'Babylonian starlight', so-called perhaps on account of the Babylonians interest in astronomy, countered the order and civilization of Greece: a light shining in an otherwise darkened sky, 'the dark of the moon'.

Kathleen Raine, in *Blake and Tradition* (i, 309), points out the similarity in theme between these lyrics and Blake's 'The Mental Traveller', a poem upon 'the cyclic nature of history':

> And if the Babe is born a Boy
> He's given to a Woman Old,
> Who nails him down upon a rock,
> Catches his shrieks in cups of gold.
>
> She binds iron thorns around his head,
> She pierces both his hands and feet,
> She cuts his heart out of his side
> To make it feel both cold and heat.

the only difference being the Woman Old (Juno) in Blake, and the 'staring virgin' (Athena) in Yeats. Although Yeats admitted he did not understand more than some of the detail in 1893 when he was editing Blake's poems, he never forgot Blake's poem, so that after further reading of Neoplatonists he is able to connect the sacrifice of Dionysus with the start of the Great Year.

In neither lyric is Dionysus considered in his position as the centre of a fertility cult, as in the actions of his followers in the play, but as a dignified saviour-god, the role which he plays later. The epilogue to the play, another octosyllabic lyric, continues the theme. Christ fundamentally pities subjective people but is unable to help them, although he himself is responsible for 'man's darkening thought'. This is the theme of Yeats's play, *Calvary*, in which Christianity is

88

shown as an objective religion with Christ unable to die for 'the white heron', subjective man. The climax of the play is referred to in the line 'He walked the room . . .' In the final stanza, the theme of the transitory nature of man's endeavours is superbly restated by the poet, in lyric poetry of unequalled beauty, leading to the final lines:

> Whatever flames upon the night
> Man's own resinous heart has fed.

This takes us back to the mention of the god's beating heart in the first lyric, with its source in the Dionysiac rites, and to the beating of the heart of Christ at the climax of the play, which finally convinces the Greek. The flames fed by 'Man's own resinous heart' is allied to a symbol from Blake: the imagination, which is the real, the eternal, the spiritual body, fed by the divine and holy essence of fire which the Creator has and which any creator must possess. Throughout the cycles of history the divine fire of the artist's imagination is thus fed by man's beating heart.

Leda and the Swan

> A sudden blow: the great wings beating still . . . .
> Above the staggering girl, her thighs caressed
> By the dark webs, her nape caught in his bill,
> He holds her helpless breast upon his breast.
>
> How can those terrified vague fingers push
> The feathered glory from her loosening thighs?
> And how can body, laid in that white rush,
> But feel the strange heart beating where it lies?
>
> A shudder in the loins engenders there
> The broken wall, the burning roof and tower
> And Agamemnon dead.
>   Being so caught up,
> So mastered by the brute blood of the air,
> Did she put on his knowledge with his power
> Before the indifferent beak could let her drop?

The Tower, 1928

In all religions there are myths of gods disguising themselves as animals. Zeus, in Greek mythology, disguised himself many times— as a bull to carry off Europa, as an eagle to abduct Ganymede, and as a swan to couple with Queen Leda. In Jungian terms, the explanation lies in man's desire to come to terms and contain his animal instincts in his own nature, which the god here represents in dream or myth. The result of Zeus and Leda coupling was two eggs, one giving birth to Helen of Troy (Love), the other to the twins (Gemini), Castor and Pollux (War).

89

Cesare da Sesto (1480–1521), Leda and the Swan *after Leonardo da Vinci. Since about 1700 Leonardo's painting has been lost, but we have this which may even have been painted in Leonardo's workshop. (1507–10)*.

In *VIS* Yeats propounds his theory of history running in 2000-year cycles, and sees in Zeus and Leda a parallel with the Holy Ghost and the Virgin Mary. Both are the end of an epoch, caused by loss of control in a civilization, 'first a sinking in upon the moral being, then the last surrender, the irrational cry, revelation—the scream of Juno's peacock'. Both also are the beginning of another era, the first giving birth to Homeric Greece, the second to Christianity. Each is therefore an incarnation or annunciation, iconographically shown in Renaissance painting as a dove for the Holy Ghost, and in classical Greek sculpture as a swan for Zeus. The germ of the idea of the parallels between pagan and Christian myths is an essay by Walter Pater, 'The Poetry of Michelangelo' which Yeats undoubtedly read.

Although in the octave of this sonnet Yeats uses violent physical imagery, the symbolism is the real heart of the matter, and that, as usual, can be taken at many levels. Louis MacNeice (in *The Poetry of W. B. Yeats*), thinks that the poem signifies Yeats's belief that 'history has its roots in philosophy, that the eternal (Zeus) requires the temporal (Leda), further (for the myth is complex) that the human (Leda) requires the animal (the swan)', the second being a part of the Jungian theory we have mentioned above. Melchiori (in *The Whole Mystery of Art: pattern into poetry in the work of W. B. Yeats*), as well as listing every possible source from medieval and Renaissance painting and sculpture for the Ledean influence on Yeats, sees Zeus and Leda in terms of a union of opposites: of 'primary' and 'antithetical', of Man and Mask, of Knowledge (Reason) and Power (Energy), which, he says, explains the penultimate line of the sonnet: 'Did she put on his knowledge with his power'. Did she see the outcome of her act in the happenings of the future? At another level, 'Leda and the Swan' is a symbolic union of Godhead and Woman, and as a result the line quoted above could again be taken as asking the question whether she became divine, and indeed whether these opposites, Power and Knowledge could ever cohabit, even though Leda could *not* fail to feel the God's heart (line 8).

To return to the myth: the result of their union was

> The broken wall, the burning roof and tower
> And Agamemnon dead

that is to say, the seizure of Helen by Paris, the Trojan Wars to get her back from Troy, and all the troubled history ending with the murder of Agamemnon, the most powerful ruler in Greece and, for Yeats, the symbol of dignity, power and majesty.

Yeats wrote few sonnets, and this one, with its phonetic sublety, its concentrated imagery, and its subject matter revealing the very core of his philosophic thought, is his finest. Listen to the polyphony of the first quatrain: the hard 't's like whips cracking in 'great', 'beating still', 'staggering', 'caught', 'breast'; the sibilation of 'sudden', 'still', 'staggering', 'things caressed', 'helpless'; the bursting of 'blow', 'beating', 'bill', 'breast', 'above'. Whatever the symbolism, there is a violence in the detonation of the sounds, which matches the violence of the imagery. The repetitions of words throughout are so placed they become incantatory: 'breast', 'how can', 'so', 'his'. Both octave and sestet end with a question; then the typographical and unique break in the eleventh line after the abrupt monosyllable 'dead', and more noticeable after the polysyllabic 'Agamemnon', preparing the way for the final question. The octave describes the physical yet symbolic action in much detail, the sestet, the philosophic explanation for that action.

The story in Renaissance painting and sculpture is not portrayed with the violence of a rape used by Yeats; Correggio, Veronese and Michelangelo all show apparent agreement on Leda's part with the god's actions—no 'sudden blow', 'burning roof', 'brute' in the violent sense in which Yeats uses the terms. So it is not surprising that in 1923, when offered the poem by Yeats for the *Irish Statesman*, AE thought his readers might not understand the symbolism, therefore was not prepared to print it. We are fortunate in having *VIS* to show us the symbolism of a moment of vision expressed in this poem in fierce sexual terms.

After Long Silence

> Speech after long silence; it is right,
> All other lovers being estranged or dead,
> Unfriendly lamplight hid under its shade,
> The curtains drawn upon unfriendly night,
> That we descant and yet again descant
> Upon the supreme theme of Art and Song:
> Bodily decrepitude is wisdom; young
> We loved each other and were ignorant.

Words for Music Perhaps 1932

The poet speaks to his lover (see below pp.153–4) in their old age, 'all other lovers being estranged or dead', and having been apart for some months, 'after long silence'. The lamplight in their room is 'unfriendly as it reveals the physical defects of age; and the world outside is also "unfriendly night".' But with age they have gained wisdom to interpret 'the supreme theme of Art and Song' from their experience. When they were young they did not bother with such descanting, but just loved each other. Wisdom and Beauty cannot go together, it seems—a paradox with which 'Sailing to Byzantium' is concerned.

Critics have maintained that poetic rhythms alone can possess aesthetic value, apart from the meaning. But this short poem is a good example to show how irregularities in metrical form must be taken in conjunction with the sense. It is written basically in iambic pentameters, but is daringly irregular in order to reproduce the rhythms of conversation and afford the greater weight to the sense and feeling. It is worth examining these irregular lines. The first is metrically as follows:

> Spéech after lóng sílence; ít is ríght,

A dramatic accent on 'Speech' to start with; then 'after' hurried over giving more weight to 'long'; followed by a trochaic foot for 'silence', without a syllable separating 'silence' and 'it'; but the semicolon takes the place of the missing syllable in slowing it up, so that the sense is strongly emphasized. Another irregular line is

> 'Bódily decrépitude is wísdom; yóung'

Here we have three unaccented syllables after 'Bod-   ', forcing one to hurry on in saying it, to arrive breathless at 'wisdom', with no apparent feeling for an iambic line. Then the monosyllable 'young' after a long pause. Why is 'young' so stressed? Because at this point it comes in contrast to all of the poem so far, which has been dealing with age. 'Young' is therefore a hinge between the two trains of thought, which takes us to the last line dealing with youth. I. A. Richards in *Practical Criticism*, by quoting a made-up nonsense poem of exactly the same number of syllables, and the same metre and rhythms as the start of Milton's 'On the Morning of Christ's Nativity', shows conclusively that there must be a 'close cooperation' of the 'form and the meaning', which those who take just sounds as meaningful might deny. Richards says the alliance between form and meaning must be 'natural and inevitable', and an examination of the metre and internal rhythms of 'After Long Silence' is valuable in showing just this: the irregular and variable metrics add to the full expression of the content. There are further metrical variations in lines three and six.

The Irish, unlike the English, do not habitually swallow the ends of their words, so Yeats would have pronounced 'ignorant' with a full emphasis on the last syllable, giving the poem a masculine finality. In reading the poem aloud, the long parenthesis, lasting from lines two to four, makes it difficult to hold together 'it is right . . . That we descant', though there is no difficulty in reading it on the page. The poem is filled with euphony of 'd's and 't's as in 'bodily decrepitude'. The rhyme scheme is as remarkable as ever for its ingenious form—as it were, almost hidden.

A Woman Young and Old

Her Vision in the Wood

Dry timber under that rich foliage,
At wine-dark midnight in the sacred wood,
Too old for a man's love I stood in rage
Imagining men. Imagining that I could
A greater with a lesser pang assuage
Or but to find if withered vein ran blood,
I tore my body that its wine might cover
Whatever could recall the lip of lover.

And after that I held my fingers up,
Stared at the wine-dark nail, or dark that ran
Down every withered finger from the top;
But the dark changed to red, and torches shone,
And deafening music shook the leaves; a troop
Shouldered a litter with a wounded man,
Or smote upon the string and to the sound
Sang of the beast that gave the fatal wound.

All stately women moving to a song
With loosened hair or foreheads grief-distraught,
It seemed a Quattrocento painter's throng,
A thoughtless image of Mantegna's thought—
Why should they think that are for ever young?
Till suddenly in grief's contagion caught,
I stared upon his blood-bedabbled breast
And sang my malediction with the rest.

That thing all blood and mire, that beast-torn wreck,
Half turned and fixed a glazing eye on mine,
And, though love's bitter-sweet had all come back,
Those bodies from a picture or a coin
Nor saw my body fall nor heard it shriek,
Nor knew, drunken with singing as with wine,
That they had brought no fabulous symbol there
But my heart's victim and its torturer.

This poem belongs to the splendid creative period of *The Tower*, being completed just before 'Sailing to Byzantium'. On superficially looking at the appearance of the poem, compared with others of *Words for Music Perhaps* and *A Woman Young and Old*, one should be able to sense it must be the most significant poem of the book, for it is written in eight-line stanzas in *ottava rima* (rhyming abababcc)

Andrea Mantegna, The Entombment. *Engraving.*

95

which Yeats often uses for his deepest philosophic and reflective poems, such as the two Coole Park poems, 'Sailing to Byzantium' and 'The Municipal Gallery Revisited'. When dealing with Mantegna's 'Agony in the Garden', a painting in the National Gallery which Yeats knew, Henn points out (*The Lonely Tower*, chapter 14) that the bird on the tree in the painting, which observes the kneeling Christ and the sleeping Apostles, is a symbol, as usual, for the solitary, subjective man, for whom Christianity means little. Yeats's play, *Calvary* is concerned with this problem, and the refrain 'God has not died for the white heron' constantly recurs. Similarly, beast symbolism is often used by Yeats for objective humanity, as Yeats remarks in his own notes to *Calvary*. The visual inspiration for 'Her Vision in the Wood' is from another work of Mantegna (Illustration p.94).

The epithet 'sacred' occurs in the second line of 'Her Vision in the Wood', and the poem is in fact concerned with much the same problem as *Calvary*. It is 'wine-dark midnight', the time both of death and visionary knowledge, and an old woman who has not come to terms with her 'withered' and 'dry' state, that is to say her age, stands in rage as she remembers the lovers of her past. At that moment she is disturbed by deafening music and singing, as a troop of men and women, bearing a wounded man on a litter, appear through the trees. Whoever the man is, whether Attis, Dionysos, Diarmuid or Christ, he is undoubtedly an archetypal sacrificial figure, who has been given a fatal wound by 'the beast'. The women in the troop, with their 'loosened hair or foreheads grief-distraught', resemble the women from *Calvary* who talk to Christ on his road:

> Martha and those three Marys, and the rest
> That live but in His love are gathered round Him.
> He holds His right arm out, and on His arm
> Their lips are pressed and their tears fall; and now
> They cast them on the ground before His dirty
> Blood-dabbled feet and clean them with their hair.

If Christ's love is taken away from them, their love becomes 'a *drowned* heron's feather/Tossed hither and thither/Upon the bitter spray', that is to say, they are objective in character and will be blown round by the wind if unsupported by Christ. Also note the similarity between the epithets in poem and play—'blood-dabbled' and 'dirty' or 'mire' in both. But the old woman who is the subject of the poem is not allied to the three Marys, although she is 'caught in grief's contagion' and sings her 'malediction' against the beast who has given the fatal wound. For when the wounded man fixes her with his 'glazing eye', that moment, which should have been symbolic of Man's knowledge (Logos) meeting Woman's relatedness (Eros) thereby securing a sacred union, brings catastrophe. She knows that they have

96

brought not a 'fabulous symbol' for her, but 'her heart's torturer'. He cannot unite body and soul for her, but only illustrate suffering and salvation, those essential elements of Christianity, which are not for her, lonely, subjective-minded as she is—the white heron for whom God has not died. Not until the Crazy Jane poems and 'The Three Bushes' does Yeats show us the unity of opposites, body and soul, the concord between brutality and beauty which could have transcended the lust and rage of the old woman. This is a very disturbing poem on account of the savage depiction of the scene, the violence of the emotion displayed, and the joyless ending.

The Three Bushes

An incident from the 'Historia mei Temporis' of the
Abbé Michel de Bourdeille

Said lady once to lover,
'None can rely upon
A love that lacks its proper food;
And if your love were gone
How could you sing those songs of love?
I should be blamed, young man.
      O my dear, O my dear.

'Have no lit candles in your room,'
That lovely lady said,
'That I at midnight by the clock
May creep into your bed,
For if I saw myself creep in
I think I should drop dead.'
      O my dear, O my dear.

'I love a man in secret,
Dear chambermaid,' said she.
'I know that I must drop down dead
If he stop loving me,
Yet what could I but drop down dead
If I lost my chastity?
      O my dear, O my dear.

'So you must lie beside him
And let him think me there.
And maybe we are all the same
Where no candles are,
And maybe we are all the same
That strip the body bare.'
        O my dear, O my dear.

But no dogs barked, and midnights chimed,
And through the chime she'd say,
'That was a lucky thought of mine,
My lover looked so gay';
But heaved a sigh if the chambermaid
Looked half asleep all day.
        O my dear, O my dear.

'No, not another song,' said he,
'Because my lady came
A year ago for the first time
At midnight to my room,
And I must lie between the sheets
When the clock begins to chime.'
        O my dear, O my dear.

'A laughing, crying, sacred song,
A leching song,' they said.
Did ever men hear such a song?
No, but that day they did.
Did ever man ride such a race?
No, not until he rode.
        O my dear, O my dear.

But when his horse had put its hoof
Into a rabbit-hole
He dropped upon his head and died.
His lady saw it all
And dropped and died thereon, for she
Loved him with her soul.
        O my dear, O my dear.

The chambermaid lived long, and took
Their graves into her charge,
And there two bushes planted
That when they had grown large
Seemed sprung from but a single root
So did their roses merge.
        O my dear, O my dear.

When she was old and dying,
The priest came where she was;
She made a full confession.
Long looked he in her face,
And O he was a good man
And understood her case.
    O my dear, O my dear.

He bade them take and bury her
Beside her lady's man,
And set a rose-tree on her grave,
And now none living can,
When they have plucked a rose there,
Know where its roots began.
    O my dear, O my dear.

Last Poems, 1936–39

Yeats 'appropriated' the draft of this poem, written by Dorothy Wellesley, in the same manner as he had Lady Gregory's play, 'The Countess Cathleen', then set his imagination to work on it, and created a poem of deep significance from apparently simple ballad diction.

The epigraph is a little joke of Yeats's: 'bourde' in French means a sham or fib, and although there apparently was an Abbé Pierre de Bourdeille in the fifteenth century, he is not known to have written a history of his times. (For this matter, see A. M. Garab's article entitled 'Fabulous Artifice' in *Criticism*, vii.3, 1965).

The 'Crazy Jane' poems, which this poem complements, can be summed up by the lines at the start of 'Crazy Jane on the Day of Judgment' (*CP*, p.291).

    'Love is all
    Unsatisfied
    That cannot take the whole
    Body and soul,'
    And that is what Jane said.

'The Three Bushes', despite the levity of the epigraph and other touches of humour, is endowed with the same theme as the 'Crazy Jane' poems, and this is a deep one. The narrative, like all the real ballads, is quite clear, but if the poem is taken as just a love story, then the lady's trickery is not easy to forgive. If she loved him, she should either have slept with him or ended the affair: her compromise is not valid. But there is more to it than this. The poem deals at another level with the allegory of love: the lady and the chambermaid are soul and body respectively, with the lover becoming the centre of gravity (in two senses of the word). As he is the singer of a story, namely a poet, it is for his songs that the lady promised to become his lover; and ironically it is on account of his songs that he died when he was recklessly galloping to reach home by midnight, having spent too long singing at the inn. Ironic also is the fact that midnight by tradition is the moment of death, and it is then that the lovers meet, though it was in the 'bridal chambers of joy' that the midnight chimes were heard. The allegory and the story are perfectly unified, and, as Jon Stallworthy writes in *Vision and Revision in Yeats's Last Poems*, pp. 80–111, they exemplify 'the union of the popular and the intellectual', the poem being sung in the streets of Dublin 'for its racy narrative', by 'many who have no inkling of the philosophic argument that occupies the few'.

The use of direct speech in the poem makes it brilliantly dramatic, and, if read aloud by three solo voices and more voices in the refrain, can be amazingly effective. With regard to the refrain (taken from a Gaelic ballad) it is necessary to work out who is speaking: lady to lover in the first two verses, lady to chambermaid in verses three and four, priest in last two verses etc. The diction is memorable, especially the passionate, slow intensity of monosyllables like 'drop down dead'; the very few and deceptively simple adjectives like 'proper food' or 'full confession', the latter with other lengthy vowels appropriately slowing up the verse; and the dramatic change of rhythm in verse seven for the men singing at the inn, similar in spirit to the essence of 'the singing masters of my soul'. Then comes the absolute rightness of Yeats's ending, with the medieval allegory of the rose tree as the symbol of love. Throughout the poem, the seriousness of the allegory continues amidst snatches of verbal punning and humour: the sixteenth-century conceit, much used by Shakespeare, on the word 'die', implying also post-coital detumescence in the male; the pun on the word 'lie' in verse four, and the implied reasons for the exhaustion of the chambermaid the next day. So that although the poem superficially resembles a ballad, with such balladry phrases as 'No, but that day they did', or 'And O he was a good man', it is really far removed from his early adjective-ridden, clichéd ballads like 'Father O'Hart' or 'Father Gilligan'. Yeats has arrived at a point at which he can compose a ballad dealing with philosophic matters from Plato, yet outwardly keep the appearance of a narrative ballad lyric. The union of body and soul, the physical and the spiritual, that union of opposites which need each other, here reaches fruition in both love and death. No other modern poet has so revealed in allegory that love is incomplete without purity of soul and intensity of passion.

Under Ben Bulben

I

Swear by what the sages spoke
Round the Mareotic Lake
That the Witch of Atlas knew,
Spoke and set the cocks a-crow.

Swear by those horsemen, by those women
Complexion and form prove superhuman,
That pale, long-visaged company
That air in immortality
Completeness of their passions won;
Now they ride the wintry dawn
Where Ben Bulben sets the scene.

Here's the gist of what they mean.

II

Many times man lives and dies
Between his two eternities,
That of race and that of soul,
And ancient Ireland knew it all.
Whether man die in his bed
Or the rifle knocks him dead,
A brief parting from those dear
Is the worst man has to fear.
Though grave-diggers' toil is long,
Sharp their spades, their muscles strong,
They but thrust their buried men
Back in the human mind again.

III

You that Mitchel's prayer have heard,
'Send war in our time, O Lord!'
Know that when all words are said
And a man is fighting mad,
Something drops from eyes long blind,
He completes his partial mind,
For an instant stands at ease,
Laughs aloud, his heart at peace.
Even the wisest man grows tense
With some sort of violence
Before he can accomplish fate,
Know his work or choose his mate.

IV

Poet and sculptor, do the work,
Nor let the modish painter shirk
What his great forefathers did,
Bring the soul of man to God,
Make him fill the cradles right.

Measurement began our might:
Forms a stark Egyptian thought,
Forms that gentler Phidias wrought.
Michael Angelo left a proof
On the Sistine Chapel roof,
Where but half-awakened Adam
Can disturb globe-trotting Madam
Till her bowels are in heat,
Proof that there's a purpose set
Before the secret working mind:
Profane perfection of mankind.

Quattrocento put in paint
On backgrounds for a God or Saint
Gardens where a soul's at ease;
Where everything that meets the eye,
Flowers and grass and cloudless sky,
Resemble forms that are or seem
When sleepers wake and yet still dream,
And when it's vanished still declare,
With only bed and bedstead there,
That heavens had opened.
Gyres run on;
When that greater dream had gone
Calvert and Wilson, Blake and Claude,
Prepared a rest for the people of God,
Palmer's phrase, but after that
Confusion fell upon our thought.

Irish poets, learn your trade,
Sing whatever is well made,
Scorn the sort now growing up
All out of shape from toe to top,
Their unremembering hearts and heads
Base-born products of base beds.
Sing the peasantry, and then
Hard-riding country gentlemen,
The holiness of monks, and after
Porter-drinkers' randy laughter;
Sing the lords and ladies gay
That were beaten into the clay
Through seven heroic centuries;
Cast your mind on other days
That we in coming days may be
Still the indomitable Irishry.

VI

Under bare Ben Bulben's head
In Drumcliff churchyard Yeats is laid.
An ancestor was rector there
Long years ago, a church stands near,
By the road an ancient cross.
No marble, no conventional phrase;
On limestone quarried near the spot
By his command these words are cut:

        Cast a cold eye
        On life, on death.
        Horseman, pass by!

Last Poems, 1936–39

This is Yeats's last will and testament, but not the last poem he wrote despite its present position at the end of *Last Poems*. Jon Stallworthy (*Yeats: Last Poems*, p.217), shows what trials Yeats endured in the creation of the poem, started in August 1938, and still being corrected in minor points only two days before he died. Stallworthy writes:

There remain twenty-six folios of manuscript and typescript working. . . . First, on nine folios of a small loose-leaf notebook Yeats made three very rough prose drafts. Then on two more folios in the same notebook his poem starts to tumble into rhyme. Phase three is a complete, but rough, verse draft on six folios of a large loose-leaf notebook. Finally, there are three typescripts, each of three quarto sheets. The prose drafts are very rough indeed: many words are—to me, at any rate—illegible.

The poem includes many of the major themes of Yeats's life and verse, a formidable list; the wisdom of the occult; the magical Sidhe of Ben Bulben; the eternities of race and soul; the vitality of conflict; the ordered tradition of the arts; the ability of the artist to bring the soul of man to God; the confusions of the modern world; the virtues of the Irish aristocrat and peasant; the horse as a symbol of nobility; the belief in the immortality of the soul and therefore the validity of an unsentimental attitude towards death.

The tone is set by prominent pontifical imperatives in sections I, III, IV and V. The start of section VI is in quiet contrast until, suddenly, the epitaph, cut 'at his command' includes two further imperatives. The contrasting moods, the diverse subject matter, changing from splendour to levity, give the poem a wildness which Yeats uses deliberately to avoid compassion or yearning.

It is written in couplets with a loose four-stresses to a line—a rare form for Yeats, which he perfected in his play, *Purgatory*. Much of the verse is uneven in quality; from the doggerel of

> Scorn the sort now growing up
> All out of shape from toe to top.

or the freakish humour of

> Michael Angelo left a proof
> On the Sistine Chapel roof,
> Where but half-awakened Adam
> Can disturb globe-trotting Madam
> Till her bowels are in heat,
> Proof that there's a purpose set
> Before the secret working mind:

The fourth line of the above sounds more effective if the final 'g' is silent in 'globe-trotting', for Yeats as an Irishman would have pronounced it in this way. Compare those lines with the sublimity of form and content in

> Where everything that meets the eye,
> Flowers and grass and cloudless sky,
> Resemble forms that are or seem
> When sleepers wake and yet still dream.

The opening verse of the poem is difficult and not made easier by eccentric syntax. The confusion lies in the repetition of the word 'spoke' which, to make sense, must have 'the sages' as its subject both times. The allusions are not familiar either. Unless you are a geographer or well-grounded in Ancient Egyptian myths, you will not know either where the Mareotic Lake is or what went on there; however, if you read Yeats's prose works in conjunction with his poetry, and on this occasion, his essay entitled 'The philosophy of

104

Shelley's poetry' from *E & I*, you will find the background to 'The Witch of Atlas', Shelley's long poem. Lake Mareotis (today called El Maryat and situated at the rear of Alexandria) was famous in ancient times for the temple to Osiris-Horus, the god-man who gave to worshippers those numinous emotions which enabled them to identify themselves with the god. The sages, the priests of Osiris, are the inheritors, therefore, of occult wisdom. Then, in line three of 'Under Ben Bulben', follows the reference to this poem of Shelley's which has a misleading title as she was not really a witch, as one currently thinks of one, but a fay, naiad, or wizard-lady; in fact, a symbol of the soul, possessing superhuman and magical powers not used for evil, who, during the poem, which is a description of an archetypal journey, visits Lake Mareotis. Shelley tells us not to 'unveil' the Witch from her light, flowing garments, by which he means we should not investigate the story in the cold light of reason and intellect. However, one must add that she lived in a cave, and, as Yeats says in his essay, 'Shelley could hardly have thought of any cave as a symbol without thinking of Plato's cave that was the world'; and, as Homer also says, caves are symbols of 'invisible power, because caves are obscure and dark, so the essence of all these powers is occult'. In Shelley's poem, Yeats found (when he read it forty years before writing 'Under Ben Bulben') the traditional details and beliefs of Platonic philosophy, including the immortality of the soul.

> She, all those human figures breathing there,
> Beheld as living spirits—to her eyes
> The naked beauty of the soul lay bare,

Yeats was immeasurably absorbed by this poem and obviously never forgot some of its details, which echo in his own writing. One such concerns a dolphin in the description of the Witch who

> would often climb
> The steepest ladder of the crudded rock
> Up to some beaked cape of cloud sublime,
> And like Arion on the dolphin's back
> Ride singing through the shoreless air;

So from the Fay to the Sidhe, the 'pale, long-visaged' horsemen of Ben Bulben, is not such a leap as it seems. What the heroic men and women who gallop through the mists of Ben Bulben stand for, when combined with the wisdom of the Mareotic Lake, is then amplified in the next section of the poem.

'Man stands between two eternities, that of his family and that of his soul', Yeats once wrote to Lady Gerald Wellesley. In this poem, family becomes country (Ireland) and its traditional folk-wisdom, and the soul implies the occult tradition. One can see, therefore, the dualism of the first two verses of the poem here drawn together in this philosophic truth, and understand the two dominant influences in Yeats's writing. This is abruptly followed in the poem by the violence of death from a rifle—a hint of what is to come in section III, but compensated for by the final couplet of II declaring the immortality of the human spirit and the unreality of death. The gravediggers

> . . . but thrust their buried men
> Back in the human mind again.

John Mitchel (1815–75), with the Young Irelanders, endeavoured to free Ireland from the political mismanagement of the English Parliament. After an abortive insurrection at about the time of the Great Famine (1845) he was tried, transported and put in jail, where he wrote a journal containing the words quoted, but later returned to become an M.P. He was, therefore, one of that long succession of Irishmen, reaching into our own times, who believe that fulfilment of an end can be achieved only by violent methods. At this point, Yeats has evidently chosen to forget his dislike of Maud Gonne's volcanic passions in politics, and to adopt his anti-mask of the soldier, which he here wears. The unsolved question with reference to the word 'laugh' is whether the fighting-mad man is laughing with or at people, and I suspect it is the latter.

In section IV we have an abbreviated history of European culture as seen through Yeats's somewhat limited vision. But he does rightly see the perfection of Phidias, who was the greatest sculptor in fifth-century Athens, responsible for the ornaments of the Parthenon and the statue of Zeus at Olympus. Also Yeats appreciates the perfection of *quattrocento* (fifteenth-century) Renaissance art in Michelangelo (or 'Michael Angelo' in the mongrel, anglicized spelling which he uses). Apart from being sculptor, draughtsman and architect *in excelsis*, Michelangelo's frescoes on the vaulted ceiling of the Sistine Chapel of the Vatican are the finest work of their kind. The panel to which Yeats refers depicts God in majestic flight sweeping through the air, awakening a naked Adam stretched on the earth, and endowing him with life by touching him with the point of His finger. Both Phidias and Michelangelo attained perfection through measurement, order and craftsmanship, a theme enlarged on in 'The Statues' (*CP*, p.375). After Yeats had seen the Sistine Chapel in February 1925 he was obsessed by the work of Michelangelo, taking home many large photographs of the frescoes. Poet and sculptor are now ordered, in 'Under Ben Bulben', to work as Phidias and Michelangelo did, thus translating a vision of perfection, bringing the soul of man to God. As Goethe said, and Yeats may well have read his words although he did not admire his work, 'Phidias created tranquil Divinities; Michelangelo, suffering Heroes'.

Then, as the gyres run on, we are hurried through the centuries to Yeats's favourite artists—a strange quartet at first sight, but all

106

painters of types of pastoral, visionary landscapes, which had influenced and enthralled him since as a young man he saw Turner's 'The golden bough'. Richard Wilson (1713–82), much influenced after a journey to Italy, by the romantic Italian landscapes of Claude Lorraine (1600–82); Edward Calvert and Samuel Palmer, English painters at the beginning of the nineteenth-century who as young men knew Blake, but it is their later romantic, pastoral etchings and engravings, which Yeats owned and is here remembering. Yeats's interests did not extend to any later artists, when 'confusion fell upon our thought'.

Section v starts with orders to Irish poets to 'sing' (repeated three times) of whatever is well made, of the peasants and aristocracy of the past, of the 'indomitable Irishry', and also of an odd lot of people including some whom Yeats can rarely have met, and to scorn 'the sort now growing up', by which he presumably means the middle-class makers of modern Ireland. It is a strangely unacceptable list, even allowing for Yeats's anti-mask.

Section vi has the simplicity of a bare statement, giving reasons for being buried at Drumcliffe; a quiet lyric in contrast with the bombastic rhetoric of the orders given to the poets in the previous section.

What the epitaph means and to whom it is addressed is anybody's guess. It has been much discussed, sometimes receiving interpretations bordering on the fantastic. For example, Virginia Moore (*The Unicorn*, pp.446–7) calls the horse a symbol of the libido, and then says she thinks it was not a horse, but a unicorn. However, one may well ask, is the horseman one of the galloping sidhe? Is he Yeats's ghost? Is he any passing rider? I take it as having multiple meaning, expressing a wish for cold, dispassionate reaction as the horseman looks at death and passes by. Conventionally, in the pastoral sentiment followed since Virgil's time, the footsore traveller (not usually a horseman), whoever he is, when viewing a tomb has been told to pause or stop—'Siste Viator'—then to consider his own mortality, remembering that as the dead man is, so will he be. In composing his epitaph, the line 'Draw rein, draw breath' was erased in an earlier draft by Yeats. This line surely would have implied that the horseman was pausing, for drawing rein means this in equestrian terms. As it now is, in the final version, the horseman is at once told to pass by. It is similar in spirit, as has been pointed out, to Swift's epitaph, which Yeats much admired; here the traveller is told to go and imitate Swift if he dare. Yeats's epitaph being so short, little pause would be required even to read it. The words look better on the printed page than on his tombstone, though the letters are well cut, because, for some reason best known to himself, the stonemason carved capitals for the initial letter of 'eye', 'life' and 'death'. This was absurd, as obviously Yeats wished to play all sentiment down, not to exalt the

Samuel Palmer, Pastoral with Horse-Chestnut, *a watercolour from his Shoreham period. (1832)*

108

inscription so that it became like any ecclesiastical convention for death, but to see life and death coldly and paradoxically balanced, an antithesis so dear to him.

I do not agree with a well-known critic that this poem is a fitting conclusion to Yeats's life and work; for there are too many diverse themes which Yeats is here bringing together. It requires a poem of more than ninety-four lines, and, unlike T. S. Eliot in *Four Quartets*, Yeats never crowned his life's work with a poem of that length. Also, the verse is uneven, and this makes the orders to the Irish poets in section v doubly unacceptable. But as Louis MacNeice wrote in his essay, 'Yeats's Epitaph', 'If you believe a man was a genius it is an insult to him to ignore his deficiencies and peculiarities'. Anyway, the magnificent lyrics in the poem (section II and VI) make up for everything. Here the heavens have indeed opened to him.

Part Three

Reference Section

Yeats's family, friends and acquaintances

James Connolly, 1868–1916
Robert Corbet, 1866
Eamon de Valera, 1882–1973
Edwin Ellis, 1848–1918
Florence Farr (Mrs Emery), 1860–1917
Iseult Gonne (Mrs Francis Stuart), 1894–1954
Maud Gonne (Madame Gonne MacBride), 1866–1953
Constance Gore-Booth (Countess de Markievicz), 1868–1927
Lady Gregory, 1852–1932
Major Robert Gregory, M.C., Légion d'Honneur, 1881–1918
Dr Douglas Hyde, 1862–1949
Augustus John, O.M., 1877–1961
Lionel Johnson, 1867–1902
Sir Hugh Lane, 1875–1915
Major John MacBride, 1865–1916
Thomas MacDonagh, 1878–1916
John Masefield, O.M., 1878–1967
MacGregor Mathers, 1855–1918
Seán O'Casey, 1880–1964
General Eoin O'Duffy, 1892–1944
Standish O'Grady, 1846–1929
Kevin O'Higgins, 1892–1927
John O'Leary, 1830–1907
Pádraic Pearse, 1878–1916
George Pollexfen, 1840–1910
Ezra Pound, 1885–1972
John Quinn, 1870–1924
Margot Ruddock, 1907–1951
George Russell (AE), 1867–1935
Junzo Sato, 1897–
Mrs Olivia Shakespear ('Diana Vernon'), c. 1867–1938
Arthur Symons, 1865–1945
J. M. Synge, 1871–1909
Dorothy Wellesley (Lady Gerald Wellesley), 1889–1956
Jack Butler Yeats, 1871–1957
John Butler Yeats, 1839–1922

> Think where man's glory most begins and ends,
> And say my glory was I had such friends.

(*CP*, p.370)

Some of his friends, like Maud Gonne and Richard Gregory, are transformed into symbol and myth. Their characters and actions are larger than life—heroic like the gods and goddesses of Greek mythology in the clarity of their affirmation of truth through experience: myths created by Yeats from his inner self and often becoming the anti-mask which he so constantly sought.

> Poet's imaginings
> And memories of love,
> Memories of the words of women,
> All those things whereof
> Man makes a superhuman
> Mirror-resembling dream.

It is his realization of these ideal figures in their loneliness, courage and pride which accounts for much of this verse. By *Last Poems* most of his friends belong to the heroic past, for which the present is no compensation for Yeats. Their attitude to life was positive, and lived with nobility and joy. Through thus revealing them to us, Yeats is declaring his own belief in the Truth which their lives embody.

James Connolly, 1868–1916

James Connolly was born in Ulster, the son of a farm labourer; in Scotland during his boyhood; married, returned to Ireland in 1896 and founded Irish Socialist Republican Party. An internationally-minded Labour leader, he was seven years in U.S.A. On his return he founded the Irish Labour Party and was one of the signatories of the Proclamation of the Irish Republic, 1916. He was in charge of operations at the G.P.O. in the Rising, and twice wounded; faced the firing squad propped up in a chair on account of a gangrened leg.

In 1897 he first met Yeats, with Maud Gonne (see below), in connection with the anti-Jubilee demonstrations when he addressed meetings. He was a member of the Memorial Committee, with Yeats, at the 1898 Wolfe Tone Centenary Celebrations. For references to him in Yeats's poems, see 'Pádraic Pearse' below. 'The player Connolly' mentioned in 'Three Songs to One Burden', III, (*CP*, p.371) is not James Connolly, but a young actor from the Abbey Theatre whom Yeats knew, and who, as the poem says, was the first man to be killed in the Rising.

D. Ryan, *James Connolly, His Life, Work and Writing* (1924) is the definitive biography, but for an objective study of his work see the recent one by Samuel Levenson (1973).

Robert Corbet, 1866

The poet's great uncle, and the owner of Sandymount Castle (see below p.161). Yeats liked to think of him as one of his ancestors who belonged to the Protestant landed gentry, and who had the characteristics of that class. In 'Are you Content?' (*CP*, p.370) Yeats asks his ancestors, including Corbet, to judge what he has done.

113

Corbet was an amiable and sociable man who in his youth had been a soldier; latterly he was interested in the arts and in landscaping his small estate in Sandymount. He became an unsuccessful stockbroker, more interested in gardening than business; so he found himself in financial difficulties, and quietly drowned himself by stepping overboard from the Dublin–Holyhead boat when out to sea.

Eamon de Valera, 1882–1973

Eamon de Valera was born in New York of a Spanish father and an Irish mother. After his father's death he was sent, at the age of three, to his mother's family in Ireland, where he was educated in school and university; later he became a mathematics teacher and university lecturer, with a passionate interest in Gaelic literature. In 1916, aged thirty-three, he was Adjutant of the Dublin Brigade of the Volunteers in the Easter Rising. His death sentence was commuted to life imprisonment, as was that of Cosgrave and Constance de Markievicz (see below p.135). In 1919 de Valera was elected President of Sinn Féin; opposed the Treaty (1921) whereby the Irish Free State was recognized (less the Six Counties in the north) as a Dominion in the British Commonwealth, and when the Dáil ratified it, de Valera resigned, as his party wished for an autonomous Republic with no oath of allegiance to the British monarchy. He was President of Sinn Féin in the Civil War, June 1922–May 1923. At the election in February 1932, he and Fianna Fail were returned to office (Yeats did not vote for him) and the Oath of Allegiance was abolished. Subsequently he was An Taoiseach (prime minister) for several terms of office; President of Ireland 1959–1973.

Yeats met him in New York in 1920 and thought him 'a living argument rather than a living man. All propaganda, no human life . . .' In 1932 he interviewed him about the importance of the Government not stopping the subsidy to the Abbey Theatre. On that occasion he was impressed by his 'simplicity and honesty', though he differed in opinion from him.

'Parnell's Funeral' (CP, p.319) is a bitter political poem in which Yeats curses those who brought Parnell's downfall. In the second part, he lists de Valera, Cosgrave and even O'Duffy, as contemporary politicians who have none of Parnell's virtues and heroic qualities; if they had Parnell's 'heart' there would have been no Civil War in Ireland, and O'Higgins would not have been assassinated.

> Had de Valera eaten Parnell's heart
> No loose-lipped demagogue had won the day,
> No civil rancour torn the land apart.

In 'The Statesman's Holiday' (CP, p.389), a very slight poem, de Valera is listed with such diverse leaders as F. E. Smith (later Lord Birken-

114

head) who in 1921 refused to negotiate with the leaders of southern Ireland; General Sir Hubert Gough who was in what was called the Curragh mutiny of 1913; George II of Greece who was exiled from his country; and Lord Nuffield (then William Morris) who 'made the motors'—all famous, but not free from worry nor leading the happy life of the retired statesman who has become a wandering balladist playing upon a one-stringed lute, a better trade than politics.

Edwin Ellis, 1848–1918

The son of a printer who worked with Isaac Pitman on his system of phonotype, a poet and painter, and a friend of Yeats's father. He collaborated with Yeats on the three-volume edition of *The Works of William Blake, Poetic, Symbolic and Critical*. London, 1893.

In May 1900 Yeats wrote in his own copy of the Blake edition:

> The writing of this book is mainly Ellis's, the thinking is as much mine as his. The biography is by him. He rewrote and trebled in size a biography of mine. The greater part of the 'symbolic system' is my writing; the rest of the book was written by Ellis working over short accounts of the books by me.

> Much of the editing of this work is inaccurate and it is full of misprints, nevertheless Yeats was the first editor to tackle Blake on his own level of thought with regard to the interpretation of the symbolism, thus the edition is of unique value.

> Miss Kathleen Raine sums this up in her introduction to *Blake and Tradition*:

> There must be few books on Blake, good or bad, which I have not since read, including Ellis and Yeats's monumental commentary, as obscure to me at first reading as Blake himself. Yet I then sensed, and have since come to be certain that, for all its inaccuracies in those mechanical matters to which the modern academic world attaches such inordinate importance, of all his commentators Ellis and Yeats (or was it above all Yeats?) most nearly shared Blake's essential premises.'

Florence Farr (Mrs Emery), 1860–1917

Yeats met Florence Farr in 1890, after a performance of a play she had been acting in at the Club House, Bedford Park (see below pp. 181–3). He was fascinated: 'Her speech was music, the poetry acquired a nobility, a passionate austerity . . .' A year later he persuaded his friend Arnold Dolmetsch, a famous maker of harpsichords and lutes, to make a psaltery with twelve strings for her.

When Florence who died a Buddhist nun,
Took up the psaltery which Dolmetsch made.

With the aid of this instrument, which was a sort of simplified lute, she half-spoke, half-sang Yeats's verse, an art which he called 'cantilating'. From Yeats's essay, 'Speaking to the Psaltery' (*E & I*, pp.13–28), one can see exactly what he intended. But there were many critics, and one of these was Bernard Shaw who said that cantilating was nothing less than 'nerve-destroying crooning like the maunderings of an idiot banshee'. The triangular relationship between the three is amusingly recounted by a friend, Clifford Bax, who edited *Florence Farr, Bernard Shaw and W. B. Yeats*, 1941.

Florence Emery was also an important committee member with Yeats of the Order of the Golden Dawn at the time of the expulsion from the temple of MacGregor Mathers. So it is perhaps surprising Yeats should later have forgotten the row they had in 1900 when he puts Florence Emery and MacGregor Mathers together in 'All Souls Night' (*CP*, p.256) among his friends who have died. However, there is no doubt of the warmth of the two splendid verses to Florence Emery compared with the grudging acknowledgement to Mathers. The second verse to her is the core of the poem, which was later the 'Epilogue to "A Vision" '.

In 1912 she went to Ceylon where she became Principal of Ramanathan College, a Vedanist seminary for girls, and translated Tamil poetry, studying under a swami. She died of cancer in 1917, after many 'foul years' of the disease, having previously written to Yeats, using words which stayed with him: 'I am always glad to hear of someone making a brave end. I came here to make mine brave and I seem to have started another incarnation.'

Iseult Gonne (Mrs Francis Stuart), 1894–1954

In the summer of 1910, when Yeats went to stay with Maud Gonne at her house in Normandy, he met her daughter Iseult Gonne who was at a convent school nearby. She was beautiful, sensitive and intelligent; for example, taking an interest in Yeats's reading a translation of Tagore's poems to the extent of asking him to get her a Bengali grammar in order that she might read the poems in the original. In 1912 Yeats paid a second visit in the summer, during which Iseult's graceful dancing on the seashore inspired him to write 'To a Child dancing in the Wind' (*CP*, p.136). Neither this nor 'Two Years Later' (*CP*, p.137) is particularly distinguished verse; in fact the poems might have been written by any minor Georgian poet, especially the latter with its clichéd theme of youth and age. In 1916, during the war, Yeats again returned in the summer to Normandy, where Maud Gonne was nursing wounded in a hospital.

He read her 'Easter 1916' on the beach of Calvados, but she thought the poem did not do justice to the martyrs of the Rising. Iseult acted as his secretary throughout the summer, and very attractive she must have been to him. 'Men improve with the Years' (*CP*, p.152) tries to work out a *modus vivendi* in their relationship: a triton is safe enough—top half man, lower half fish. But the solution is not so simple. Can he really be 'delighted' with just wisdom?

> O would that we had met
> When I had my burning youth!

This is the same sentiment as he expressed some years later in 'Politics' (*CP*, p.392), another slight poem. Later in the year, Iseult, now aged twenty-two, arrived in London, where Yeats felt responsible for her. 'Presences' (*CP*, p.174), indicates his state of mind, which is hardly suitable for responsibility for anybody. Jeffares (*W. B. Yeats: Man and Poet*, p.190) points out that 'To a Child Dancing in the Wind', 'Two Years later' and 'Presences' all contrive to contrast Iseult's youthful innocence with Maud Gonne when young, and this is the obvious trend of Yeats's thought. More and more Iseult comes to represent what her mother had been to him.

In 1917 he again returned to Normandy in the spring. On this occasion he proposed marriage to Iseult more than once; but she refused 'Uncle Willie', as she called him. Later in the year he found her a job as assistant librarian in the School of Oriental Languages in London, and on 21 October he married Miss Hyde-Lees. A few days after his marriage he wrote 'Owen Aherne and his Dancers' (*CP*, p.247), in which the duologue between I and the Heart reveals Yeats's realization of the inappropriateness of the whole affair with Iseult. The verse has a new strength in comparison with the washy lyrics about Iseult.

> The Heart behind its rib laughed out. 'You have called
> me mad, it said,
> 'Because I made you turn away and run from that
> young child;
> How could she mate with fifty years that was so wildly
> bred?
> Let the cage bird and the cage bird mate and the wild
> bird mate in the wild.'

But in 'Two Songs of a Fool' (*CP*, p.190) he still shows responsibility for Iseult, the hare, although he is now married to the 'speckled cat'. (Note that many poems in *CP* are not placed in the order they were written: for example, this poem is dated 1918.)

'O let her choose a young man now and all for his wild sake', says the Heart. She chose to marry, in the 1920s, an erratic, unsettled adventurer, by name Francis Stuart, and when Yeats met her, at

Glendalough in 1929, she had a child of 'about three'. (She parted from her husband some years later.) In *Last Poems* Yeats remembers

> A girl that knew all Dante once
> Live to bear children to a dunce;

(CP, p.388)

None of the poems relating directly to Iseult is more than a charming lyric in either *Responsibilities* or *The Wild Swans at Coole*. But the whole affair is of interest, if only to show how much we owe to Mrs Yeats.

Maud Gonne (Madame Gonne MacBride), 1866–1953

Maud Gonne's autobiography, *A Servant of the Queen* (1938), referring not to Queen Victoria but to Cathleen ni Houlihan, gives much of her background, though little about Yeats for the first 250 pages. Professor Jeffares, in *W. B. Yeats: Man and Poet*, devotes more words to her than to any other friend of the poet. Yeats was twenty-three when he met her at the family house in Bedford Park; he had never seen in a 'living woman so great beauty'—complexion like 'the bloom of apples', divine stature (six feet tall), graceful movement, charm and vitality. She brought into his life 'an overpowering tumult', by which he meant he was wildly in love with her. Until 1903, when she married John MacBride, Yeats had hoped he would marry her and repeatedly proposed marriage to her.

Her sole purpose in life was concentrated in the attainment of an Irish nation. She came from the same Anglo-Irish stock as Constance Gore-Booth, and she also rejected all that that social group stood for, with a compulsive energy. Among other projects, she travelled throughout Ireland to help evicted tenants against landlords; organized the Friends of Irish Freedom, a revolutionary group in Paris, against England; lectured to Young Ireland Societies; briefly joined the I.R.B. (so she said); helped to promote the Wolfe Tone Centenary celebrations; and established Inghinnide na hÉireann (Daughters of Ireland). But she was not content with just lecturing: any methods to rid Ireland of its English oppressors were to be encouraged. Yeats often allied himself with the proud and strong hero as a type, but he was not then in favour of violence. Maud Gonne made a cult of violence into which she swept him, culminating in the Jubilee riots of 1897 in Dublin. I do not think the ferocity of these has been sufficiently commented upon. On the night of the celebrations, Yeats was at her side in the National Club in Rutland Square (now Parnell Square), outside of which hung a huge screen on which were large photographs of eviction scenes and of men who had been executed or had died in the cause of Irish freedom. Electric cables were cut to prevent Unionist shops having loyalist lighting displays; a coffin with black flags and the words 'British Empire' on it, accom-

118

Maud Gonne, aged about thirty, wearing the same hat of feathers as in her portrait by Sarah Purser.

119

panied by a brass band playing the Dead March, was thrown into the Liffey on the orders of James Connolly, who thought the police were about to seize it; huge crowds assembled in the evening outside the National Club, arrests were made, and the police charged; after which it was discovered that an old woman had been killed. When Maud Gonne went out, a voice cried out: 'This is your work, Miss Gonne, I hope you are satisfied.' The news of the old woman's death spread, and that night £2000-worth of plate glass windows were broken—in fact, every window in Dublin with Jubilee decorations.

In the next year Yeats travelled with her on a lecture tour in England and Scotland to promote the 1898 Wolfe Tone Association and Irish nationalist celebrations. He afterwards declared they were the worst months of his life, and henceforward he refused to be drawn into her political schemes. In 1900, during Queen Victoria's visit to Dublin, in reply to a Dublin Unionists' gathering of 12,000 children in a grandstand, from which they might cheer the passing Queen, Maud Gonne marched another 40,000 children out to a field at Drumcondra where, in the presence of priests, they swore an undying hatred for England until freedom had been won. 'How many of these children will carry bomb or rifle when a little over thirty?' Yeats asked. The Easter Rising in 1916 was to answer his question.

No poet has celebrated a woman's beauty to the extent Yeats did in his lyric verse about Maud Gonne. From his second book to *Last Poems* she becomes the Rose, Helen of Troy (the Ledaean Body), Cathleen ni Houlihan, Pallas Athene, and Deirdre. The following list of poems gives some idea of the references to her, either in poems directly addressed to her, or in others about her; but even this list is not complete. (The *CP* page reference is given for each poem.)
The Rose, 1893
The Rose of the World (p.41)
The Pity of Love (p.45)
The Sorrow of Love (p.45)
When you are Old (p.46)
The White Birds (p.46)
The Countess Cathleen in Paradise (p.48)
The Two Trees (p.54)
'A symbol of spiritual love and supreme beauty' is how Yeats describes the Rose, and he also combines it with themes concerned with ancient Irish heroes, so it comes to mean both Maud Gonne and Ireland. 'The Rose of the World' is a typical Pre-Raphaelite poem showing a view in which sex and religion are inextricably mixed in unrequited love, similar in many ways to Rossetti's 'The Blessed Damozel'; filled with dreamy, sleepy imagery, 'pale waters', 'passing stars', 'dim abode', and archaic diction like 'betide'. This poem culminates in an image of Maud Gonne 'lingering' by God's throne, which AE described as a 'ridiculous' view of experience.

The Wind among the Reeds, 1899
He hears the Cry of the Sedge (p.75)
He thinks of those who have Spoken Evil of his Beloved (p.75)
The Secret Rose (p.77)
The Poet pleads with the Elemental Powers (p.80)

The themes of the sacredness of passion and of the Rose have not changed since *The Rose*, nor has the diction.

In the Seven Woods, 1904
In the Seven Woods (p.85)
The Arrow (p.85)
The Folly of Being Comforted (p.86)
Never Give all the Heart (p.87)
Adam's Curse (p.88)
Red Hanrahan's Song about Ireland (p.90)
O Do Not Love Too Long (p.93)

Yeats has arrived at the Coole period, and through the influence of the environment there and all that it stood for, has managed to reject

> The unavailing outcries and put away the old bitterness
> That empty the heart

This does not refer to Maud Gonne's marriage, for the poem was written in August 1902, but to the eleven years of loving her. These are beginning to have their effect, especially in 'The Folly of Being Comforted'.

Between 1899 and 1910, Yeats was occupied with the Abbey Theatre, writing and producing his plays, so there are only fourteen poems. in *In the Seven Woods*, one a ballad. Those concerned with Maud Gonne are therefore over half the total.

The Green Helmet, 1910
A Woman Homer Sung (p.100)
Words (p.100)
No Second Troy (p.101)
Reconciliation (p.102)
King and No King (p.102)
Peace (p.103)
Against Unworthy Praise (p.103)

After Maud Gonne's marriage and his struggles in the Abbey Theatre, Yeats was bitter and distressed. However, his verse takes on a new strength; no longer the vague twilight suggestions of the previous volumes, but taut, lambent statements, often in three or four-stressed lines, with controlled rhythms to match. In 'Words' he realizes it is Maud Gonne who has made him into a poet whose words now obey his call. But, fortunately, she did not understand them, otherwise he might have 'thrown poor words away' and been content to marry her. 'No Second Troy' (1908) consists of four rhetorical questions that are absolutely sure in their strong rhythmical variation and diction, in fact, as Louis MacNeice pointed out, are 'counterpointed' like Gerard Manley Hopkins's verse. How wrong were contemporary critics not to sense this development in Yeats's work, instead of condemning him as a poet who had said all he had to say in his previous lyric verse:

Responsibilities, 1914
Untitled prefatory poem (p.113)
When Helen Lived (p.124)
Fallen Majesty (p.138)
Friends (p.139)
That the Night Come (p.140)
The Cold Heaven (p.140)

Henceforward the number of poems about Maud Gonne decreases. The 'barren passion' of line 19 of the Untitled prefatory poem is bitter, so are many memories of his unrequited love:

> And what of her that took
> All till my youth was gone
> With scarce a pitying look?
> How could I praise that one?

Ultimately, however, the memory is therapeutically bitter-sweet. The one superbly constructed sentence of 'That the Night Come' is dramatically right for the terse passion it expresses. In 'The Cold Heaven', a boreal celebration of Maude Gonne's marriage, Yeats recalls what she meant to him. The poem's long complex rhythms, counterpointing the alexandrines, are a preview of what is to come in his mature verse.

The Wild Swans at Coole, 1919
The Wild Swans at Coole (p.147)
The Living Beauty (p.156)
His Phoenix (p.170)
Her Praise (p.168)
The People (p.169)
A Thought from Propertius (p.172)

Yeats is now recalling Maud Gonne in small parts of the poems: in the bitterness of verse three of 'The Wild Swans'; in realizing he is growing old in 'The Living Beauty' (1915), another poem with a splendidly counterpointed long sentence; and in the refrain of 'His Phoenix'. 'The People' sums up the wasted years in Dublin politics with Maud Gonne, when he might have been writing verse in the Urbino-like setting of Coole Park.

Suddenly he comes to see how political opinions destroy a woman, and states it with one of these rhetorical questions that he now can manage so well:

> An intellectual hatred is the worst,
> So let her think opinions are accursed.
> Have I not seen the loveliest woman born
> Out of the mouth of Plenty's horn,
> Because of her opinionated mind
> Barter that horn and every good
> By quiet natures understood
> For an old bellows full of angry wind?

But it is really not so sudden. Ten years previously he had written to Synge: 'Women, because the main event of their lives has been a giving themselves and giving birth give all to an opinion as if it were a terrible stone doll.' Both Maud Gonne and Constance Markievicz had found themselves in Holloway prison, and as they grew old their bitterness and hatred hardened them. A few years later Seán O'Casey describes Maud Gonne, now in her sixties, at a meeting at which he was required to tell a hostile audience why he wrote critically of the Irish in *The Plough and the Stars* (1926):

> She was clad in a classical way, with a veil of dark blue over her head, the ends flowing down over her shoulders. She turned slowly, only once, to glance at him [O'Casey] and Seán saw, not her who was beautiful, and had the walk of a queen, but the poor old woman, whose voice was querulous, from whom came many words that were bitter, and but few kind . . . This was she for whom Yeats had woven so many beautiful cloths of embroidered poetry. She, too, was changed, changed utterly, for no ring of glory now surrounded that wrinkled, querulous face. Shadows now were all its marking, shadows where the flesh had swelled or where the flesh had sagged. This is she who, as Yeats declared,
> *Hurled the little streets upon the great.*
> She had never done that, for her knowledge of the ways of the little streets was scanty, interesting her only when they issued from their dim places headed by a green flag. She never seemed to have understood Yeats the poet. Indeed, she could not, having little of the poet in herself, so that she never felt the lure of melody . . . Here she sat now, silent, strong; waiting her turn to say more bitter words against the one who refused to make her dying dream his own.

Yeats, now sixty years of age, looks on the children in the 'long school-room', and is reminded of his own schooldays and of a story that Maud Gonne told him about hers. Was she similar to these children? Then he sees in his mind her 'present image', and so to the picture of every mother dreaming of her own children—a bitter thought to imagine them at sixty years old. In 'A Man Young and Old' the image of stone again appears when he thinks of her. It is the regret of an old man; but is also the start of Yeats's great creative period.

The Winding Stair, 1933
Quarrel in Old Age (p.286)

Beyond the 'distorting days' of 1931, when he temporarily quarrelled with her, he remembers her youth and beauty once again.

Last Poems, 1936–39
Beautiful Lofty Things (p.348)
A Bronze Head (p.382)

The former has been discussed in this section with reference to the other heroic characters mentioned (O'Leary, Lady Gregory, J. B. Yeats, Standish O'Grady.) Here he remembers Maud Gonne as Pallas Athene, but evidently in her role as a goddess of war, rather than as patron of the arts or possessor of all wisdom and knowledge. As a virgin divinity she was inaccessible to the passion of love. Maud Gonne certainly fulfilled the second state with regard to Yeats. 'A Bronze Head' refers to the bronze-painted plaster bust of her, now in the Municipal Gallery, Dublin. The poem once again declares her superhuman qualities. In actuality, the bust shows a tight-lipped old woman, with eyes downcast, almost as if she was determined not to communicate with the sculptor, so evident is her withdrawal.

Lady Gregory, 1852–1932

Born Augusta Persse, a Connachtwoman of the Protestant landed class from nearby Roxborough House, she had a culturally impoverished childhood, without many books, but was fortunately introduced to Irish myth and history, and taught some Gaelic by Mary Sheridan, who for forty years was nurse to her family. At the age of twenty-eight she married Sir William Gregory, the Governor of Ceylon, aged sixty-three, who owned Coole Park. Twelve years later he died, and as a widow—like Queen Victoria she always dressed in black—she devoted herself to making Coole a place where writers could gather and discuss, or work in peace undisturbed.

Before her marriage, the drawing room at Coole had had no books in it. But she gradually slipped into its 'idle elegance' certain very personal books. Her literary friends, who gave their works, included Wilfrid Blunt, AE, Masefield, Douglas Hyde, George Moore, Synge, Seán O'Casey and Theodore Roosevelt. And, of course, a shelf-load of all but the earliest Yeats, who dedicated some of his books to her, and wrote poems in that very room. Round this room were MS letters in various caskets and boxes: a poem written out for her by Robert Browning at Christmas 1884, letters from Thomas Hardy, Bernard Shaw, Henry James, Bret Harte and Mark Twain.

The walls of the breakfast room were lined with engravings of eighteenth- and nineteenth-century friends of the Gregorys, one especially fine engraving of Sir Joshua Reynolds's portrait of Edmund Burke. Under this was a letter from Burke to a Robert Gregory urging him to consider the natives first in India. How much must Yeats have been influenced by Lady Gregory's attitude to these portraits as she looked up at them with 'increase of pride in the ancestral eye and hand that chose these memorials of high company to bring to his home, to put before the eyes of his successors'. In *The Oxford Book of Modern Verse* (1936) Yeats significantly includes both the Coole Park poems among his own work which he selects.

Yeats's love and admiration for Lady Gregory and all she stood for at Coole are interwoven into the fabric of his verse for many years.

> If you, that have grown old, were the first dead,
> Neither catalpa tree nor scented lime
> Should hear my living feet, nor would I tread
> Where we wrought that shall break the teeth of Time.
> Let the new faces play what tricks they will
> In the old rooms; night can outbalance day,
> Our shadows rove the garden gravel still,
> The living seem more shadowy than they.

These lines, published in *The Tower* (1928; *CP*, p.238), were written in 1912. Earlier, in 'A Friend's Illness' (*The Green Helmet*, 1910; *CP*, p.109) and in 'Friends' (*Responsibilities*, 1914; *CP*, p.139) he acknowledges that Lady Gregory enabled him to write verse, or, as he puts it,

> So changed me that I live
> Labouring in ecstasy.

In collaboration with Yeats she wrote *Cathleen ni Houlihan* and *The Pot of Broth*; her own output included numerous folk tales, more than twenty-five plays, editing an *Autobiography* (1894) of Sir William Gregory; *Our Irish Theatre* (1913); *Hugh Lane's Life and Achievements* (1921); her own *Journals 1916–1930*; and *Coole* (1931). Her collections of Irish tales are the best of many translations from the Gaelic, and should not be missed by anyone wishing to enjoy reading the background to the myth used by Yeats; they include *Gods and Fighting Men: the story of the Tuatha de Danaan and of the Fianna of Ireland*; *A Book of Saints and Wonders*; *Cuchulain of Muirthemne*; these and her other books have all been republished in the 1970s. These tales, some-

Lady Gregory in the field in front of Coole House.
126

times taken from the songs and stories of travelling men and beggars at Coole, or from the cottagers in the Kiltartan district (while Yeats, not speaking Gaelic, sat on the wall outside) are miraculously welded to the earlier scholarly translations of Standish O'Grady or Douglas Hyde.

Seán O'Casey, in his autobiography, *Inishfallen, Fare Thee Well* also describes her when he met her in the early 1920s; she was then over seventy:

> A sturdy, stout little figure soberly clad in solemn black, made gay with a touch of something white under a long, soft, black silk veil that covered her grey hair and flowed gracefully behind half-way down her back. . . . Her face was a rugged one, hard, as that of a peasant, curiously lit with an odd humour in the bright eyes and the curving wrinkles crowding around the corners of the firm little mouth. She looked like an old, elegant nun of a new order, a blend of the Lord Jesus Christ and of Puck, an order that Ireland had never known before, and wasn't likely to know again for a long time to come.

He goes on to describe his visit to Coole in much detail (p.127–254).

Lady Gregory was the modern example of the Protestant from the Irish landed class who was 'inevitably on the side of the people', and this often meant she was against England. After she had lost her fight to get the pictures of her nephew, Hugh Lane, for Dublin, Yeats showed his admiration for the patrician virtues based on honour which he knew she had:

> Bred to a harder thing
> Than Triumph, turn away
> And like a laughing string
> Whereon mad fingers play
> Amid a place of stone,
> Be secret and exult,
> Because of all things known
> That is most difficult.
>
> (*CP*, p.122)

In the Civil War in the 1920s, Roxborough House, her old home, was burnt to the ground. Soon the fine beech trees had been cut down, the river was choked by weeds and the garden became a wilderness. After a visit, Lady Gregory said she felt like Oisin on his return from Almhuin, 'for as he was the last of the Fianna, so am I of my generation the brothers, the sisters; and now the homestead that had sheltered us all a deserted disconsolate ruin'. Throughout 1931 she suffered much pain from a malignant cancer, which she bore courageously, and was angry with Yeats for recording her illness in 'Coole Park and Ballylee, 1931':

Sound of a stick upon the floor, a sound
From somebody that toils from chair to chair;
Beloved books that famous hands have bound,
Old marble heads, old pictures everywhere;
Great rooms where travelled men and children found
Content or joy; a last inheritor
Where none has reigned that lacked a name and fame
Or out of folly into folly came.

She died in May 1932, aged eighty. Her name lives on in Yeats's verse, and in her own work.

Major Robert Gregory, M.C., Légion d'Honneur, 1881–1918

Lady Gregory's only son, born in London, was a classical scholar to Harrow School, learnt Gaelic at Coole, and became an excellent stage designer for Yeats's plays at the Abbey Theatre. He was married and had three children.

Two other poems beside 'An Irish Airman foresees his Death' refer to his death, 'In Memory of Major Robert Gregory' (*CP*, p.148) and 'Shepherd and Goatherd' (*CP*, p.159). Both are very different from the two great English classical elegies, in which the poet immediately calls upon the reader to weep for the sad death:

Shelley's *Adonais*, on the death of Keats:

I weep for Adonais—he is dead!
O, weep for Adonais! though our tears
Thaw not the frost which binds so dear a head!

or Milton's *Lycidas* who

Must not flote upon his watry bier
Unwept, and welter to the parching wind
Without the meed of some melodious tear.

In 'Shepherd and Goatherd' Yeats is restrained and, according to Henn (*The Lonely Tower*, p.123), 'the Shepherd is Yeats in youth, the Goatherd himself in age', though obviously at another level the poem is referring to Robert Gregory's characteristics. 'In Memory of Major Robert Gregory' is more concerned with showing Robert as the twentieth-century example of the universal man, in the footsteps of Sir Philip Sidney, the perfect Renaissance man.

Soldier, scholar, horseman, he
As 'twere all life's epitome.

For a detailed study of these poems, see Frank Kermode, *The Romantic Image*, pp. 30–42.

Dr Douglas Hyde, 1862–1949

Son of the Protestant rector of Frenchpark, County Roscommon. When he was an undergraduate at Trinity College he met Yeats, learnt Gaelic, wrote folk tales and verse in it. He possessed a gentle temperament, was diplomatic, and a man who made no enemies. He visited Coole when Yeats was there in the summer 1899, having previously published *A History of Gaelic Literature* (1892) and been Founder and first President of the Gaelic League (1893) (*Dramatis Personae*, pp.216–19, for Yeats's account of meetings with him.) The sonnet, 'At the Abbey Theatre' (*The Green Helmet*, 1910; *CP*, p.107) was written at a time when Yeats was disillusioned with the audiences' reactions to some of the plays produced at the Abbey Theatre. He thinks that Douglas Hyde, whose pseudonym was Craoibhin Aoibhin (pronounced Crievin Eving), the Gaelic for 'the delightful little branch', being closer to the countryfolk, may be able to explain the reasons for the fickleness and ignorance of the mob. From 1908 to 1932, Hyde was Professor of Modern Irish at University College, Dublin; Senator 1932–37 and then, by unanimous consent of all parties, first President of Eire, 1939–45.

Yeats seemed to envy his ability to write fresh Gaelic verse, and wrote of him: 'He had the folk mind as no modern man had it. . . . He wrote in joy and at great speed because emotion brought the appropriate word. Nothing in that language of his was abstract, nothing worn out.'

Augustus John, O.M., R.A., 1878–1961

A Welshman, with a striking appearance—Viking yellow hair and vivid blue eyes—Augustus John trained at the Slade School of Art, where as a student, he showed his superb draughtsmanship. He became a brilliant portraitist in the grand manner, with colour tonally high and a somewhat Impressionist handling of paint. He travelled much in a rather gypsy fashion. Yeats met him at Coole in 1907 when he sat for a portrait which when finished Yeats did not much like on account of its heavy shading and his untidy appearance, with windswept hair, which he thought was not typical. The portrait reveals him as the dreamer of Celtic twilight no more, but as the fighter for the Abbey Theatre and man of the world. Yeats describes this visit by Augustus John to Coole, in a letter to Florence Farr, which, as well as revealing some of John's characteristics shows Yeats's sense of humour and his extraordinary spelling.

Coole Park,
Gort. Co. Galway.

My dear Florence Emery:

Agustus John has just left and I have time for letters. He has done numberless portraits of me to work up into an etching—all powerful ugly gypsey things. He behaved very well here, did the most wonderful acrobatic things on the floor and climbed to the top of the highest tree in the garden [the Autograph Tree, see Gazetteer, Coole Park] and did not talk much about his two wives and his seven children. Lady Gregory was always afraid some caller would say 'How many children' 'Seven' 'You must have married very young' 'About four years'. 'Twins I suppose' 'Oh no but—' and then all out. He wore hair down to his shoulders and an early victorian coat with a green velvet collar. Robert watched him with ever visible admiration and dicipleship.

In June 1930 John painted another portrait of Yeats, seated with hat on lap, legs wrapped in a fur rug, in the open air at Renvyle, on the edge of the Atlantic in Connemara. This fine portrait is poorly reproduced as a frontispiece to *AU*, disgracefully cut down at the top and bottom, so that the artist's careful relationship of figure to landscape is distorted, making Yeats look shorter than he really was.

Lionel Johnson, 1867–1902

In 'Modern Poetry', *E & I*, p.491, Yeats describes the Rhymers Club of poets who in the 1890s used to meet at 'The Cheshire Cheese' just off Fleet Street, to read and discuss their verse. One of these was Lionel Johnson, a Catholic convert, 'determined, erect, his few words dogmatic, almost a dwarf but beautifully made, his features cut in ivory'. He had had a classical education (Winchester College and Oxford), was of Irish extraction, a minor poet but major critic, interested in the Irish Literary Renaissance and Celtic legend. Between 1890 and 1895 Yeats got to know him well, dedicating *The Rose* (1893) to him. No doubt Yeats envied his scholarship and his assured manner when dealing with people. But there was a conflict in Lionel Johnson's life, which was to be his undoing, a struggle to achieve a Unity of Being in a world which shunned the artist. He wished to be a solitary man, yet had not the strength to be; to make his life a ritual devoted to art, a follower of Walter Pater, yet he could not separate art from life satisfactorily. But he certainly did not hold with 'Art for art's sake' as a doctrine. 'I have spent years in trying to understand what is meant by that imbecile phrase', he told the Irish Literary Society in 1894. His lack of inner strength lead to mental instability, to insomnia, and then to a chronic alcoholism resulting in his early death. Yeats remembers him in 'The Grey Rock.' CP, p.115.

130

> Since, tavern comrades, you have died,
> Maybe your images have stood,
> Mere bone and muscle thrown aside,
> Before that roomful or as good,
> You have to face your ends when young—
> 'Twas wine or women, or some curse—
> But never made a poorer song
> That you might have a heavier purse,
> Nor gave the loud service to a cause
> That you might have a troop of friends.
> You kept the Muses' sterner laws,
> And unrepenting faced your ends,
> And therefore earned the right—and yet
> Dowson and Johnson most I praise—
> To troop with those the world's forgot,
> And copy their proud steady gaze.

Later in life, Yeats discovered that Johnson had never met the people he claimed to have done, that

> he never met anybody, because he got up at nightfall, got drunk at a public-house or worked half the night, sat the other half, a glass of whisky at his elbow, staring at the brown corduroy curtains that protected from dust the books that lined his walls, imagining the puppets that were the true companions of his mind.

He died in hospital after he had slipped on the polished floor of an inn, fracturing his skull. In 'The Tragic Generation' (*AU*, IV), Yeats wonders why so many of these poets of the 1890s made such a mess of their lives, and he comes to the conclusion that 'souls turned from practical ends become contemplative but not yet ready for the impress of the divine will, an unendurable burden'.

Lionel Johnson receives a final tribute in 'In Memory of Major Robert Gregory' (*CP*, p.148), along with John Synge and George Pollexfen, thereby witnessing to the deep influence which these three had on Yeats's life.

> They were my close companions many a year,
> A portion of my mind and life, as it were,
> What portion in the world can the artist have
> Who has awakened from the common dream
> But dissipation and despair?

('Ego Dominus Tuus', *CP*, p.180)

Ellmann (*Yeats: the Man and the Masks*, p.75) is less than fair when he writes of the nineties: 'The last decade of the century is thronged by extravagant poseurs.' Beardsley's graphic brilliance of line in his black and white drawings dominated the nineties, and Johnson, as well as being an excellent literary critic, wrote lyric verse which Yeats thought worthy to be included in *The Oxford Book of Modern Verse*, singular though his selection sometimes was. Their aesthete philosophy was derived from the example of the writings of Walter Pater. Yeats, shy and diffident as a young man, felt inferior to Johnson when he first met him. In 'The Grey Rock' he acknowledges the real integrity of these men who, like himself, were dedicated poets.

Sir Hugh Lane, 1875–1915

Hugh Lane was born at Ballybrack, County Cork, the son of a penniless parson who had married Adelaide Persse, Lady Gregory's sister. His parents separated and it was left to Lady Gregory to plan his future. She arranged for him to be trained at Colnaghi, the Fine Art dealers in Old Bond Street, London. In a short time he had shown much talent and had started his own gallery, where he was able to sell Old Masters and to buy French Impressionists. Soon he was arranging exhibitions of the work of Irish artists, including Jack Yeats, in Dublin and London. In 1908 he became the founder of a Gallery of Modern Art in Dublin, bequeathing 154 works, but specifying that a special gallery should be built to house them. Lady Gregory in her *Journals, 1916–1930* (edited by Lennox Robinson, p.284) writes thus of Lane, her favourite nephew:

> His career was meteoric; it reads like a Balzac novel. Spending nothing on himself (except perhaps on his clothes, for I always remember him as immaculately dressed), lunching on a bun and cup of tea, living in his lovely house in Chelsea, he would not afford a fire in his bedroom, though downstairs there would be hanging a noble Titian . . . one of the most lovely Goyas in existence, and other pictures worth thousands of pounds—nor would he afford himself a taxi. In 1909 he was knighted.

This description of him goes some way to explain Yeats's phrases about Parnell, Lady Gregory and Lane—'All that delirium of the brave', that frenzied excitement in living, that quality of 'passionate serving'. This contrasted with the mediocrity of Dublin Corporation, which refused to provide money to house thirty-nine of his best pictures, including Renoir's magnificent *Les Parapluies*. Lane in consequence left them to the National Gallery, London. However, in subsequent years, relations with Dublin improved, and as most of his collection in London, including the Renoir, was being housed in cellars, Lane wrote a codicil to his will in February 1915, reversing his decision to bequeath the pictures to London, giving them to Dublin instead. Unfortunately, he failed to get a witness to his signature. Coming back from U.S.A. in May of that year, he was drowned in the *Lusitania*, the liner torpedoed by a German submarine.

Yeats saw Lane as a proud man, arrogant to his enemies, and defeated by the meanness of popular passions. Like Parnell he was hounded by men of small minds who placed little value on what he stood for: a heroic figure therefore. So in 'An Appointment' (*Responsibilities*; *CP*, p.141), Yeats shows his contempt for the representatives of petty bureaucracy. Meanwhile, as Lane's Trustee, Lady Gregory was labouring to get the pictures back to Dublin, but English lawyers eventually declared that the unwitnessed codicil was legally valueless. (Not until 1959 was agreement reached: the collection now is half in Dublin and half in London, exchanges taking place, though it is still owned by the National Gallery, London.) In five poems (*CP*, pp.119–23) Yeats sears the hated bourgeoisie who have opposed his heroic figures. 'To a Wealthy Man who promised a Second Subscription to the Dublin Municipal Gallery if it were proved the People wanted Pictures' makes it clear that Yeats thinks that in aesthetic matters the people have to be led. He is no believer in democracy in art, and cites the work of three autocratic Italian Renaissance rulers, including Guidobaldo da Montefeltro, of Urbino (see below p.188) 'September 1913' (*CP*, p.120) compares the Ireland of the 1898 rebellion with the contemporary dried-up state, in Yeats's white-hot rhetoric, which upset so many of the Irish political leaders of the time.

> Was it for this the wild geese spread
> The grey wing upon every tide;
> For this that all that blood was shed,
> For this Edward Fitzgerald died,
> And Robert Emmet and Wolfe Tone,
> All that delirium of the brave?
> Romantic Ireland's dead and gone,
> It's with O'Leary in the grave.

'To a Friend whose Work has come to Nothing' is addressed to Lady Gregory, after her failure over the pictures. 'Paudeen', like all these poems, has a reference to loneliness and solitariness as an integral part of heroic strength—the curlew in this poem; the wild geese, the Irish exiles after the Boyne, in 'September 1913'; the eagle's nest in 'To a Wealthy Man . . .'. 'To a Shade' sums up the qualities which Parnell, Lane and Lady Gregory showed in their life work: 'their children's children loftier thought'. Yeats outlines the background to these poems in a note, *CP*, pp.529–31. Lady Gregory may have failed in her task, but at least she failed triumphantly, and Hugh Lane has achieved an immortality in these poems which he would not otherwise have gained.

Major John MacBride, 1865–1916

Described in *Hone* as 'a red-headed, high-spirited Celt', he was born at Westport, County Mayo; when a boy, joined the I.R.B.; was second-in-command of the Irish Transvaal Brigade against the British in the Boer War; married Maud Gonne in 1903; legally separated from her two years later. He knew nothing of the preparations for the Easter Rising, but when the G.P.O. was fortified he immediately offered his services to Thomas MacDonagh at his post; possibly the only leader who had been under fire before; court-martialled and shot.

Yeats had first proposed marriage to Maud Gonne in 1891, and when he received news in U.S.A. of her marriage to John MacBride, he was overwhelmingly shocked, especially as both he and her friends thought it a most unsuitable match—which it certainly was. But after MacBride's execution by the firing squad in 1916, Yeats includes him with the heroes to be remembered, even though he was 'a drunken, vainglorious lout' who had done Yeats 'most bitter wrong'.

> He, too, has resigned his part
> In the casual comedy;
> He too, has been changed in his turn,
> Transformed utterly:
> A terrible beauty is born.
>
> (*CP*, p.203)

Thomas MacDonagh, 1878–1916

In 'Easter 1916' (*CP*, p.202) MacDonagh is the first of the four heroes; mentioned also in verse two of 'Sixteen Dead Men' (*CP*, p.205). He was born in County Tipperary, father a schoolteacher, mother English. When in his early twenties he lived more than a year in Paris, and spoke fluent French. He was on the staff at St Enda's (see below, p.143) from 1908, Gaelic speaking therefore; University College lecturer; wrote *Literature in Ireland*; married, two children. A leader of the I.R.B. and one of the signatories of the Proclamation; executed with the others—a tragic loss: a poet, scholar, musician, just 'coming into his force'.

Yeats first met him in 1909 and thought him 'a man with some literary faculty which will probably come to nothing through lack of culture and encouragement' ('Estrangement', *AU*, p.488). At the time, 'The Green Helmet' period, Yeats was bitter about Ireland, and this is scant praise for MacDonagh; however, he does go on to say, 'in England this man would have become remarkable in some way'.

Countess de Markievicz, 1868–1927

Constance, the elder of the two Gore-Booth sisters whom Yeats visited at Lissadell House (see below pp.178–9): married in 1900 a Polish artist, Count Casimir de Markievicz. A daughter Maeve (born in 1901), was brought up by her grandmother, Lady Gore-Booth, and saw her mother so little she did not recognize her in 1921. Constance was temperamentally a rebel against the Anglo-Irish landed class into which she had been born, and always backed the underdog with passionate and fiery intensity. Devoted her life from 1908 to the welfare of the Irish poor and freeing Ireland from English rule. Supported James Connolly in the transport workers' strike in 1913; and in the Easter Rising 1916 was second-in-command at the post on St Stephen's Green. She was sentenced to death for her part in the Rising, but the sentence was commuted to life imprisonment ('On a Political Prisoner', *CP*, p.206). She was released in 1917 and for the next ten years, until her death, she played a part in Irish politics. Was Secretary for Labour in the Dail cabinet in 1920; backed the Republicans ('Irregulars') in 1922; eventually supported de Valera on how a settlement should be made with England, thereby being opposed to Yeats. In addition, Yeats was appalled at her downfall, as he thought, from the beautiful and courageous rider with the County Sligo Harriers to the conspirator among ignorant men. Maybe the Easter Rising 'changed, changed utterly' her as well as the other leaders, but he regrets it in her case as a betrayal of her tradition:

> That woman's days were spent
> In ignorant good-will,
> Her nights in argument
> Until her voice grew shrill.
> What voice more sweet than hers
> When, young and beautiful,
> She rode to harriers?

She died in a hospital in a slum quarter of Dublin, at her own wish among the poor, thousands of whom followed her coffin at a public funeral. There is a limestone bust of her on St Stephen's Green; of two biographies the first, by Anne Marreco, *The Rebel Countess*, is inclined to gloss over her faults; the second, by Seán O'Faoláin, *Constance Markievicz*, is more objective.

John Masefield, O.M., 1878–1967

Masefield first met Yeats in the 1890s when he used to attend the 'Monday evenings' at Woburn Buildings (see below, pp.183–5). But he had seen much of life before that, having left school at the age of fifteen to become an apprentice on a windjammer which sailed round

Cape Horn; subsequently he was for three years in New York. He was invited to Coole by Lady Gregory, who liked him as a person but was not impressed by his poetic talents. His full and successful life as poet, editor, critic, novelist and autobiographer is well known. In 1930 he became Poet Laureate on the death of Robert Bridges; in 1935 was awarded the Order of Merit.

Masefield's *Some Memories of W. B. Yeats* (1940) is the best account of the Woburn Buildings house and its visitors. When the Yeatses were at Broad Street, Oxford (see below, p.185), Masefield lived on Boar's Hill nearby, and used to visit them and invite them to his home. He and his wife also visited the Yeatses at Riversdale, Rathfarnham, in 1935, for the Irish poet's seventieth birthday party (13 June). In 1963, at the age of eighty-five, he went to London to protest against the possible demolition of 18 Woburn Buildings, but was reassured that the interior of Yeats's sitting-room would be preserved as far as possible, despite extensions to an hotel. His final tribute, 'On what he was', are lines full of warmth, written in the Georgian poetic style one associates with Masefield. Very different was W. H. Auden's 'In Memory of W. B. Yeats' (1940), in which such lines as 'for poetry makes nothing happen', a sentiment far removed from Yeats's philosophy, though integral to Auden's, are typical of Auden's egocentric approach throughout the poem. Similarly, we are shocked by Auden's 'You were silly like us', for Yeats may have been silly, but never like Auden. On the other hand, Masefield's sensitive relevance sounds a sympathetic note, though Yeats would not have agreed that beauty was one of the mainsprings of his poetry:

> He died far from the trotting of the donkeys
> With the turf-creels; far from the smell of peat,
> And Sligo pier, where the ear-ringed pilots talked;
> Far from those sea-marks which henceforth all seamen
> Will note with thought of him.
>   By the bright sea
> He changed this life, beside a dancing-floor
> Where beauty is created day by day.

MacGregor Mathers, 1855–1918

'A well-read man, keen of visage, who talked in a deep voice and pretended to know more than he did' is how *Hone* describes him, and Yeats in 'The Trembling of the Veil. Four Years 1887–1891' *AU*, says he had 'much learning but little scholarship, much imagination and imperfect taste'. When Yeats first saw him he was copying

Constance Gore-Booth dressed for a Ball at Dublin Castle.

ancient manuscripts from occult books in the British Museum Reading Room, and later, after an introduction, he told Yeats of the Order of the Golden Dawn and the temple of the Order he had founded in London (see below p.45). Mathers was the author of *The Kabbalah Unveiled* (1887) in which he tried to prove that the learning of the Jews from Moses, passed down in Jewish tradition, had, through white magic, influenced Egyptian occult thought and, later, Pythagoras—an enthusiastic but inaccurate estimate.

Yeats met Mathers twice in Paris, where he had gone to live: in 1894 and two years later to discuss with him an Order of Celtic Mysteries (see below, p.47). In 1900 they had a quarrel about the organization and control of the Order of the Golden Dawn in which Yeats and Florence Emery were the equivalent of committee members, and thereafter Yeats never saw Mathers again. He died in Paris and was survived by his wife who was clairvoyante and the sister of Henri Bergson, the philosopher. The extent of his influence on Yeats's thought was considerable, so he was included with Florence Emery and W. T. Horton, a fellow adept, in 'All Souls Night' (*CP*, p.265).

Seán O'Casey, 1880–1964

There are no direct or indirect references to O'Casey in *CP*, but his views of Yeats and Lady Gregory in the six volumes of his *Autobiography*, show how he appreciated their personal virtues and the excellence of their work, although he himself came from a totally different background.

He was born in a Dublin tenement, of Protestant parents, and had a rough early life earning just enough money to keep himself alive in a variety of jobs. After initial failures he got *The Shadow of a Gunman* (1923) accepted by the Abbey Theatre, and afterwards *Juno and the Paycock* (1924): both tragi-comedies of slum life, with witty, shrewd dialogue, strong characterization, and much sardonic criticism of Irish weaknesses. On account of the last characteristic they were not popular with Irish audiences, and riots, similar to those during Synge's *Playboy of the Western World*, took place in the theatre. Lady Gregory and Yeats backed him fully, and in his autobiography, *Inishfallen, Fare Thee Well* there are warm references to Lady Gregory. (see above, p.127):

> I owe a great deal to you, Lady Gregory, to Mr Yeats, and to Mr Robinson [the Director of the Abbey Theatre], but to you above all. It was you said to me, 'Mr O'Casey, your gift is characterization'; and so I threw away my theories, worked at characters, and *The Shadow of a Gunman* is the result.

Unfortunately, Yeats and Lady Gregory refused to have O'Casey's

138

The Silver Tassie for the Abbey Theatre, a decision they afterwards regretted, as did O'Casey who refused to see Lady Gregory in London some years later (1929).

Fundamentally, O'Casey was a rebel, as was Lady Gregory, and he had a faith in life, as had Yeats.

General Eoin O'Duffy, 1892–1944

After Eamon de Valera and Fianna Fail, the Republican party had won the election in the Irish Free State in February 1932, certain members of the I.R.A. were released from prison. But they were suspected of having Communist sympathies, and indeed some of them had been to Moscow. To counteract this, in common with Germany and Italy, a movement grew in the country to oppose these tendencies. It had as many as 30,000 members, who wore blue shirts, drilled and saluted in a Fascist manner. Its leader was General Eoin O'Duffy, who for twelve years had been Police Commissioner of the Irish Free State government before being dismissed by de Valera. O'Duffy openly sought the end of parliamentary democracy (which he called an English growth), and described Hitler and Mussolini as great leaders. Then he formed a National Guard, blueshirted, which, incidentally, received the backing of the Church. By 1938 de Valera's law courts had imprisoned many of the Blueshirts as well as I.R.A. officers, and the former movement fizzled out, O'Duffy going off to Spain to support Franco abortively in the Spanish Civil War. For more information, see Maurice Manning, *The Blueshirts*, 1970.

In 1933, Yeats was momentarily interested in the movement. A Blueshirt friend, Captain Dermot MacManus, who often visited Riversdale, brought with him once, and once only, General O'Duffy, to whom Yeats on this occasion talked philosophy, which O'Duffy would certainly not have understood. But Yeats wrote for him at his request 'Three Songs to the Same Tune' (*CP*, p.320), which he rewrote when he discovered that the new party's ideals were not his, as *Hone* says (p.436), 'increasing their fantasy, their extravagance, so that no party could sing them'. And it would certainly not have been possible to march to them, even in their revised version, 'Three Marching Songs' (*CP*, p.377).

Other than wanting a political party which had a disciplined way of life, Yeats realized in his old age that he had had enough of politics. He makes this position absolutely clear in a letter to a friend:

> Do not try to make a politician out of me, even in Ireland I shall never I think be that again—as my sense of reality deepens & I think it does with age, my horror at the cruelty of governments grows greater, . . . Communist, fascist, nationalist, clerical, anti-clerical are all responsible according to the number of their victims. I have not been silent, I have used the only vehicle I

possess—verse. If you have my poems by you look up a poem called 'The Second Coming'. It was written some sixteen or seventeen years ago & foretold what is happening. . . . I am not callous, every nerve trembles with horror at what is happening in Europe 'the ceremony of innocence is drowned'.

However, the Fascist label stuck to Yeats, and Edward Norman, author of *A History of Modern Ireland* (1971), recently wrote, without any further qualification: 'And the Blueshirts had, predictably, got the support of those who watched over Ireland's culture. Yeats was a firm supporter.' Dr Norman must be thinking of those beautiful sky-blue shirts which Yeats often wore, as Richard Ellmann says, not for political but aesthetic reasons.

Standish O'Grady, 1846–1928

From the Protestant landed class, O'Grady was educated at Trinity College, Dublin. He wrote a *History of Ireland* (1881), mostly about the old Irish heroes, Finn, Oisín and Cuchulain, with very little history. However, he was the real creator of the Gaelic revival, his translating of the Irish legends, though not so able as Lady Gregory's subsequently, bringing the Celtic past to the ordinary reader for the first time. Similarly, such books as his *Early Bardic History* (1879) really started the Celtic revival.

Louis MacNeice (*The Poetry of W. B. Yeats*, p.74) points out an important difference between the Irish and the English in their attitude to their folk legends; and MacNeice, with his split Irish and English background, understands both peoples. He thinks that these imaginative periods from folk times

> are not in fact separated from modern Ireland by the same great gulf that separates modern England from the Round Table. Ireland has remained a far more primitive country in which the primitive saga-virtues still awake echoes among the people at large. It is not a mere affectation that a statue of Cuchulain stands in the Dublin Post Office as a memorial to the 1916 rebels.

Furthermore, there are countless native legends in Ireland, whereas King Arthur seems to be the sole English one. Also, long ancestral memories so common in Ireland are virtually unknown in England: for example, I once talked with an Irish countrywoman about Oliver Cromwell as if he had been living recently.

According to AE, O'Grady was 'the most conscientious and honourable man in public life in Ireland', and John Quinn ranks him with Douglas Hyde as being one of only three people in the Dublin literary world 'who did not say anything malicious about others'. So the position of O'Grady as the third of the Olympians in

'Beautiful Lofty Things' (*CP*, p.348), is not strange. In each case Yeats remembers the person by his bearing at one particular moment, and especially in the position of his or her head, implying pride, control, inner strength and magnanimity. The fact that Yeats is able to exalt such banal subjects as awaiting a local train or speech-making at a banquet, shows how marvellously by *Last Poems* he manages his verse, in this case in alexandrines. In *AU* (p.422), Yeats gives an account of Standish O'Grady speaking at a dinner given for the poet. Like the rest of the guests, O'Grady had had plenty to drink, yet he never betrayed it, for he spoke with style and wit, in a low, sweet voice, with noble gesture.

> Standish O'Grady supporting himself between the tables
> Speaking to a drunken audience high nonsensical words.

Kevin O'Higgins, 1892–1927

Kevin O'Higgins was born in County Leix. After taking his B.A. at University College, Dublin, he became a lawyer, and later a minister in the first Free State Government under Cosgrave, 1922. The country was then in a state of civil war, guerrilla forces of the I.R.A. being in arms against Government troops. But the Government somehow managed to preserve the upper hand, and the Senate, with Yeats as a member (see Gazetteer, 'Dublin. Merrion Square' below), was convened at the end of the year, although the rebels declared they would shoot all senators at sight. Yeats's friend, Senator Oliver Gogarty was taken off by armed men, but managed to escape by jumping at night into the swollen waters of the Liffey; and the houses of thirty-seven senators were burnt to the ground, including Renvyle, Gogarty's house in Connemara, where Yeats had been staying when Augustus John painted his portrait. In May 1923 there was a cease-fire and the government started on constructive plans for the future. O'Higgins was the outstanding minister of this Government and showed statesmanlike judgment in trying for a rapprochement between Ulster and the Free State; he also made a major contribution to the drafting of the Statute of Westminster at the Imperial Conference (1926).

He was altogether exceptional: an honest, liberal-minded politician, who fearlessly spoke out and would act if he thought it right, whatever the cost. Winston Churchill described him as 'a figure from the Antique, cast in bronze'. Yeats knew him well as a personal friend, his wife and he often visiting Mr and Mrs O'Higgins's house in Dublin. He also admired O'Higgins's writing and speeches in the Dail, which he thought resembled those of Burke in the eighteenth-century tradition. On 10 August 1927 as O'Higgins walked to Mass he was brutally assassinated by terrorists. The whole of Ireland, and,

141

of course, Yeats, were profoundly shocked by this savage murder of a man who showed such promise for the future. 'Death' (*CP*, p.264), directly deals with O'Higgins's heroic qualities in the face of death, the sibilants hissing his disdain:

> A great man in his pride
> Confronting murderous men
> Casts derision upon
> Supersession of breath.

Some years later, as Yeats walks round the Municipal Gallery, he comments on O'Higgins's portrait among those of the makers of modern Ireland (*CP*, p.368). 'Blood and the Moon' (*CP*, p.267), is influenced by O'Higgins's murder in glorifying the tower and the winding-stair, those symbols which Yeats uses not only for himself but also for the four Anglo-Irish writers, Goldsmith, Swift, Berkeley and Burke, whose qualities he most admires. He was not listed by Yeats with de Valera and Cosgrave, those politicians who were unable to 'eat' Parnell's heart, that is to say, take on some of the great qualities of Parnell (*CP*, p.320). O'Higgins, the 'sole statesman' would not have died had they inherited some of Parnell's virtues.

John O'Leary, 1830–1907

Born in County Tipperary, O'Leary became a medical student at Trinity College, where he joined the revolutionary Fenian Brotherhood, and edited *The Irish People*, official Irish Republican Brotherhood newspaper. In 1863, after a trial, being convicted of treason and felony he was sentenced to twenty years penal servitude in England, but was released in 1870 on condition he did not return to Ireland for fifteen years. On his return after his exile, he met Yeats and seemed venerable to the young poet, although he cannot have been more than in his middle fifties. A wonderful friendship grew up between the two despite their difference in age: O'Leary respected Yeats's integrity, Yeats acknowledged that 'from O'Leary's conversation and from the Irish books he lent or gave me has come all I have set my hand to since'. The poems of Thomas Davis (1814–45) and other patriotic literature of the eighteenth and nineteenth centuries were chief among these.

> Nor may I less be counted one
> With Davis, Mangan, Ferguson,
> Because, to him who ponders well,
> My rhymes more than their rhyming tell
> Of things discovered in the deep
> Where only body's laid asleep.

Thus in 'To Ireland in the coming times' (*CP*, p.56) Yeats allies himself with the Irish patriot poets, but also adds, in the last couplet, his indebtedness to magic, of which O'Leary disapproved. So Yeats wrote to him to allay his suspicions: 'If I had not made magic my constant study I could not have written a single word of my Blake books, nor would The Countess Cathleen have ever come to exist. The mystical life is the centre of all that I do and all that I think and all that I write.'

O'Leary possessed a generosity of spirit, bred in suffering, which Yeats immediately recognized as the opposite of an ambitious politician. He was venerable and bearded, a sage, who was the subject of more than one portrait by J. B. Yeats. Of ancient Roman virtue and moral integrity, he became for Yeats the personification of god-like nobleness; one of the heroic, lonely figures, first in the ranks of the Olympians: 'Beautiful lofty things: O'Leary's noble head.'

In 1889 he helped Yeats by being chiefly responsible for obtaining subscribers to enable him to have published *The Wanderings of Oisín*; in 1891 Yeats was sharing lodgings with him in Dublin when the news of Parnell's death in Brighton reached them; at that time O'Leary was President of the newly formed Irish Literary Society (see *AU*, p.209 ff). He was President of the Supreme Council of the I.R.B. until his death, on St Patrick's Day 1907. Six years later Yeats thought of it as the end of an era:

> Romantic Ireland's dead and gone,
> It's with O'Leary in the grave.

> 'September 1913' (*CP*, p.120)

Pádraic Pearse, 1880–1916

Pearse's father was a Devon man who had settled in Dublin as a monumental mason, and married an Irish country-woman. Pádraic, the eldest of four children, became a member of the Irish Bar, an enthusiastic supporter of the Gaelic League, a fine Gaelic scholar, a passionate orator, and founder (1908) and headmaster of St Enda's School for boys, one of the few lay schools in the country, and one which Yeats visited. He seems to have been dedicated from his early years to the freeing of Ireland from the English, and his life showed certain austere features fitting this dedication. In his lectures to American audiences when he was touring U.S.A. 1932–33, Yeats spoke of Pádraic Pearse and his younger brother, William:

> Three or four years after the betrayal of Parnell two little boys, sons of a Dublin stone mason, knelt down beside their beds and prayed that they might sacrifice their lives for Ireland. In their early

143

twenties, I saw them occasionally: they would come to the Abbey Theatre for some reason or other. I think they hired it for some concert or public meetings.

More likely it was hired for political meetings, as Pádraic rarely relaxed socially or visited a theatre, never drank alcohol or smoked, and was unmarried.

The fixation of a Blood Sacrifice was to be consummated sooner than anyone expected. In 1913 the Irish Volunteers were formed after a large meeting in Dublin, the committee including Pearse and The O'Rahilly. Soon 10,000 had enrolled, Eamon de Valera, a mathematics teacher among them. The movement went from strength to strength, despite not receiving official backing from the Irish Republican Brotherhood; and the Gaelic League became political as well as literary (see Gazetteer, Dublin, Trinity College, below, for Pearse and Yeats speaking at the Antient Concert Rooms in 1914). In April 1916, after a meeting in Liberty Hall, Dublin, the Volunteers, led by Pearse as Commander-in-Chief, issued a Manifesto, obviously written by him, to the people of Ireland declaring a Provisional Government of the Irish Republic 'as a Sovereign Independent State'. On Easter Monday, about sixty armed Volunteers entered the General Post Office, ejected the staff and civilians who happened to be there and fortified the building. At the same time, other strategic positions in the city were occupied. The week of the Rising has been well documented and photographed: *Protest in Arms* by Edgar Holt, and *Easter Rebellion* by Max Caulfield both give admirable accounts. After five days, about 2000 rebels with rifles only had held at bay nearly ten times that number of British troops armed with machine-guns, artillery and a gun-boat. But the Rising was not generally popular on account of the material damage done to the city, and on the Thursday, Pearse in the G.P.O. realized it was ultimately doomed. At the end of the week the rebels capitulated. Then followed, from 3 May to 12 May, a protracted series of courts-martial which produced a violent revulsion of feeling as two or three of the leaders were executed each day. Pearse knew they would be more powerful in death than life and declared at his trial: 'We seem to have lost, but we have not lost; we have kept faith with the past and handed on a tradition to the future.'

Yeats was in England and wrote at once to Lady Gregory at Coole: 'I have little doubt there have been many miscarriages of justice. ... I am trying to write a poem on the men executed "terrible beauty has been born again" ... I had no idea that any public event could so deeply move me and I am very despondent about the future.'

The General Post Office after the Easter Rising, 1916.

Yeats was then more than fifty years old, and had obviously never lost that awareness of responsibility which he had had as a young man after the Jubilee riots in which Maud Gonne was concerned. In 'The Man and the Echo', Yeats emphasizes this point many years later:

> All that I have said and done,
> Now that I am old and ill,
> Turns into a question till
> I lie awake night after night
> And never get the answers right.

(CP, p.393)

In September, he finished 'Easter 1916' (*CP*, p.202), the first of the four poems of homage to the Easter martyrs. He starts by thinking of his meeting these men in ordinary life in Dublin, and speaking 'polite meaningless' words to them. Then abruptly he changes the tone, switching to the incantatory refrain of the poem:

> All changed, changed utterly:
> A terrible beauty is born.

He later used this powerful oxymoron 'terrible beauty' when he was commenting upon a short story of Oscar Wilde's, which he quotes in its original form, before Wilde lengthened it, in *The Trembling of the Veil*, IV (*AU*). In both this poem and the Wilde story there is a narrative of tragic action, having its tragedy in the ambiguity of its motivation, concerned with death, and set in a street. Yet the meaning of 'terrible' is not altogether clear, for the word has become threadbare through colloquial usage—a long way from the soul-searing *terribilità* of Dante's vision. In the second stanza of 'Easter 1916', Yeats outlines the characteristics of the four leaders whom he knew. In the third he compares the rock-like integrity of their hearts with the mutations of natural phenomena. The 'terrible beauty' is the result of their single-ness of purpose and dedication—especially in the case of Pearse—which changes them utterly. They become terrifyingly strange and cold in their beautiful unity of mind and action with regard to their consecrated task.

> Hearts with one purpose alone
> Through summer and winter seem
> Enchanted to a stone
> To trouble the living stream.

Natural life, 'the living stream', changes by the minute; but not these passionate, devoted men and women. He accounts for this in one of the many memorable poetic phrases which make 'Easter 1916' one of the greatest poems of this century:

> And what if excess of love
> Bewildered them till they died?

He answers with the final prophetic refrain, uttered with granite certainty:

> I write it out in a verse—
> MacDonagh and MacBride
> And Connolly and Pearse,
> Now and in time to be,
> Wherever green is worn,
> Are changed, changed utterly:
> A terrible beauty is born.

In the short, ballad-type poem, 'Sixteen Dead Men' (*CP*, p.205), he is again concerned with the correctness of the timing of the Rising. But he decides that heroes are men who would not consider the matter in the same light as we who 'meddle with give and take', for they converse 'bone to bone'—an image like that of stone which Yeats constantly uses for hard, essential matters. 'The Rose Tree' (*CP*, p.206), written in 1920, is introduced as a duologue between Pearse and Connolly. The politicians (de Valera and Lloyd George?) have caused the Rose Tree to wither, and there is bitterness in the final verse of the poem.

The ennoblement of the heroes of the Rising rings out in Yeats's verse until 'Last Poems'. The detail of 'The O'Rahilly' (*CP*, p.354)— his not being told of the Rising, his arrival in Dublin, his mortal wound from which he wrote his signature in blood—is told with a ballad simplicity which is very moving, because the miracle of transmutation in sacrifice is still the key:

> What remains to sing about
> But of the death he met
> Stretched under a doorway
> Somewhere off Henry Street;
> They that found him found upon
> The door above his head
> 'Here died the O'Rahilly.
> R.I.P.' writ in blood.
> *How goes the weather?*

The refrain, conventionally used by seamen upon the ship's bridge before a possible storm, implies heroic action, but also may be taken like Plato's ghost's question, 'What then?', to express doubt in the future of the political climate.

Finally, in 'The Statues' (*CP*, p.375), the heroic Pearse is chosen as the supreme prototype of action rather than thought. 'Few men have passed from thought to action with so deadly a thoroughness and sincerity'. Yeats takes classical statuary as philosophy in action, governed as it is by measurement in which every feature is planned with Pythagorean wisdom, though now submerged in the dark sea of the modern world. In the final stanza, Greek myth and Irish legend are combined, and time is foreshortened.

Yeats saw the Easter Rising not as the work of politicians, but of heroes who in the moment of death transcended all their intellectual limitations and found themselves complete. As Cuchulain, fastened to a pillar when dying, was surrounded by the spirit presences of Ireland, so with the martyrs of the Rising. This was not the intellectual nationalism of the politician but the moment of fulfilment of the hero, and that for Yeats was sole reality.

> Some had no thought of victory
> But had gone out to die
> That Ireland's mind be greater,
> Her heart mount up on high;
> And yet who knows what's yet to come?
> For Patrick Pearse had said
> That in every generation
> Must Ireland's blood be shed.
> *From mountain to mountain ride the fierce horsemen.*

(CP, p.373)

George Pollexfen, 1840–1910

Yeats's bachelor uncle with whom he used to stay at Sligo from childhood on for many summers—in fact until he was invited to Coole by Lady Gregory in 1896. Uncle George had been a fine amateur rider and still kept a racehorse, but he had given up riding by the time Yeats was a young man, and the eccentric, unbalanced strain in the Pollexfens had started to appear in his acute hypochondria and the wilful discomfort of his living conditions, despite his being a rich man. He was always interested in astrology and the Kabbala, as well as horoscopes which he could make; all this much absorbed Yeats when he visited him. Verse five of 'In Memory of Major Robert Gregory' (*CP*, p.149), written in 1918, mentions George Pollexfen's decline from equestrian activity to a 'sluggish and contemplative' life.

'In Memory of Alfred Pollexfen' (*CP*, p.176), written three years earlier, and a somewhat undistinguished poem, is an early indication of Yeats's ancestor worship, particularly for the Pollexfen relatives at Sligo; Old William Pollexfen and his sons—John, 'the sailor John' referred to, George and Alfred, his younger brother. The poem is written in four-footed lines, which was to become a constant feature of his later verse with a rhyme scheme which was much more skilfully concealed by enjambement and internal rhythms than this is:

148

> And Masons drove from miles away
> To scatter the Acacia spray
> Upon a melancholy man
> Who had ended where his breath began.

Yeats describes the funeral in 'Reveries over Childhood and Youth'
(*AU*, pp.67–74). He was much moved by the simplicity of the
ceremony, although there were two thousand people present and it
was the largest funeral at Sligo in living memory. Many freemasons
cast 'acacia spray' in the tomb in St John's churchyard, with the
words, 'Alas my brother so mote it be'; and after it Yeats wrote to
Lady Gregory comparing the ceremony with Synge's recent funeral,
attended 'by none . . . after some two or three but enemies or conventional images of gloom'.

George left £50,000 to his brothers and sisters, all of whom were
well-off, but none to any of Yeats's relations, much to the disappoint-
ment of Yeats's father, who was his brother-in-law and oldest friend,
and much in need of money at the time.

Ezra Pound, 1885–1972

Pound first met Yeats in London in 1908 and declared him to be the
only contemporary poet worthy of serious study, regarding him as a
bridge between the Symbolists and Mallarmé. He often went to
Yeats's Monday evenings at Woburn Buildings in the winter of
1912–13 (see below pp.183–5). Having persuaded Yeats to contribute
to *Poetry*, October 1912, as editor he made changes in the poem
'Fallen Majesty' (*CP*, p.138), which Yeats sent (see Ellmann, *Eminent
Domain*, p.64). Yeats visited Pound at Stone Cottage (see p.186) during
the winters of 1913, 1914 and 1915. Pound's *Pisan Cantos*, Canto
LXXXIII refers:

> so that I recalled the noise in the chimney
> as it were the wind in the chimney
> but was in reality Uncle William
> downstairs composing.
>
> . . .
>
> at Stone cottage in Sussex by the waste moor

Pound edited Professor Ernest Fenellosa's translations of the Japanese
Noh plays, which were to have much influence on Yeats's playwriting.
In April 1914 he married Dorothy Shakespear, the daughter of
Olivia Shakespear. He was best man to Yeats at his wedding in
London; met Yeats in Paris, 1922; in Sicily, 1925; in Rapallo, 1928,
1929–30 and 1934; and again in London in 1938.

After Synge's death, Pound took his place as Yeats's major friend.
Though he was twenty years younger, and referred to Yeats as
'Uncle William' or 'Old Billyum', the relationship was on equal

terms, each taking notice of the other's suggestions, despite Pound being poetically more experimental than Yeats, and therefore less apt to take advice. Canto LXXXIII was never seen by Yeats, but he would have liked

the sage

delighteth in water
the humane man has amity with the hills

as the grass grows by the weirs
thought Uncle William . . .

John Quinn, 1870–1924

There is no direct or indirect reference to Quinn in *CP*, but for many years he was a friend and patron in New York of Yeats and his brother Jack, of AE, Douglas Hyde and Lady Gregory. The son of Irish immigrant parents, he became a very rich man through a successful practice as a financial lawyer in New York. He arranged Yeats's 1903 lecture tour in U.S.A.; helped him financially, bought some of his MSS and his brother's pictures; supported J. B. Yeats in U.S.A. by finding him rich sitters for portraits; played a leading part in the Irish Literary Society in New York. Visited Coole in 1903 and 1904, and, after his return to New York, his letters (unpublished) to Lady Gregory reveal the deep intimacy of their friendship.

He was somewhat dictatorial in manner; but was generous, well-read and able to hold his own in literary and philosophic discussions with AE and Yeats. He had a fine sense of a worthwhile painter, even if in an avant-garde style, and owned many fine modern pictures. He was invaluable to Yeats, Eliot, James Joyce and Jack Yeats as a patron.

Margot Ruddock, 1907–1951

Margot Ruddock first met Yeats in 1934; she was an actress and poetess engaged in establishing a theatre for poetic drama, in which T. S. Eliot was interested; she also knew Purohit swami, who taught her. Yeats and she met often in 1935 and corresponded about her poetry until he went to Majorca (see below pp.192–3).

While he was in Palma with the swami, she suddenly appeared, having had a mental breakdown in London caused by spiritual problems and domestic worries. When under stress she had shown signs of schizophrenia for some years. Yeats describes her arrival in a letter to Olivia Shakespear:

> She walked in at 6.30 [a.m.], her luggage in her hand, and, when she had been given breakfast, she said she had come to find out if

150

her verse was any good. I had known her for some years and had told her to stop writing as her technique was getting worse. I was amazed by the tragic significance of some fragment and said so. She went out in pouring rain, thought, as she said afterwards, that if she killed herself her verse would live instead of her, went to the shore to jump in, then thought she loved life and began to dance. . . . Next day she went to Barcelona and there went mad. . . . The British Consul at Barcelona appealed to me, so George and I went there, found her with recovered sanity sitting up in bed at a clinic writing an account of her madness.

'A Crazed Girl' (*CP*, p.348) describes the incident:

> That crazed girl improvising her music,
> Her poetry, dancing upon the shore,
> Her soul in division from itself
> Climbing, falling she knew not where,
> Hiding amid the cargo of a steamship,
> Her knee-cap broken, that girl I declare
> A beautiful lofty thing, or a thing
> Heroically lost, heroically found
>
> No matter what disaster occurred
> She stood in desperate music wound,
> Wound, wound, and she made her triumph
> Where the bales and baskets lay
> No common intelligible sound
> But sang, 'O sea-starved, hungry sea.'

The octave of this sonnet in tetrameters has all the details of her behaviour, then the unexpected and sudden declaration:

> A beautiful lofty thing, or a thing
> Heroically lost, heroically found.

Why does Yeats group her as a 'beautiful lofty thing' with his other personal friends? What qualities had she in common with Lady Gregory and Maud Gonne, the two women he includes in 'Beautiful Lofty Things'? (*CP*, p.348). Fundamentally it must have been her heroic courage, which saved her from grave despair and melancholy, for the sestet of the sonnet enlarges on these qualities. As a young dancer and poetess she also had a beauty, wildness and grace—further qualifications for inclusion. The phrase 'O sea-starved, hungry sea' is difficult. But I think the poor woman is identifying herself with the sea, which in her mind is itself 'starved' by its own shortcomings and loneliness. The phrase is originally Margot Ruddock's own (see *Ah, Sweet Dancer. A Correspondence*, edited by Roger McHugh, p.97).

In 1937, after she had recovered, Yeats arranged for her to be the chief speaker in three BBC broadcasts of his poems, because she possessed one quality which he much valued—the ability to pass naturally from speech to song for the refrain of these poems. Hand-drums were used to accentuate rhythms, and the refrains were most moving when sung by her unaccompanied voice, especially in 'Sweet Dancer' (*CP*, p.340), which he wrote for her. This is an infinitely sad poem in two seven-line stanzas, with grave, slow rhythms, describing the melancholy scene as men come to take her away. Yeats shows his admiration for her, and regret that it should have happened; regret being the more important reaction, because he was worried he might have caused her final breakdown soon after the broadcasts, when she was taken to a mental home, where she died in 1951. If you look at 'The Man and the Echo' (*CP*, p.393) you will find that Yeats's conscience, when he is an old man near to death, is much troubled by his often telling Margot Ruddock to concentrate on her poetic technique, and eventually, in Majorca, suggesting to her she should stop writing.

> Did words of mine put too great strain
> On that woman's reeling brain?

George Russell, 1867–1935

(pseudonym 'AE', for 'Aeon')

An Ulsterman who was a fellow student of Yeats at the Metropolitan School of Art in Dublin in 1884. Later became a painter of mystical landscapes, rather like inferior Corots; a poet with a genuine mystical and visionary bias, but lacking precision or vitality, with a somewhat loose and archaic diction, not unlike *The Wind in the Reeds* period of Yeats; an active supporter of the Irish Literary Renaissance; interested in theosophy, though not in magic, anticipating Yeats in investigating Indian thought; editor from 1910 of *The Irish Statesman*, for which he refused to publish 'Leda and the Swan' (*CP*, p.241), as it might be misunderstood; a prolific essayist, and, it is hard to believe, an effective and practical civil servant in the Department of Agriculture, organizing cooperative dairies..

AE was a most likeable and magnanimous man who lived nearly all his life in Dublin and used to hold weekly 'evenings' for discussion similar to Yeats's in Merrion Square, but attended by a rival literary clique, which James Joyce's Stephen Daedalus irreverently referred to as 'The yogibogeybox in Dawson Chambers'. He was Yeats's oldest friend to whom he dedicated his prose romance, *The Secret Rose* in 1897, but they frequently quarrelled, for they were poles apart in character, as Mrs Yeats realized when she spoke of him as 'the nearest to a saint you or I will ever meet'. He died of cancer. Yeats attended his funeral in Dublin.

Junzo Sato, 1897–

In March 1920, Junzo Sato, a young Japanese diplomat, was attending a business course at Portland, Oregon. As a member of the Yeats Society of Japan he had enjoyed reading Yeats's poetry, and was therefore delighted when he had an opportunity to hear the poet lecture on the Irish Literary Renaissance. His own words, quoted by Shotaro Oshimo, *W. B. Yeats and Japan* (1965) reveal his next step:

> I wished to express in some way how deeply moved I was. And after reflecting all night, I decided to present Yeats with my favourite short sword, forged by Bishū Isafuné Motoshigé. For it seemed to me that there was nothing more suitable than this sword as a present to Yeats, who had a keen appreciation of and an ardent longing for Japanese art.

Yeats accepted the 650 year-old Sato family sword, subsequently giving Junzo Sato a copy of his *Complete Works*, and later dedicating *The Resurrection* to him.

This perfect weapon of Motoshigé's (Yeats misspells his name) became for Yeats an emblem of Self (Ille) when rejecting a life of mysticism. *A Dialogue of Self and Soul* (*CP*, p.265), at the climax of the 'Tower' period, is Yeats's affirmation of life lived to the full, which he describes in a letter: 'I am writing a new Tower poem . . . which is a choice of rebirth rather than deliverance from birth. I make my Japanese sword and its silk covering my symbol of life.' 'Symbols' (*CP*, p.270), is but a shorthand of the same theme. For the samurai and Yeats, the sword was more than just a razor-sharp weapon; it possessed a spiritual quality. In Japanese poetry it was often a symbol of determination to fight for a noble cause. Thus the splendidly positive declaration by *My Self* in the poem, almost as if he had the sacred sword in front of him while he speaks:

> I am content to follow to its source
> Every event in action or in thought;
> Measure the lot; forgive myself the lot!
> When such as I cast out remorse
> So great a sweetness flows into the breast
> We must laugh and we must sing,
> We are blest by everything,
> Everything we look upon is blest.

Olivia Shakespear ('Diana Vernon'), 1867–1938

From 1894 until her death Yeats wrote fuller letters to Olivia Shakespear than to any of his friends, male or female, discussing in detail

Olivia Shakespear. 'She was not more lovely than distinguished—no matter what happened she never lost her solitude'.

what he was reading, the poems he was writing, his reactions to personal and political events, and constantly seeking her advice. Many of the letters are quoted in *Wade*, but after her death when Ezra Pound, her son-in-law, returned many, Yeats burnt them. Nevertheless, from those we have, it is possible to fill in the gist of her responses; and remarkably intelligent she was in her critical comments, and well-read in English, French and Italian literature— apart from being a novelist herself. From her photograph and from the descriptions of those who knew her, there is no doubt of her serene beauty, which reflected a gentle, contemplative and still temperament.

She was the cousin of Lionel Johnson, the Rhymer, who had introduced her to Yeats. At that time he was swirling in the waters of his unrequited affair with Maud Gonne, which naturally led to eddies with regard to 'Diana Vernon', as he called Olivia Shakespear until her husband, an aged solicitor, died. 'The Lover Mourns for the Loss of Love' (*CP*, p.68) is a short, explicit statement of the situation. 'He Bids his Beloved Be at Peace' (*CP*, p.69), reveals more sensuality than some of his contemporary love poems (Professor Jeffares says he has counted twenty-three references to the hair of the beloved in these poems). 'The Travail of Passion' (*CP*, p.78), with its Rossetti-like imagery, has another of these hirsute attributions. He includes

154

Olivia Shakespear ('Diana Vernon') in a trio with Lady Gregory and Maud Gonne in 'Friends' (*CP*, p.139):

> Three women that have wrought
> What joy is in my days:

And later he writes of her face as an inspiration of the primary imagination, as it was in some of Shakespeare's sonnets. The short poem, 'A Deep-sworn Vow' (*CP*, p.174) exemplifies this.

In December 1929 he met her in London after a gap of some months, and then wrote 'After Long Silence' (*CP*, p.301). After her death he wrote to Dorothy Wellesley: 'For more than forty years she has been the centre of my life in London, and during all that time we have never had a quarrel, sadness sometimes, but never a difference.'

Arthur Symons, 1865–1945

Poet, playwright and critic, he introduced Yeats to the French Symbolist school, which he discusses in *The Symbolist Movement in Literature* (1899), a book in which Yeats had a hand. After the friendship between Yeats and Lionel Johnson had lessened, Symons became Yeats's closest friend, being an especially sympathetic listener. A most important influence on Yeats in the nineties, helping on Yeats's use of symbolism, already started in *The Wanderings of Oisin*. A member of the Rhymers Club; visited the Aran Islands and Coole Park with Yeats in 1896. No specific reference to him in *CP*.

J. M. Synge, 1871–1909

Although Synge, born in County Dublin, educated Trinity College, was one of Yeats's nearest friends from 1896 until his early death from cancer in 1909, their common interests concerned only the drama. The notorious '*Playboy*' riots in 1907 at the Abbey Theatre were but the climax of the Dublin reaction to Synge's criticism of the weaknesses in Irish character expressed in *In the Shadow of the Glen*, an earlier play. Yeats's memories of this occasion gave birth to the bitter, epigrammatic, 'On those that hated "The Playboy of the Western World", 1907' (*CP*, p.124), in which he scorns the emasculated reaction to the play: also to the section of 'Beautiful Lofty Things' (*CP*, p.348), when he remembers his father addressing the audience after the play. Synge was thought by the '*Playboy*' audience to be unpatriotic and a blasphemer:

> 'Is it killed your father?'
> 'With the help of God I did, surely, and that the Holy Immaculate Mother may intercede for his soul.'

And, incredible though it now seems, the spark which started the fiery riot, after which the actors could not be heard for the rest of the play, was the line: 'a drift of chosen females in their shifts'—a shift being a chemise which it was then considered obscene to mention. Yeats's drama is outside the scope of this present book, but it is impossible to excise such incidents in Yeats's life for they build up the picture of that 'rooted', 'solitary', and 'enquiring' man John Synge as an heroic figure who had the courage to expose unpleasant traits of personality, and weaknesses in Irish life, often with savage humour.

When they met in Paris in the 1890s, Yeats advised Synge to leave and go to the Aran Islands: 'Live as one of the people themselves; express a life that has never found expression.' Synge took his advice, so totally altering the direction of his life, and the journey became for Yeats an archetype like that of Dante and Bunyan—a spiritual journey through life in which Synge found fulfilment:

> And that enquiring man John Synge comes next,
> That dying chose the living world for text
> And never could have rested in the tomb
> But that, long travelling, he had come
> Towards nightfall upon certain set apart
> In a most desolate stony place,
> Towards nightfall upon a race
> Passionate and simple like his heart.

The discovery by Synge of the tough peasantry and their violent lives was to influence Yeats vitally. Henceforward disillusion and violence figure in his own verse, and sometimes sections of his poems such as 'The Hour before Dawn' (*CP*, p.130):

> The beggar in a rage began
> Upon his hunkers in a hole
> 'It's plain that you are no right man
> To mock at everything I love
> As if it were not worth the doing.

or 'The Three Hermits' (*CP*, p.127), might be Synge's own:

> While he rummaged rags and hair,
> Caught and cracked his flea, the third,
> Giddy with his hundredth year,
> Sang unnoticed like a bird.

Yeats has left the aesthetes in the Pre-Raphaelite room, where he sat dreaming in the 'aureate' Celtic twilight, for the beggars in the fresh Easter wind. The 'Crazy Jane' poems and many of *Last Poems* later indicate this influence of Synge's thought on Yeats's verse, so it is in 'The Municipal Gallery Revisited' he writes his final tribute:

John Synge, I and Augusta Gregory, thought
All that we did, all that we said or sang
Must come from contact with the soil, from that
Contact everything Antaeus-like grew strong.
We three alone in modern times had brought
Everything down to the sole test again,
Dream of the noble and the beggar-man.

Synge exemplified for Yeats his theory of the mask, perhaps was even his own mask, his Anti-Self. For Synge, the gentle, shy and sick man, created and perfected his art revealing life in its brutality and harshness—the opposite of all he was in daily life: one aspect of the 'double soul' discussed by Ellmann in *Yeats: The Man and the Masks* pp.174–9 ff. See also 'The Mask' (*CP*, p.106), written not long after Synge's death, and showing, in its conversation between the lovers, the difficulty in revealing true identity behind the mask.

Yeats chose eight of Synge's poems for the *Oxford Book of Modern Verse*, after having referred very briefly to Synge's verse in his introduction—a 'perverse judgement' as T. R. Henn calls it in his excellent chapter on Yeats and Synge in *The Lonely Tower*; but there is no doubt that Synge's poetry is inferior to his plays. It is the years at the Abbey Theatre which Yeats thinks should be remembered: 'I think when Lady Gregory's name and John Synge's name are spoken by future generations, my name, if remembered, will come up in the talk, and that if my name is spoken first their names will come in their turn because of the years we worked together' ('The Bounty of Sweden', *AU*, p.553).

Dorothy Wellesley (Lady Gerald Wellesley), 1889–1956

For details of her house and Yeats's visits to it during the last four years of his life, see below p.186. Like Lady Gregory she gave Yeats friendship, through which he was able to discuss, either at Penns or by letter, his poetry and hers. The relationship was one of master to pupil, and she as a minor poet benefited from his advice, while he thrived on the peaceful setting which enabled him to write. Kathleen Raine, a poet herself, who understands the mythological and mystical background to Yeats's verse better than Dorothy Wellesley did, sums up the relationship between them in her Introduction to *Letters on Poetry from W. B. Yeats to Dorothy Wellesley*:

The letters throw light upon the aims Yeats set himself as a poet during the last years of his life, the years in which he wrote his play *Purgatory* (he knew it for a masterpiece) and his last volume of poems, some of them his finest. They remind us that the soil from which great poetry grows is remote from these aridities which occupy the pens of critics; the beauty of woman, the charm of her house and her companionship, friendship, dreams and kindness, these nourish immortal poetry.

Jack Butler Yeats, 1871–1957

Six years younger than the poet, he also spent his childhood in Sligo. Unlike his elder brother, he had a cheerful, open disposition which enabled him to get on with people easily, and especially with his Pollexfen grandfather, whose favourite he was. Sligo with its ships, fairs, races and circuses, and the variety of men and women associated with them, was an inspiration for his drawing from 1887 until he started his career as an art student in London, following in the footsteps of his father. 'In half of the pictures he paints today I recognize faces that I have met at Rosses or the Sligo quays', wrote the poet in *AU*.

By 1910 he was happily married and had had seventeen exhibitions, with patrons including Lady Gregory and Robert Gregory, John

Jack Yeats and W. B. Yeats. Photo taken outside 'Gurteen Dhas', the house of Lily and Lollie Yeats at Dundrum, about five miles from the centre of Dublin. It is the last photo taken of the two brothers together.

Quinn and John Masefield, who shared his enjoyment of the vigorous life and also his delight in story-telling. Previous to 1905 when he left watercolours for oil painting, his best work had been for illustrations to *The Aran Islands* and a tour which he made with J. M. Synge in Connemara. His strength of line was especially suitable for drawing the poverty-stricken peasants leading their hard life on poor land along the shores of the wild ocean.

His later work, after 1924, which does not reproduce well in black and white, became much more romantic, freer with broader pigments, and outlines receding, at times almost abstract Impressionist. He also wrote numerous plays, novels and articles. In 1948 he told a friend: 'In writing, as in my painting, my inspiration has always been affection wide, devious, and, sometimes, handsome . . . in every book there is somewhere in it a memory of Sligo . . . to which lovely place the beak of my ship ever returns.

The wild faces of horsemen, the quiet dignity of tinkers and wanderers, set against tumultuous skies which flash and dance with colour, are transformed in his imagination; and that, after all, is what his brother achieved in poetry often having that very subject matter.

John Butler Yeats, 1839–1922

The poet's father was brought up in a large family at Tullynish in Ulster, where his father was the 'red-headed' Rector. His early days were happy, except for the horrors of a private school in the Isle of Man, from which he returned home only for six weeks in the summer. His life there was redeemed by the excellence of the art teacher who realized he had talent. George Pollexfen was a schoolfellow, but had none of the brilliance of J. B. who was always top of his class. Following in the family tradition, he entered Trinity College in 1857, reading Classics, and, afterwards, Law. When he married Susan Pollexfen at Sligo in 1863 the Pollexfens were pleased: a handsome young man, who might be a brilliant barrister, and who had already inherited Butler lands in County Kildare, suited them. Their hopes were dashed. Having been called to the Irish Bar in 1866, J. B. decided not to practise, but to train to be an artist in London, to the disgust of the practical, worldly-wise and ambitious Pollexfens. His wife, doubtless influenced by her family, at first refused to follow him or even to acknowledge his existence as an artist, and with five children and no commissions for five years his lot was not enviable.

J.B.'s anxiety about the influence of the Pollexfens while Willie was in Sligo has been discussed (see above, pp.11–12). Dreading the thought of the Pollexfen characteristics—taciturnity, melancholia and inarticulateness—coming out in Willie, J. B. removed him to London where he decided to help to educate him personally. When J. B.

returned to Dublin in 1880, he was responsible for the poet attending the Metropolitan School of Art, which had a lasting effect on him, for he developed the ability to observe closely, despite his short sight, and this is a rare quality in academically trained people. As a result of help from Hugh Lane who recognized J. B.'s worth, he painted many portraits of leaders in Irish literary and political life, two of which were hung in a Royal Academy exhibition. Professor Bodkin (Honorary Professor of Art, Trinity College) thought the portraits of John O'Leary, Standish O'Grady and George Russell had 'an air of mingled intimacy and dignity that no other painter of modern times surpasses'. On J. B.'s return with his family to Bedford Park, his literary and artist friends, most of whom were minor Pre-Raphaelite painters, had some influence on the poet's thought, though by then he was trying to break away from his father. On the other hand, his younger brother Jack was even then showing signs of draughtsmanship and painterly ability which was encouraged by J. B.

Throughout his life he never made much money, as he never thought it right to live with that end in view. He was a brilliant conversationalist with great intellectual curiosity, an avid reader, totally unselfish and unambitious, but incapable of planning or organization. His delightful wry humour is illustrated in the anecdote of the 'plaster Saints' in 'Beautiful Lofty Things' (*CP*, p.348):

> My father upon the Abbey stage, before him a raging crowd;
> 'This land of Saints,' and then as the applause died out,
> 'Of plaster Saints'; his beautiful mischievous head thrown back.

Though as J. B. remembered this incident, from the *Playboy* riots (1907) after nine years it was slightly different, yet still showing his humour.

> I began with some information about Synge which interested my listeners and then: 'Of course I know Ireland is an island of Saints, but thank God it is also an island of sinners—only unfortunately in this Country people cannot live or die except behind a curtain of deceit.' At this point the chairman and my son both called out, 'Time's up, Time's up.' I saw the lifted sign and like the devil in *Paradise Lost* I fled. The papers next morning said I was howled down. It was worse, I was pulled down.

In December 1907 he went to New York with his daughter Lily, and thereafter refused to return to Ireland, despite repeated requests from his family. He painted portraits and lectured, sometimes receiving financial help from John Quinn (see above, p.   ) as well as from the poet himself. All his life he wrote many letters, and there are said to be 5000 as yet unpublished, apart from those in *J. B. Yeats. Letters to his son, W. B. Yeats and others*, edited with a Memoir by Joseph Hone (1944).

Gazetteer

Ireland

Sandymount Castle, Dublin
When the poet's family were living at 'Georgeville', 1865–66, this castle nearby was owned by Robert Corbet, the poet's great-uncle. J. B. Yeats had lived there when an undergraduate at Trinity College, sometimes rehearsing Greek plays in the drawingroom, and now the poet himself was wheeled in his pram in the extensive grounds. The castle was an eighteenth-century house, gothicized beyond recognition by Abbotsford-type battlements, tower and cloister. The gardens were large (five gardeners) and it was landscaped in the eighteenth-century manner by Robert Corbet, with vistas to the sea, a lake and a small deer park. After Corbet's death it was sold. The poet visited it again in 1900, but could scarcely recognize the grounds. It has now been built on, forming part of the seaside suburb of Sandymount.

Georgeville, No. 2 Sandymount Avenue, Dublin
This was where the poet was born at midnight on 13 June 1865. Described by *Hone* as 'a recently-built, six-roomed, semi-detached house at the head of Sandymount Avenue . . . the most genteel house in the avenue, with stone steps up to the hall door, and plate-glass windows'. Uncle Corbet was a snob and used to address letters to 'The Quarry Hole' because the house had been built on a quarry site. It is still there, though now No. 5, with its name inscribed on the stone wall.

Trinity College, Dublin
Founded in 1592 by Queen Elizabeth I for the education of Protestants. Not until 1873 did Catholics gain completely equal privileges with Protestants. The Roll of famous Trinity men includes Jonathan Swift, Oliver Goldsmith, Edmund Burke, George Berkeley, Wolfe Tone, Henry Grattan, J. M. Synge and Oscar Wilde. The buildings, with their splendid classical façades and elaborate interior plasterwork, flanked by extensive playing-fields, occupy a large area in the very centre of Dublin. The Library houses Ireland's greatest collection of books and MSS, including the famous illuminated eighth-century gospel book, *The Book of Kells*.

The poet's great-grandfather, grandfather and father had all been undergraduates there, and it was hoped he might follow them. But he realized his Latin and Mathematics would not be up to the standard of the entrance examination, so he went to an Art School. When he was involved in the romantic Celtic revival in the 1890s, he made long attacks on Protestant Ireland as exemplified by Trinity College, in his introduction to *A Book of Irish Verse* (1895). 'No Irishman', he wrote, 'living in Ireland has sung excellently of any but a theme from Irish experience, Irish History or Irish tradition.' Further on he pointed to Trinity College as 'an enemy of all enthusiasms; because all enthusiasms seemed her enemies she has taught her children to look neither to the world about them nor into their own souls where some dangerous fire might slumber'. He then added that the products of English universities, and of Trinity College which aped them, were ignorant of the very names of the best writers in *A Book of Irish Verse*. A decade later he had modified his views slightly, and later in life he came to admire profoundly the work and thought of Trinity College's most famous eighteenth-century graduates—Swift, Goldsmith, Berkeley and Burke.

Yeats came up against Trinity College traditions in 1914 when Pádraic Pearse, who was then considered a revolutionary, both politically and in being a Gaelic scholar, had been invited to address the Gaelic Society of the College at a commemoration of the centenary of the Irish poet, Thomas Davis. The Vice-Provost, Dr Mahaffy (elected Provost in November), dissolved the Society and closed the gates of the College to them. Yeats, who was also giving a lecture on this occasion, decided he and Pearse should go ahead, so they lectured in the Antient Concert Rooms in Brunswick Street, later renamed Pearse Street.

Earlier in the same year Yeats had applied for permission to read in the library of the college. As was customary, he had to take an oath, to be read out in Latin, before the Vice-Provost, swearing not to damage the books. In due course Yeats was sent a copy of the oath with the stresses and quantities of the Latin words marked by Mahaffy, who added, according to Gogarty, 'for I have a sensitive ear'. Yeats could not read Latin, and Mahaffy's method of showing Yeats he knew this was the action of an academic snob—arrogant and insensitive.

All was forgotten by 1922 when Yeats was honoured by a D.Litt. degree from the College.

St Patrick's Cathedral (Protestant), Dublin
The largest church ever built in Ireland. On the site of a pre-Norman church, which legend associates with the Saint. Rebuilt in the twelfth century, most of it is thirteenth-fourteenth century, with an eight-bay nave, four-bay choir, Lady Chapel and Baptistery. The 100-foot granite spire was built in 1750. The cathedral is much restored, 1864–69, money being given for that purpose by Sir Benjamin Lee

Guinness, whose statue stands outside. It is filled with tombs of many who have served Ireland, including Jonathan Swift, Dean of the Cathedral Chapter 1713–45, and of Esther Johnson (Swift's Stella). The Latin epitaph for his wall monument was composed by Swift himself. Yeats used to 'wander and meditate' in the cathedral, or sit by this monument in the gloom, Swift for him being 'always just round the next corner'. Perhaps he thought out his famous verse based on the epitaph, with which he had difficulty before it reached its final version (*CP*, p.277).

> Swift has sailed into his rest;
> Savage indignant there
> Cannot lacerate his breast.
> Imitate him if you dare,
> World-besotted traveller; he
> Served human liberty.

Immediately after Yeats's death in the south of France in 1939, the Dean of the Cathedral wrote to Mrs Yeats suggesting a final resting place for the poet in the cathedral—the first offer of this kind for a hundred years. But Yeats had signified he wished to be buried among his ancestors at Drumcliffe, County Sligo, so she refused the honour.

The General Post Office, O'Connell Street

Amidst cinemas, ice-cream parlours and cheap hotels, the classical columns of the façade of the General Post Office (1814–18) by Francis Johnston, one of Ireland's finest architects, stand in lone and majestic dignity. As a result of being the headquarters of the 1916 insurgents, who proclaimed the Irish Republic there, and being bombarded again in 1922, all that survives of Johnston's work is the O'Connell Street (Sackville Street till 1916) front. In the main hall, as you buy a stamp, you pass the 1916 memorial statue, *The Death of Cuchulain* in bronze, by Oliver Sheppard, a sculptor whom Yeats knew at the Metropolitan School of Art. The analogy for Yeats between the heroic figures of the Easter Rising and those of Irish myth often occurs in his writing, and so accounts for such lines as those from 'The Statues':

> When Pearse summoned Cuchulain to his side,
> What stalked through the Post Office? . . .

The question sounds stronger if the stresses are right: the Irish pronounce it Post Óffice, whereas the English usually say Póst Office.

82 Merrion Square, Dublin

The Yeatses and their children lived in this house from September 1922 to May 1928. It was built in the last twenty years of the eighteenth century, during the time of Grattan's Parliament that Yeats so much admired. Merrion Square, with its central garden, is the most handsome Georgian square in Dublin, second only in size to St Stephen's Green. This house, like others in the square, is of maroon-coloured brick, with a large front door, flanked by elegant Ionic pillars supporting pretty fanlight tracery. Inside there are some vast rooms, including a double drawing-room which was useful when the poet held literary evenings at which he read his latest work such as his play *The Resurrection*. Also, he could pace up and down whilst he dictated his Senate speeches to his wife who typed.

Yeats was elected a member of Seanad Éireann (the Irish Senate) during this period, and as the Civil War was raging, there were guards outside the house, for many senators' houses in the country had been blown up or burnt by Irregulars. To be living in such a house, with its high rooms, marble chimneypieces and rococo plasterwork was a matter of much pride for Yeats. But when his term of office as a 'green-robed senator' was about to come to an end he realized he couldn't afford to go on living there without a senator's salary, so they moved. As it was they had to let the top storey and Cuala industries (weaving) was in the basement. Even then the size of the house must have been inconvenient for easy domesticity. V. S. Pritchett in his autobiography, *Midnight Oil*, vol. 2, describes an afternoon call he paid on Yeats:

> The exalted voice flowed over me. The tall figure, in uncommonly delicate tweed, walked up and down, the voice becoming more resonant, as if he were on a stage. At the climax of some point about the Gaelic revival, he suddenly remembered he must make tea, in fact a new pot, because he had already been drinking some. The problem was one of emptying out the old teapot. It was a beautiful pot and he walked the room with the short steps of the aesthete, carrying it in his hand. He came toward me. He receded to the bookcase. He swung around the sofa. Suddenly, with Irish practicality, he went straight to one of the two splendid Georgian windows of the room, opened it, and out went those barren leaves with a swoosh, into Merrion Square.

Riversdale, Willbrook, Rathfarnham, County Dublin
A stone house with an estate of about four acres, which the Yeatses went to in July 1932 and owned until his death. Found by Mrs Yeats, it was ideal: a pleasant, well-stocked garden, a walled orchard, croquet lawn and gardener's cottage; with views to the Dublin mountains, standing a mile beyond the village of Rathfarnham, four miles south-west of Dublin. But doubts in Yeats's mind were evidently raised by the cynical question of Plato's ghost, the daimon who takes part in the conversation of the soul with itself, when death is approaching:

All his happier dreams came true—
A small old house, wife, daughter, son,
Grounds where plum and cabbage grew,
Poets and Wits about him drew;
'What then?' sang Plato's ghost. 'What then?'

'The work is done', grown old he thought,
'According to my boyish plan;
Let the fools rage, I swerved in naught,
Something to perfection brought';
But louder sang that ghost, 'What then?'

(*CP*, p.347)

One would have liked to have thought of Yeats happy and settled at
Riversdale at the end of his life, but obviously the Platonic voice in the
poem disturbs his peace.

Coole Park, County Galway

For two hundred years until 1932 the Gregory family lived at Coole.
This stone house, which has been demolished, was neither grand nor
imposing, a simple three-storeyed cube of six bays with a semicircular
Palladian window above a square porch. In its setting of open park-
land it had a sturdy plainness which did not give the impression of its
having been built for defence like so many Irish houses, but rather as
an accessible dwelling where all were welcome. On the West side,
Victorian bay windows looked down to the lake; not far off was the
stable block, ruined now, but still having a magnificent dovecot in a
gable which soars above the trees. The estate is wooded and picturesque, the Cloon river flowing under high poplars on a steep bank by
the rocky wood, Páirc-na-Carraig, through a causeway bridge of vast
limestone flags, to join a wild lake edged in brown and velvet moss.
After which it plunges underground to flow into Galway Bay twenty
miles to the west. All this under the shadow of the Dun of the legendary King Guaire. It was here, according to ancient legend, that King
Guaire, having heard a child would be born who would be greater
than he, planned the murder of the child's mother. So King Guaire's
people 'took her and tied a heavy stone about her neck and threw her
into the deep part of the river where it rises within Coole. But by the
help of God the stone that was put about her neck did not sink but
went floating upon the water, and she came to the shore and was
saved from drowning.' The name of the child who was born in the
parish of Kiltartan was Saint Colman, afterwards famed for his good
works throughout Ireland.

From the days of Richard Gregory, who collected the fine library
in the eighteenth century, the house was always a place of peace: the
home of a Protestant family living in amity with tenants and peace

165

The East front of Coole in 1888. Robert Gregory, the child on the left; his mother seated and his father on the extreme right.

with Catholic neighbours. And thanks to Lady Gregory one of the few houses in Ireland unscarred by the Troubles and Civil War in the 1920s. Yeats remembers it in 'Beautiful Lofty Things' (*CP*, p.348):

> Augusta Gregory seated at her great ormolu table,
> Her eightieth winter approaching: 'Yesterday he
>   threatened my life.
> I told him that nightly from six to seven I sat at this table,
> The blinds drawn up';

Adjoining the house was a walled garden of about three acres, planted with trees, ornamental shrubs and flowers. At the end of a flowered-bordered gravel walk, at the lower part of the garden beyond the Vineries, stood, on a simple plinth, a large bust of Maecenas brought from Italy by Richard Gregory, in the 1790s. Near the middle of the garden alongside the gravel walk was a copper-beech, called the Autograph Tree, on which famous visitors were invited to inscribe their initials, whilst others were discouraged from inserting them. Although the tree was mutilated after Lady Gregory's death, it is still possible to see the initials of W. B. Yeats, his father and his brother, Jack; the lyre-cipher of John Synge, and G.B.S. Lady Gregory and her husband Sir William continually planted, and in 1898, at the centenary celebrations for the Rebellion of the United Irishmen, she recommended that every Nationalist should 'plant at least one tree . . . and every Unionist in 1900, and every waverer or indifferent person in the year that separates them'.

It was fitting she should have arranged to meet Yeats in the centenary year to discuss the founding of the Irish National Theatre. A few days after this meeting Yeats went to Coole, which virtually became his home for many years. In 1898 he was physically sick, poor and homeless. Augusta Gregory nursed him back to health, lent him money and gave him ideal conditions in which to work. 'I found at last', he wrote, 'what I have been seeking always, a life of order, and of labour, where all outward things were the image of an inward life.' So one finds in his verse written during the next thirty years much of the imagery inspired by the experience of living at Coole: the wild swans 'mysterious, beautiful', so different from the tame and protected English kind, first as symbols of passion and beauty, then to betoken inspiration in the later poem, 'Coole Park and Ballylee, 1931' (*CP*, p.275):

> That stormy white
> But seems a concentration of the sky;
> And, like the soul, it sails into the sight
> And in the morning's gone, no man knows why:

The Seven Woods, first in their tragic sublimity reflecting the loneliness in which Yeats felt the eternity of nature, later became a mirror of his mood as he reflects on the tragedy of Coole. Even the 'Great Wind', the hurricane of 1903, which 'blew down so many trees, troubled the wild creatures and changed the look of things' became a symbol for what had happened to him after his beloved Maud Gonne had unexpectedly married. From direct experience of the Coole garden and the wood Pairc-na-Lee arose his sonnet 'In the Seven Woods' (*CP*, p.85), in which the pigeons in the woods, and the bees in the lime-tree flowers could make him forget the bitterness of his love for Maud Gonne, as well as the futilities of the coronation festivities of Edward VII.

It was at Coole that Yeats saw the continuance of eighteenth-century traditions of courage, intellect and imagination. Whether from Swift at the beginning or Grattan at the end of the century, the pace of life induced a quietness of thought which in turn engendered a Unity of Being, as in 'Coole Park, 1929' (*CP*, p.274):

Great works constructed there in nature's spite
For scholars and for poets after us,
Thoughts long knitted into a single thought,
A dance-like glory that those walls begot.

Coole embodied ceremony, order and freedom, and he remembered these when he gave a talk for the B.B.C. entitled 'My own poetry again' in October 1937:

> From my twenty-seventh year until a few years ago all my public activities were associated with a famous country house in County Galway. In that house my dear friend, that woman of genius, Lady Gregory, gathered from time to time all men of talent, all profound men, in the intellectual life of modern Ireland.

In 1921 the excessive Irish land rates had forced the Gregory family to sell some of the land, and ultimately Coole was doomed, though there had been 'no country house in Ireland with so fine a record'. In 1927 it was sold to the Ministry of Lands and Agriculture, but Lady Gregory was allowed to live there on payment of a small rental. Yeats knew the house could not survive long: it would become, he wrote (*EX*, p.319) 'an office and residence for foresters, a little cheap furniture in the great rooms, a few religious oleographs its only pictures'. In 1941, after Lady Gregory's and Yeats's deaths, it was sold to a building contractor who pulled it down for the value of the stone. Nothing remains but the garden walls, the ruins of the stable block, and a few floor tiles. It is almost impossible to visualize the garden, as the great catalpa has already gone, the box hedges are eye-level, and rows of so-called Christmas trees are rising high. When I was there recently an Irishwoman poetically summed it all up: 'The trees,' she said, 'are full of tears.'

Thoor Ballylee, Gort, County Galway
Sturdy, stone towers, with six-foot thick walls, built in medieval times, sometimes ruined, firmly punctuate the Irish landscape. Thoor Ballylee, within walking distance of Coole House, and once a part of the demesne, is typical. It guards a small stone bridge which was a fording place over a swift-flowing stream. The interior is simple: four storeys, each one large room, a narrow stone stair cut into the walls, and battlements as parapet. He first went to Ballylee, while staying at Coole in the 1890s, and described it in 'Dust hath closed Helen's Eye', an essay published in October 1899.

Thoor Ballylee. Engraving by Alan Fenn from a drawing made while the roof of the cottage was being repaired.

I have been lately to a little group of houses, not many enough to be called a village, in the barony of Kiltartan in County Galway, whose name Ballylee, is known through all the west of Ireland. There is the old square castle, Ballylee, inhabited by a farmer and his wife, and a cottage where their daughter and their son-in-law live, and a little mill with an old miller, and old ash trees throwing green shadows upon a little river and great stepping-stones. I went there two or three times last year to talk to the miller about Biddy Early, a wise woman that lived in Clare some years ago, and about her saying 'There is a cure for all evil between the two mill-wheels of Ballylee', and to find out from him or another whether she meant the moss between the running waters or some other herb. I have been there this summer and I shall be there again before it is autumn, because Mary Hynes, a beautiful woman whose name is still a wonder by turf fires, died there sixty years ago; for our feet would linger where beauty has lived its life of sorrow to make us understand that it is not of the world.

When he was at Coole during many subsequent summers, he must have seen the tower and the cottages gradually becoming ruinèd after the farmer and his family had left them. The setting and its Gaelic associations with Mary Hynes, the local miller's daughter whom the blind poet Raftery had sung of and loved, held him fascinated. In 1917, even though the floors were rotten and there was no roof on the tower, he made a bid for the property, then owned by a government department oddly called the Congested Districts Board. As no one wanted it he managed to buy it and the two cottages for £35. Then he set to work to have repairs done, and sturdy elm furniture designed and made on the spot by a local craftsman from Gort. After Yeats's marriage in October 1917 it was important to get the work finished. But he was not able to take up residence until the summer of 1919. Even then only the ground and first floors of the tower were finished, though one of the cottages enabled him to have a study to work in. The roof was eventually cemented, despite his wish to have it covered in 'sea-green slates' which he had paid for as they had been recommended by the famous architect Sir Edwin Lutyens. But the local builder considered they would not withstand Atlantic gales, although they are certainly used in Scotland in similar circumstances. The verse (CP, p.214) now carved on an outside wall of the tower remembers them. Henceforward the tower becomes a recurrent and paramount symbol in his verse as in 'A Prayer on going into my House' (CP, p.183):

> God grant a blessing on this tower and cottage
> And on my heirs, if all remain unspoiled,
> No table or chair or stool not simple enough
> For shepherd lads in Galilee; and grant

> That I myself for portions of the year
> May handle nothing and set eyes on nothing
> But what the great and passionate have used
> Throughout so many varying centuries
> We take it for the norm; . . .

As the tower's ground floor room was flooded when the river was high, and always was rather damp, he could live there for only very limited 'portions of the year'. Not until 1922, when the Yeatses had their Merrion Square house, was a large bedroom on the second floor completed. During the Civil War, on one occasion when the Yeatses were living there the tower was surrounded by Irregulars who blew up part of the bridge ('The Tower', v; *CP*, pp.229), and again, when they were not there, was occupied temporarily by Free State soldiers.

For some years previously the symbol of the tower had been used by Yeats. Two poems written in 1915 show what it then meant to him. The first, 'Ego Dominus Tuus' (*CP*, p.180), is a dialogue between *Hic*, signifying the objective self, and *Ille*, the subjective self: a clash or struggle between these two, which have been termed the self and the anti-self of the same personality. Between, for example, the characteristics of the philosopher-scholar or imaginative artist and the man of action, the soldier or politician. *Hic* opens the poem:

> On the grey sand beside the shallow stream
> Under your old wind-beaten tower, where still
> A lamp burns on beside the open book
> That Michael Robartes left, you walk in the moon,

Michael Robartes is a fictional figure, the solitary scholar, perhaps one of the subjective sides of Yeats's personality. The symbol of the search for wisdom, of the lamp burning in the darkness of the night, is further developed in the second of the two poems, 'The Phases of the Moon' (*CP*, p.183), when Robartes says to Aherne, another fictional scholarly character, also representing a part of Yeats's subjective side:

> We are on the bridge; that shadow is the tower,
> And the light proves that he is reading still.
> He has found, after the manner of his kind,
> Mere images; chosen this place to live in
> Because, it may be, of the candle-light
> From the far tower where Milton's Platonist
> Sat late, or Shelley's visionary prince:
> The lonely light that Samuel Palmer engraved,
> An image of mysterious wisdom won by toil;
> And now he seeks in book or manuscript
> What he shall never find.

Samuel Palmer (1805–81), the artist referred to, late in life took to etching on copper (not to engraving, as Yeats says), achieving some fine work when he illustrated Milton's poem 'Il Penseroso'. Yeats had a copy of this etching on a wall of his room at Woburn Buildings. He must have been very fond of it, for he had it beside him when he read in the Bodleian Library, Oxford, in 1920. Palmer himself always kept a small copy of Milton's poems in his pocket and was obsessed by 'Il Penseroso', and while he was working on his etching, 'The Lonely Tower', which illustrated this poem, he wrote to a friend:

> You ask me to show you anything which especially affects my inner sympathies. Now only three days have passed since I did begin the meditation of a subject which for twenty years has affected my sympathies with sevenfold inwardness, though for the first time I seem to feel, in some sort, the power of realizing it. It is from what Edmund Burke thought the finest poem in the English language. The passage includes 'the bellman's drowsy charm'. I never artistically knew such a sacred delight as when endeavouring, in all humility, to realize, after a sort, the imagery of Milton.

The tower in Palmer's etching (reproduced as a frontispiece in *Henn*) 'on a plat of rising round', is near human habitation, the roof and gable of a cottage being visible on the skyline. Although it is night, it is not dark, for the moon and stars shine brightly, while *il penseroso* reads Plato by the light of his lamp which can be seen from far off, through the window. Two shepherds, possibly symbolizing the objective anti-self, are separated by a deep chasm from the tower, but they are gazing at its light, their day's work being finished. An owl, Athene's bird of wisdom, flies toward them from the direction of the tower, above which, can be seen the constellation of Ursa Major —the Bear, which the Platonist often 'outwatches'. Here is 'the image of mysterious wisdom won by toil' as seen by Samuel Palmer and so communicated to Yeats. Also mentioned is Shelley's visionary prince, named Prince Athanase, who 'sate Apart from men as in a lonely tower'.

After the summer of 1929 the Yeatses did not again live in Thoor Ballylee, and although they owned it nothing was done to keep it in repair. Yet compared with Coole House its subsequent history is heartening. By 1952 it had really fallen into decay: Virginia Moore (*The Unicorn*, p.282) describes it as 'a barn for cattle and a rallying place for crows'. Vandals had torn planks from the oak door, and water had leaked through the roof. But then in 1961 a newly founded Kiltartan Society, aided by Bórd Fáilte Éireann (the Irish Tourist Board), started to restore it, and Mrs Yeats and her children placed it in a Trust's hands. Although all the furniture has not yet been remade, the buildings are in excellent condition: weatherproof, cottages re-thatched and walls repainted. If you go there in early morning or late evening, when there are no other visitors, and stand at a window overlooking the bridge, the light from the water dances on the ceiling, and no sound breaks the silence except the stream splashing over the stones, or the wind in the big ash trees.

Lough Key, County Roscommon: The Castle of the Heroes

One of the landscapes in Ireland which combined Christian and pagan mythology, and which much appealed to Yeats, was at Lough Key, near Boyle, County Roscommon. The shores of this romantic lough are indented with many coves, and its surface dotted with islands. On Trinity Island the White Canons had compiled the *Annals of Loch Cé* in Tudor times, and the ash trees still entwine their branches across the graves of the star-crossed lovers, Una MacDermott, daughter of the last chieftain of the Rock, and the MacCostello of Moygara. On Castle (Rock) Island, the MacDermotts had once entertained the poets of all Ireland, and there Yeats dreamed of founding a mystical cult based on druidic mysteries combined with Christianity. He relates in *The Trembling of the Veil* III (*AU*, p.253), how the idea occurred to him:

> When staying with Hyde in Roscommon, I had driven over to Lough Kay [sic], hoping to find some local memory of the old story now called *Proud Costello, MacDermot's Daughter, and the Bitter Tongue*. I was rowed up the lake that I might find the island where he died; I had to find it from Hyde's account in the *Love-Songs of Connacht*, for when I asked the boatman, he told the story of Hero and Leander, putting Hero's house on one island, and Leander's on another. Presently we stopped to eat our sandwiches at the 'Castle Rock', an island all castle.... The situation in the centre of the lake, that has little wood-grown islands, and is surrounded by wood-grown hills, is romantic, and at one end, and perhaps at the other too, there is a stone platform where meditative persons might pace to and fro. I planned a mystical Order which should buy or hire the castle, and keep it as a place where its members could retire for a while for contemplation, and where we might establish mysteries like those of Eleusis and Samothrace; and for ten years to come my most impassioned thought was a vain attempt to find philosophy and to create ritual for that Order. I had an unshakable conviction, arising how or whence I cannot tell, that invisible gates would open as they opened for Blake ... and that this philosophy would ... set before Irishmen for special manual an Irish literature, which ... would seem the work of a single mind, and turn our places of beauty or legendary association into holy symbols.

It was arranged that Maud Gonne should be one of the leaders of this cult and AE another. But unfortunately Maud Gonne thought it a good idea if it was organized politically so as to hasten Ireland's freedom from English domination. Yeats did not see it in this way, but as a nexus with the Irish Literary movement, and as an expression, as he says, of those symbols associated with certain holy places in Ireland, which he was in any case to develop in his verse. After some years the rites of the cult had not been worked out, and under the influence of Lady Gregory at Coole he started instead to devote his energies to the Irish National Theatre, and the writing of plays.

The whole project is very typical of Yeats's wish to find and use legendary symbols for Ireland. It is fortunate that Lady Gregory diverted his energies into play-writing, otherwise we might have been left with occult mysteries of minor importance rather than some splendid plays which went far to incorporate the spirit of those mysteries.

Knocknarea, County Sligo

Crowned by Miosgán Meabha (Queen Maeve's cairn), Knocknarea is the most conspicuous and memorable mountain in County Sligo. It was Maeve of Connacht who, after years of bitter fighting, defeated Cuchulain and the Red Branch Knights of Ulster. Legend says that near her tomb on the mountain is a smaller tomb of Eoghan Bel, a warrior knight who was buried upright, A.D. 537: a gesture of heroic despair against Fate such as Cuchulain's in tying himself to a column at the moment of death, and similar to the attitude shown by the soldiers in 'The Black Tower' (*CP*, p.396), when they know they will continue to guard the tower although the King will never come again:

> There in the tomb stand the dead upright,
> But winds come up from the shore:
> They shake when the winds roar,
> Old bones upon the mountain shake.

Yeats was haunted by the mythology connected with Knocknarea from the day when he first stayed as a small boy at 'Merville', his grandparents' house at the foot of the mountain. It was much with him when he wrote *The Wanderings of Oisin* (1886–88; *CP* p.409) within sight of the mountain at George Pollexfen's:

> Caoilte, and Conan, and Finn were there,
> When we followed a deer with our baying hounds,
> With Bran, Sceolan, and Lomair,
> And passing the Firbolgs' burial-mounds,
> Came to the cairn-heaped grassy hill
> Where passionate Maeve is stony-still:

In fact, the 'grey cairn on the hill', on which the wind has 'thrown the thunder', was Ireland itself for Yeats: the burial mounds, the thorn-trees, the waterfalls and the sidhe speak to Red Hanrahan, and through him to us.

174

Ben Bulben, County Sligo
Like Knocknarea, this long, flat-topped limestone mountain (1,750 feet) with its precipice to Glencar, has long figured in Irish legend. In the best-known Irish epic tale, Diarmuid, lover of Grainne, was mortally wounded on its slopes by Finn MacCumhal's enchanted boar, after being chased by Finn throughout Ireland (see Lady Gregory, *Gods and Fighting Men*). The mountain looms large in Yeats's childhood: the smoking cataract of 'The Mountain Tomb' (*CP*, p.136), that same Glencar waterfall 'That all my childhood counted dear', in 'Towards Break of Day' (*CP*, p.208); and again when he is parodying Wordsworth in 'The Tower' (*CP*, p.218):

> No, not in boyhood when with rod and fly,
> Or the humbler worm, I climbed Ben Bulben's back
> And had the livelong summer day to spend.

Lastly, in his final confession of faith, 'Under Ben Bulben' (*CP*, p.397):

> From mountain to mountain ride the wild horsemen.

Jack Yeats, On Drumcliffe Strand *(1918) during a race meeting. The man in the foreground is a Volunteer, and the country woman seems to be regarding him seriously. Queen Maeve's cairn at the top of Knocknarea is clearly visible on the skyline.*

Lough Gill and Innisfree, County Sligo

Lough Gill, near Sligo, flanked by mountains and woods is nearly as unspoiled today as it must have been two hundred years ago. Dramatic emerald isthmuses, covered with holly, bay and arbutus trees, stretch out into the lough, which is studded with islands. Among the smallest is Innisfree (the Heather Island), and jutting out into the lough opposite another larger island is Dooney Rock, near which the fiddler used to play and the folk danced (*CP*, p.82). On one occasion when Yeats was staying with his uncle, George Pollexfen, in the summer of 1889, he decided he would walk round the lough, spending the night out while doing so. He gives an account of his ventures in *Reveries over Childhood and Youth (AU)*.

The book, which inspired Yeats to think of Innisfree as a place to live in, was *Walden* by Henry Thoreau (1817–62), the American poet and philosopher who chose Walden Pond, then a remote spot in the woods near Boston, Mass., in which to live in solitude. Some of the passages which Yeats heard his father read from *Walden* explain the author's reasons: 'I went to the woods because I wished to live deliberately to front only the essential facts of life, and see if I could not learn what it had to teach, and not, when I came to die, that I had not lived.' The actual writing of the poem by Yeats was prompted by an incident which he relates in *The Trembling of the Veil (AU)*. He was very homesick for Sligo, and as he walked through Fleet Street, London, he 'heard a little trickle of water and saw a fountain in a shop-window which balanced a little ball on its jet, and began to remember lake water. From the sudden remembrance came my poem *Innisfree*, my first lyric with anything in its rhythm of my own music.'

The poem was more popular in Yeats's lifetime than any other of his poems, so that he grew to dread being asked to recite it. Once he had to endure hearing hundreds of Boy Scouts saying it in unison, and Dorothy Wellesley records that he frowned all the time he was reciting it to her, after she had asked him to do so. Yeats never allowed Robert Louis Stevenson's words of admiration to appear in any work of his, but they can be read in Stevenson's *Letters*. From Samoa he wrote: 'It is so quaint and airy, simple, artful and eloquent to the heart.' Yeats afterwards declared the first line of the poem had an archaic diction which he would not then use, and he also disliked the inversions. Yet much critical nonsense has been written about the poem, and it seems fashionable to decry it. Stephen Spender in *The Destructive Element* (p.117) says the poem 'calls up the image of a young man reclining on a yellow satin sofa', presumably surrounded by his fellow-aesthetes in London. This surely is tantamount to accusing Yeats of insincerity. He really did wish to get away from 'the pavements grey', the poem being written in 1890 in his study at Bedford

Lough Gill, County Sligo. Innisfree is about 1½ miles up the lough to the right of the photo.

177

Park and, as Louis MacNeice points out in *The Poetry of W. B. Yeats*, County Sligo is fact, not fiction.

If you ever have a chance in summer when you are in Sligo, it is worth while rowing a boat out to Innisfree and staying there for an hour or two. You will be surprised how amazingly accurate was the poet's aural memory: the wild bees hum in the heather, the low, buzzing stridulation of the crickets surrounds you, and 'peace comes dropping slow' with the sound of the gentle lapping of the lake water.

Yeats's recording of the poem (now out of print) read in his unique monotonic voice, brings out the variety in the vowel music, which has been remarked on by critics, although Yeats later said that he hardly knew what a vowel was at the time he wrote the poem. John Masefield used to attend the Monday evening sessions at Woburn Buildings and often heard Yeats read. In *Some Memories of W. B. Yeats* he describes the experience: 'His reading was unlike that of any other man. He stressed the rhythm till it became almost a chant; he went with speed, marking every beat and dwelling on his vowels. That wavering ecstatic song, then heard by me for the first time, was to remain with me for years.'

Lissadell House, County Sligo

An austere stone house in the neoclassical Grecian style, built 1832–34 for Sir Robert Gore-Booth, the grandfather of Eva and Constance whom Yeats knew. It stands at the end of a long drive alongside the bay, almost on the seashore in the woods at the foot of Ben Bulben. Its south front with the great bay windows, looks over Rosses Point across the water to Knocknarea. In 1894 Yeats visited the Gore-Booths when he was staying with his grandmother in Sligo. It is the first of those houses where he found gracious and ordered living, presided over by members of the Protestant ascendancy. Consequently it is not hard to imagine the impression left on this middle-class young man who had not been used to the style of living of the 'gentry': a hundred-foot-long gallery with columns and a floor of Kilkenny marble, with similarly magnificent rooms, as a worthy setting for the two beautiful girls who listened to his poetry and his plans for the Irish Literary movement.

> The light of evening, Lissadell,
> Great windows open to the south,

A visit which he remembered over thirty years later when he wrote this elegy (*CP*, p.263), after their storm-ridden and tragic lives had ended. The house where they were brought up is now an 'image of such politics'—sadly decayed, with the surrounding woods decimated.

The Quays, Sligo

After sailing up the long, twisting estuary of the Garavogue, the

178

moment of disembarking from their grandfather's steamship at the Quays, busy with boats, was a lifelong memory for the Yeats children. During the holidays, as Willie grew older, he would stroll along the quayside among the sailors and fishermen, sometimes hearing McCoy, a crazy ship's carpenter, as he read the Scriptures and denounced his neighbours from an old ship's boiler left on the Quay—'very big, very high, the top far out of reach, and all red rust'. 'Why should not Old Men be Mad?' (*CP*, p.388) may be using this memory as an exemplar of the inexorable whims of Fate, or Yeats may be thinking of William, his Pollexfen uncle, who had designed the Quays but who lingered in a mental home until he died in 1913. Yeats certainly remembers the ship's carpenter when he names his last prose work, *On the Boiler* (1938), which has a cover design, by Jack Yeats, of the bearded old man struggling to the top of the boiler to preach.

Despite his shyness, Jack as a boy mixed more with the people of the Quays than did the poet, and even on one occasion organized donkey races for the children of the sailors. In Jack's paintings, the pilot with the peaked cap becomes a regular theme; in W. B. Yeats's writing, the Quays epitomize the Pollexfen physical vitality and strength, which, combined with the literary and artistic gifts of the Yeatses, made the poet often think, as in 'Under Saturn' (*CP*, p.202), of his childhood vow 'sworn in vain Never to leave that valley his fathers called their home'.

Drumcliffe
In the Drumcliffe valley, three and a half miles from Sligo, shadowed by Ben Bulben, Rector Yeats lived in the tall Rectory across the road from the plain church (1809), whose square tower rises among the trees: the home of many of the poet's Anglo-Irish ancestors on both sides of the family, whom he sings of in 'Are you Content?' (*CP*, p.370):

> He that in Sligo at Drumcliff
> Set up the old stone Cross,
> That red-headed rector in County Down,
> A good man on a horse,
> Sandymount Corbets, that notable man
> Old William Pollexfen,
> The smuggler Middleton, Butlers far back,
> Half legendary men.

The limestone precipices of Ben Bulben and King's Mountain form a dramatic back-drop, and, nearer, the Celtic Cross and the lower part of a Round Tower alone remain of Saint Columba's monastery. The dualism of the mythology of Ireland, Christian and pagan, is here centred. So it was Yeats's wish to be buried near the church,

179

though the proud epitaph on his tombstone is unusually pagan. Here
he would join his ancestors and the heroic figures of Irish legend.

> No marble, no conventional phrase;
> On limestone quarried near the spot
> By his command these lines are cut:
>> *Cast a cold eye*
>> *On life, on death,*
>> *Horseman, pass by!*

England

Bedford Park, Chiswick

From 1876–80 the Yeats family lived at 8 Woodstock Road, Bedford
Park, the forerunner of all redbrick garden suburbs, then being built
on the north side of the Hammersmith Road. Its constulant architect
was Norman Shaw, and with its well designed houses, pleasant
winding roads and a green, lined by mature trees, it was certainly an
improvement for the Yeatses on the London and Dublin terrace
houses in which they had been living. Many of the inhabitants were
artists and writers, and gradually Bedford Park became a self-
contained residential unit, with its own cultural, religious and social
activities: Chiswick School of Art, which Jack Yeats briefly attended,
a new church, and an inn with stores, as well as a club house in which
plays could be performed. From the ages of nine and eight Willie and
his sister Lily visited their father's friends and talked freely, with
Irish accents and turns of phrase learnt from the old coachman and
the stable-boy at the Pollexfens. Although they both longed to return
to Sligo, the four years at Bedford Park, except for the unpleasantness
at school, were enjoyable.

Then J. B. Yeats led his family off to Dublin, where he tried to sell
his pictures, with little success. So at the end of 1887 he returned with
his family to No. 3 Blenheim Road, a tall redbrick house with a large
horse-chestnut tree shading the garden. The poet's mother was then
suffering from the results of a stroke from which she never recovered
before she died in 1900. For the period 1888 to 1896 Yeats lived with
his family; but then decided to have his own rooms in Woburn
Buildings, Euston. Thanks largely to J. B. Yeats's temperament and
fortunes, they had been a rootless family, except, of course, for Sligo,
so Bedford Park provided a more stable existence for them. In this
house Yeats met Madame Blavatsky, the founder of the Theosophical
Society, MacGregor Mathers, the magician, Maud Gonne and
Florence Farr, whom Yeats saw playing the lead in May 1890 in a

*Ben Bulben from Drumcliffe churchyard. Yeats's grave is
in the immediate foreground.*

performance of *A Sicilian Idyll* at the Club House, the play being written by an Irish college friend of his father's, Dr Todhunter, who was a neighbour in Bedford Park. But Yeats was away for long periods in Sligo, Dublin, Paris and Coole Park, and also he was out of sympathy with many of his father's friends who, on the whole, were naturalistic as painters and realist as writers. His interest in Blake and the symbolists had moved him from their positivist and rationalist point of view with which he found nothing in common.

> Then, too, they were very ignorant men; they read nothing, for nothing mattered but 'knowing how to paint', being in reaction against a generation that seemed to have wasted its time upon so many things. I thought myself alone in hating these young men, their contempt for the past, their monopoly of the future, but in a few months I was to discover others of my own age who thought as I did.

Thus does Yeats sum up in *AU* the painters from the Paris art schools who were the younger friends of his father. The older men whom the poet met at Bedford Park were equally limited: York Powell, Oxford Professor of History, who 'cared nothing for philosophy, nothing for economics, nothing for the policy of nations', or the painter with the model railway running round his studio or the decorative artist who had placed a great lychgate, bought from some churchyard, at the entrance of his garden. G. K. Chesterton's ridicule of 'Saffron Park', as he called it in *The Man who was Thursday* (1908) was from his inside knowledge, as he was married there, a ceremony all the Yeatses attended.

However, there was what the Danish architect, Rasmussen, calls 'a stamp of unity' about this garden suburb, and maybe Yeats benefited from an environment, when he was a boy, in which there were Morris wallpapers and de Morgan tiles. But he had outgrown it by their second stay.

18 Woburn Buildings (now 5 Woburn Walk), London W.C.1
From 1895 to 1919 Yeats occupied this terraced house near St Pancras church, on the north side of what might now be called a 'pedestrian precinct', then a stone-flagged alley. The houses were built in the early nineteenth century, and the area had evidently come down in the world. In fact, according to *Hone*, Yeats was known as 'the toff wot lives in the Buildings', as he was said to be the only person in the street who ever received letters. It was convenient for him as it was near the British Museum, where he was reading, and many of his friends lived fairly near. Ezra Pound sometimes attended Yeats's Monday evenings, when he was at home to his friends (8 p.m. until

No 5 Woburn Walk, London WC.1.

2 a.m. or later). According to Douglas Goldring, *South Lodge* (1943, p.49), the young Pound used to dominate the room as he took it upon himself to distribute Yeats's cigarettes and Chianti, laying down the law about poetry as he did it. John Masefield, also young, but gentler mannered, describes the house in *Some Memories of W. B. Yeats*:

> On entering the house, you went along the hall to the stair, which led inwards, then curved, and brought you to the landing on which he lived. On this, the second floor, he had a biggish front sitting-room and a small back kitchen. On the floor above, he had corresponding rooms, in which he slept.
>
> His sitting-room was papered with brown paper; the window was hung with dark curtains; brown baize at one time; later a dim blue.

Masefield goes on to list the pictures: a large portrait of the poet painted by his father; 'Memory Harbour' (Sligo) by Jack Yeats; Blake's first Dante engraving, 'The Whirlwind of Lovers'; some more Blake engravings, including 'The Ancient of Days'; two of the poet's own pastels of the lake and hills at Coole; and a Beardsley poster for Florence Farr's production of *The Land of Heart's Desire*. He continues:

> The table stood in the centre of the room during meals, and was then lifted to the side. At meal-times it bore upon it a little curved metal gong or striker of an unusual design (with some scarlet colour on it), which he struck to summon Mrs Old [she and her husband, a carpenter, were Yeats's landlords who looked after and 'did' for him.] After meals, the table bore dark glasses, brown or green, and a dull red-clay tobacco-jar (with an oriental dragon embossed on it), containing cigarettes. The chairs were dark, the effect of the room was sombre. After 1904–5, he added to the room a big, dark blue lectern, on which his Kelmscott Chaucer stood, between enormous candles in big blue wooden sconces. These candles stood about four feet and were as thick as a ship's oar. The dim dark blue of this lectern was the most noticeable colour in the room. He added curtains to match it.
>
> This sitting room has been described in detail because it was the most interesting room in London.

After Yeats's marriage, Mrs Yeats got going on the room and obviously cleaned it up in the then current taste. Swept away were the dark and sombre objects and Pre-Raphaelite blues, to be replaced by the later Voysey influence of unstained wood and earthenware bowls. In a letter to Lady Gregory, written in November 1917, Yeats describes the transformation:

I wish you could see Woburn Buildings now—nothing changed

in plan but little touches here and there, and in my bedroom (the old Bathroom) with furniture of unpainted, unpolished wood such as for years I have wished for. Then there is a dinner service of great purple plates for meat, and various earthenware bowls for other purposes.

After twenty-four years Woburn Buildings was given up when the Yeatses decided to live in the summer at Thoor Ballylee. There is no doubt of the importance of this house set, as it was, in the middle of all those other influences brought in by his friends in London.

Nos 45 and 4 Broad Street, Oxford

Although both these houses were pleasant examples of late seventeenth-century town architecture, they have been demolished since the Yeatses lived in them; the first for the New Bodleian Library building, the second for a department store.

Yeats first stayed in Oxford in 1888 with his father's friend, Professor York Powell. He read in the Bodleian Library, walked much in the unspoiled Oxford countryside, and wrote to Katharine Tynan: 'One understands English poetry more from seeing a place like this. I wonder anybody does anything in Oxford but dream and remember the place is so beautiful.'

In early 1918 when Woburn Buildings had been let, Mrs Yeats found rooms in No. 45 Broad Street just over the road from the Bodleian. In October 1919 the Yeatses rented No. 4 at the other end of the street near the Cornmarket corner. It was a quieter city then, so Yeats would have had no difficulty in hearing Great Tom of Christ Church tolling the curfew on All Souls Night, when he was to remember those friends of his from the time of his first Oxford visit— Horton, Florence Farr and MacGregor Mathers, all dead by 1919.

After an extended lecture tour in the U.S.A. in 1920, they again settled at No. 4, at which in 1921 he wrote some of 'Meditations in Time of Civil War' (*CP*, p.225). He used to visit Garsington Manor, Lady Ottoline Morrell's house near Oxford, the gardens of which are still much the same, though the vast industrial complex of Cowley has crept up over a lane along which Yeats and his friends used to walk back to Oxford. In the garden by the house the 'indifferent garden deities' on the terraces still stare down in stony silence, but the tiny fountain pouring from a carved stone shell into a small basin, by which Yeats must have sat, has ceased to run. Perhaps this in itself is symbolic of the lost values of Coole and other such houses.

At No. 4 he held his 'Monday evenings' for undergraduates and friends. After attending these, L. A. G. Strong would return to the Dragon School in North Oxford, where he was then teaching, 'exhilarated, walking on air, upheld and inspired by the knowledge, which rapidly became incredible during the week, that life could be lived on such a plane of thought and at such a pitch'.

During the winter of 1920–21 while the Black and Tans were carrying out their murderous campaign in Ireland, Yeats addressed the Oxford Union denouncing the Government's policy. He held an audience of undergraduates spellbound as he paced up and down the aisle of the Union debating hall, and for many it was an occasion they would never forget.

After a brief stay in a small rented house called Minchen's Cottage, on the main road at Shillingford, Oxfordshire, and a few months in the summer of 1921 at Thame, also in Oxfordshire, where his son Michael was born, Yeats decided it was time to return to Ireland, so bought the house in Merrion Square. He had enjoyed his time in Oxford, especially the visits of his friends, including among many others Maurice Bowra, Robert Bridges and John Masefield (who lived nearby on Boar's Hill). He was not to return until May 1931 when he received a doctorate of Letters from the University. This was his last visit to the city.

Stone Cottage, Coleman's Hatch, Hartfield, Sussex

Pleasantly situated on a private road, it still overlooks a typically unspoilt heath valley in East Sussex. Now slightly enlarged on what it was in Yeats's time, nevertheless it is sturdily built of dressed stone quarried on the spot in about 1820. When Yeats was staying nearby in 1913 with his friends the Tuckers (whose daughter married Ezra Pound), he found Stone Cottage and settled there with Pound in the autumn of that year. It was quiet and not too inaccessible—about an hour to London. There he prepared his American lecture tour, wrote and read much. He spent the winters of 1913, 1914 and 1915 there, during which time Lady Gregory sometimes came down at the weekends bringing with her intelligent and attractive women whom she thought might be suitable for Yeats. Eventually she arrived with Miss Georgie Hyde-Lees, whom Yeats had met previously with the Tuckers. Ezra Pound was the best man at their wedding at the Register Office in Harrow Road, London, on 20 October 1917, and some days of the honeymoon were spent in Stone Cottage.

Penns-in-the-Rocks, Withyham, Sussex

This was the home of Lady Gerald Wellesley (Dorothy Wellesley, the poetess). It is an elegant, part-Georgian house of rose-red brick, set in a large garden with rocky sandstone outcrops, lake and small classical garden temple, much admired by Yeats. He stayed at Penns in April and May 1937 for about a week at a time, and for similar periods in March and April 1938, his last visit being in July of that year. It provided him with an aristocratic cultured setting like Coole Park; and, like Lady Gregory, Dorothy Wellesley invited mutual friends over to meet him to discuss his schemes for words and music. He once wrote to her in a thank-you letter that he 'found great peace and contentment' among beautiful things and in her company.

During his last years he was physically weak though mentally active. Dorothy Wellesley relates how they used to walk together in the old walled garden, accompanied by her Great Dane, Brutus. In 'To Dorothy Wellesley' (*Last Poems, CP,* p.349) Brutus receives an honourable mention:

> Climb to your chamber full of books and wait,
> No book upon the knee, and no one there
> But a Great Dane that cannot bay the moon
> And now lies sunk in sleep.

Although Yeats was not especially fond of dogs, he had observed, according to Dorothy Wellesley, Brutus's 'great majesty, form and conduct' (see *Letters on Poetry from W. B. Yeats to Dorothy Wellesley,* p.145):

> When Yeats seemed too tired to reach a garden seat, the three of us would walk abreast, Yeats's hand and part of his great weight supported on my right shoulder, while my left hand and shoulder was supported by the great dog. I was always afraid of a landslide, but the great hound pacing slowly beside me never let me down. The seat was reached, the end achieved, and the tremendous Dane would settle down and turn into a piece of black and white marble until, our conversation ended, he would help us back again to the house.

It was Sir William Rothenstein, R.A. who had originally introduced Yeats to Dorothy Wellesley, and in his autobiography, *Since Fifty* (p.249), he describes the physical appearance of the young and the old poet at Penns-in-the-Rocks:

> Dorothy, slight, fair, with deep violet eyes and auburn hair . . . next to Yeats, dressed in crimson shirt, flowing coloured tie, now in his later years, brown-skinned under his crown of white hair, his dark eyes aslant, broad-shouldered and ample of form—he once so pale and lanky.

Once, on his way back to London from Penns, Yeats made a remark to Rothenstein which explains much in his later poetry: 'When I was young my mind was a grub, my body a butterfly, now in my old age, my body is a grub, my mind a butterfly.'

Italy

Urbino

In April 1907 Yeats joined Lady Gregory and Robert at Venice, after which they visited Florence, Milan (which he disliked), Urbino, Ferrara and Ravenna. At Urbino he saw the great ducal palace, described by Castiglione in *The Book of the Courtier* (1528) which he and Lady Gregory had read in Thomas Hoby's translation, at Coole before they went to Italy on this trip. In 'The People' (*CP*, p.169), Yeats describes the setting briefly:

> . . . the steep street of Urbino
> To where the Duchess and her people talked
> The stately midnight through until they stood
> In their great window looking at the dawn;

Here, at the end of the fifteenth century, Duke Federigo da Monte-feltro had had the fortress redesigned as a palace, 'a city within a city', in 'proud, golden Urbino' as Dante described it. From the courtyard ascends a monumental staircase to the living-rooms. It was there that the Duke founded his schools of Art and Poetry, Mathematics and Humanism; the library, in its day being more complete than that of Florence or Oxford University. In this vast, but beautifully proportioned building, dominating Urbino, flourished a vigorous intellectual life, led by Duke Federigo, an honest *condottiere*, compassionate in war, a patron of the arts, well-read in the classics, educated in music, poetry, grammar, maths, painting, and skilled in dancing and riding, possessing an international reputation as a fine ruler of a flourishing duchy.

In *The Courtier* Castiglione gives a detailed and personal account, in four sections, of discussions which took place in the palace on four evenings in March 1507, presided over by the Duchess Elizabetta who was married to Guidobaldo, Federigo's son. The subjects discussed cover a wide field—the responsibilities of rulers, the nature of love, the Wheel of Fortune, women's liberation, and the moral and aesthetic standards fitting to a gentleman. Some of the thirty characters who take part in the arguments show such individual traits that one feels one gets to know them by the ideas they express and the way they speak. It is therefore a surprise when at the beginning of the fourth section, Castiglione suddenly says they are now all dead. Yeats was much moved by this. In his *Diary*, kept in 1909 (*AU*, p.478), he wrote:

> All Wednesday I heard Castiglione's phrase ringing in my memory, 'Never be it spoken without tears, the Duchess, too, is dead', and that phrase, which—coming where it did among the numbering of his dead—often moved me till my eyes dimmed, brought before me all his sorrow and my own, as though one saw the worth of life fade for ever.

The way of life at Urbino in Duke Federigo's time stood for Yeats as the keystone in a Unity of Being in which *cortesia* found its full realization. It engendered the virtues of the Renaissance idealized figure: a mixture of good scholar, soldier, classical hero, Christian believer, having a virtuous mind, a dignity, a mannered elegance and virtue in the service of his prince. And Yeats was not slow to compare this with the politicians and rich men of his contemporary Ireland. In 'To a Wealthy Man who promised a second Subscription . . .' (*CP*, p.119) he compares the Renaissance rulers who supported the arts with a Dublin art patron who refused to give more money for Sir Hugh Lane's new picture gallery. Duke Guidobaldo da Monte-feltro is referred to

> when he made
> That grammar school of courtesies
> Where wit and beauty learned their trade
> Upon Urbino's windy hill,

It was not surprising that Yeats never forgot this palace at Urbino, or his admiration for the best qualities of Renaissance rulers.

Ravenna, Sicily and Rome
During this visit in 1907 Yeats also visited Ravenna where he saw the superb sixth-century Byzantine mosaics. But, according to D. J. Gordon and Ian Fletcher (*Images of a Poet*, p.82), the visit did not 'appear to have left a decisive impression on his work: his interest was concentrated on Italian painting, particularly of the Renaissance'. However, Jon Stallworthy (*Between the Lines*) thinks that Yeats's visit to Ravenna in 1907 was the main source of his interest which culminated in the Byzantium poems. Both 1907 and 1925, when he saw more Byzantium mosaics, are important.

From December to March 1924–25 the Yeatses visited Sicily and Rome on a prolonged holiday, during which he finished *VIS*. On this holiday he examined Byzantine mosaics in Sicily and in early Christian churches in Rome, taking photographs home with him. For many years he had been reading about Byzantine art, but it must have been during these visits that he finally decided to use Byzantium as the symbol for art itself in the city of Holy Wisdom, in which the soul is transfigured to a state 'out of nature'. Byzantine mosaics, from the sixth to the eleventh century, were often placed in cross-in-square churches with a central cupola or dome, and they pictured the Kos-mos (paradise) at the highest point of the church, descending to the terrestrial world in hierarchical order. One sees huge images of God the Father (Pantocrator) looking down on man placed in descending order; first on Christ, the image of God, then on the saints and martyrs, then on the animal and vegetable world.

Mosaic at its best is on curved and vaulted surfaces, especially in the upper parts of a church—flat surfaces do not reflect light as much, appearing duller. But on the curvature of domes, on the opposite sides of niches and angles, or when encased in cupolas, pendentives

and vaults, the cubes of gold mosaic glitter, and the enamel sparkles. The golden ground which entirely surrounds the figures, has an aura of sanctity in this setting of brilliant reflections, and golden grounds are common in all the great Byzantine mosaics.

> O sages standing in God's holy fire
> As in the gold mosaic of a wall,

In 'Sailing to Byzantium' (*CP*, p.217–18), the word 'holy' is repeated three times; and it is worth noting that, in the process of making the gold and enamel cubes, fire is used to purify the colour. When mosaic figures of saints are placed in a dome or cupola, as in the two Baptisteries at Ravenna, they stand frontally, as it were like spokes in a great wheel, and as one looks up at them from beneath, they appear to whirl in their circular and rhythmic relation to the other mosaics in the church. The dome comes to possess a magical dancelike rhythm as one moves one's head up or walks forward to view the figures. Similarly, in certain mosaics in the cathedral at Monreale, Sicily, which Mrs Yeats told Jon Stallworthy had much affected Yeats, the perspective seems to be upset by the curves and angles of the tympanum, and this gives the same gyring effect, as it were including the beholder in the movement which appears to continue into the spatial unit between him and the mosaic.

Yeats also saw the Norman twelfth-century palace of La Ziza, Palermo, which has a remnant of a secular mosaic showing much of oriental influences, such as peacocks (emblems of immortality), in stylized trees with tendril branches, fantastic animals and archers, like a Persian tapestry. This has no parallel with religious mosaics, but may well have interested Yeats in its iconography.

Finally, Professor Gordon and Dr Fletcher (*op. cit.* p.83) note that the ninth-century church of S. Prassede in Rome has 'striking counterparts of the sages in their golden fire'. This refers to the mosaics on the raised tribune (platform) in this church. Over the grand arch, separating nave from choir, is a mosaic of the New Jerusalem of the Apocalypse; within the tribune, Christ in golden classical robes, and the saints and martyrs amidst trees of paradise, together with the twenty-four elders and the symbols of the Evangelists, all under a vaulted blue heaven. The Yeatses certainly visited this church, and also the basilica of S. Clemente where the vault of the tribune is covered by a twelfth-century mosaic of a great cross from heaven to earth, springing from a stylized vine, together with Christ and the saints, alongside the rivers of paradise and trees with birds in the foliage. 'The hammered gold and gold enamelling', 'the sages standing in God's holy fire', the marbles on the dancing-floor (the

The dome of the Ortodossi baptistery at Ravenna.

pavement of the raised tribune) and the golden bird, 'planted on the star-lit golden bough', in the mosaics are all present in the context of these churches with the Byzantine art which so stimulated Yeats's imagination.

It is also possible he may have attended the Easter Eve service (1925) at S. Prassede in Rome. At this ceremony in the darkened church at night the priests bless and light the great paschal candle from the flame of a brazier in the starlit court outside. Then the interior of the church is slowly filled with pin-points of light as the congregation, in procession to the altar, light their own candles from the paschal candle. When this is completed, floodlights suddenly illuminate the golden splendour of the mosaics, and the choir sings a triumphant *Exultet*. That is indeed a moment of joy when Yeats could have felt the sages becoming the singing masters of his soul.

Majorca

Palma, Majorca

In December 1935, to 'escape telephones and foul weather', Yeats went by sea to Palma, accompanied by the Indian swami, Shri Purohit, whom he had met the previous year, and with whom he proposed to collaborate on a translation of the Hindu Upanishads. Purohit was a mendicant Brahmin monk, aged about fifty, a scholar, a Yogi, who for nine years had been wandering with his begging-bowl. His grandfather had been a Marátha millionaire, but Shri Purohit had renounced all worldly goods and become a Brahmin priest. Yeats admired him, questioned him on Hindu philosophy and had written an introduction to his autobiography, *An Indian Monk: his life and adventures*, 1932 (see *E & I*, pp.426–37 and 449–85 for further details). In 1935, when they arrived at Palma, Yeats was suffering from the rigours of a very rough sea voyage, and Purohit from the austerities of his religious life.

For about forty years Yeats had heard AE constantly quoting from the Hindu Upanishads, using an awful translation, as Yeats says, with 'latinized words, polyglot phrases, sedentary distortions of an unnatural English', including 'muddles muddied by "Lo! Verily" and "Forsooth",' which, said Yeats, 'could not represent what grass farmers sang thousands of years ago, what their descendants sing today'. Upanishad is doctrine or wisdom of the holy books, the Vedas, sung at the feet of a holy man or Master present or in the spirit. Shri Purohit used to sing an Upanishad every morning in Sanskrit, and Yeats quickly sensed its beauty even from Purohit's translation and so collaborated with him to produce *The Ten Principal Upanishads*, published in 1937. In a letter to Dorothy Wellesley he describes their progress:

> I am delighted with my life here. I breakfast at 7.30 and write in bed until 11 or 11.30. From 3 to 4 I help Purohit Swami to translate

the Upanishads. It is amusing to see his delighted astonishment when he discovers that he can call a goddess, 'this handsome girl' or even 'a pretty girl' instead of a 'maiden of surpassing loveliness'. I say to him 'think like a wise man but express yourself like the common people' and the result is that he will make the first great translation of the *Upanishads*. He takes great care of me and always walks slowly up and downstairs in front of me, very wide and impassable in his orange robe, for fear I may walk too fast for my heart.

Yeats is here being modest. It is *his* translation which is the 'first great translation of the *Upanishads*'. Whether it accurately translates the Sanskrit I do not know, but it has a simplicity and purity of diction which is similar to Eliot's in *Four Quartets* when he has similar philosophic themes to express. The Kena-Upanishad 2, is one of the shortest but shows these qualities fully:

'If you think that you know much, you know little.
If you think that you know It from study of your own mind
                    or of nature, study again'.
The enquirer said: 'I do not think that I know much, I
         neither say that I know, nor say that I do not'.
The teacher answered: 'The man who claims that he knows,
                                    knows nothing;
but he who claims nothing, knows. The ignorant think
         that spirit lies within knowledge, the wise man
                    knows It beyond knowledge.
Spirit is known through revelation. It leads to freedom.
                    It leads to power.
Revelation is the conquest of death.
'The living man who finds Spirit, finds Truth. But if he
fail, he sinks among foul shapes. The man who can see
the same Spirit in every creature, clings neither to this
nor that, attains immortal life'.

These translations of the Upanishads, in superb poetic prose, have been much neglected by Yeats scholars, and, like his translation of Sophocles's *Oedipus Rex* (wonderful to hear in Sir Laurence Olivier's production), have not received true recognition.

During his work with the swami, Yeats's physical condition grew worse, and Mrs Yeats went out to Palma in February 1936. She found him better, but thought it would be a long convalescence, as he was suffering from nephritis, the kidney complaint from which he eventually died. He bore it with courage and humour, although it involved discomfort. Gradually his condition improved and he and the swami finished the translation, after which the swami returned to India and the Yeatses to England.

Sweden

Stockholm

In his essay 'The Bounty of Sweden' (*AU*, p.531), Yeats describes in great detail his visit to Sweden to receive the Nobel Award for Literature in 1923. The presentation ceremony took place in the Hall of the Swedish Academy on 10 December, and the dignity of the occasion, especially of 'the old King, intelligent and friendly like some country gentleman who can quote Horace and Catullus', much impressed Yeats. The whole setting reminded him of Castiglione's description of the Court of Urbino; and even the French Renaissance architectural detail of the huge eighteenth-century Royal Palace made him think of the Ulster Bank in Sligo, which he had not seen for many years, showing what an astonishing visual memory he had. He regrets that such architectural details—in this case, it was semi-circular headed windows flanked by classic pilasters—should have since been used 'for all sorts of purposes, as if they had come out of a child's box of wooden bricks'. It certainly is a decline from the Royal Palace to the small two-storeyed bank on the street corner at Sligo. Before Yeats returned, he delivered a lecture on 'The Irish Theatre', at the Swedish Royal Academy, and saw a performance of *Cathleen ni Houlihan*.

United States of America, and Canada

Hone lists five lecture tours by the poet:

1. 1903–04, for three months in the winter, giving thirty lectures to universities, colleges and Irish societies. He earned about 3,200 dollars so was able to repay Lady Gregory what he owed her. During the tour he received a cable from Maud Gonne telling him of her marriage.

2. 1911, with the Abbey Theatre company; but after the first performance at Boston, Mass., he left for home, leaving Lady Gregory to manage the tour.

3. 1914 (February and March), misleading in *Hone*, as the chapter discussing it is headed '1916'.

4. 1919–20 (November–May). With Mrs Yeats. Met his father for the last time, in New York. When in Portland, Oregon, he was presented by Junzo Sato with his samurai's sword.

5. 1932–33 (October–January). Without his wife, but he had a friend as secretary and 'nurse'. When in New York stayed at the luxury Waldorf-Astoria hotel. He was able to make enough money to pay for improvements at Riversdale, and to endow an Irish Academy of Letters.

The strain of lecturing on tour in the U.S.A. has damaged the health of many a stronger man than Yeats, but he seems to have survived the rigours very well. He addressed audiences ranging in numbers from twenty to two thousand, and was always a cool, systematic and professional performer who was able to adapt his style appropriately. He travelled by train from the East coast to California, from the Gulf to Canada, lecturing in the first two tours mostly on the Irish Literary Renaissance, but later, after Synge's *Playboy of the Western World*, performed by the Abbey Players had enraged Irish-American audiences, he read his poems and talked about them (see Henn, *The Lonely Tower*, p.240) as well as showing slides illustrating Blake's *Book of Job*, and Calvert's and Palmer's etchings, including, of course, 'The Lonely Tower'. He was a great success, and John Quinn thought after one of the earlier tours that 'no Irishman since the time of Parnell's great trip' had made so 'grand an impression'. *Hone* (pp.201–2) describes his public speaking:

> He had the lower lip which reveals the born orator and the born pugilist; a certain disdain, a certain pugnacity, is necessary both to the pugilist and the orator. In addressing large audiences he was sometimes uneasy at the start, and would stride up and down the platform in a rather surprising manner before he attained to his natural distinction of bearing, his gravity of utterance and his rhythm. His voice was musical, touched with melancholy, the tones rising and falling in a continuous flow of sound. He lingered on certain words to avoid as it were a hiatus, but the pauses when they occurred were timed and still full of sound, like the musical pauses in the execution of a master. This cadenced utterance was most characteristic. When emphasis was needed he would introduce a hard metallic note, and this when passion intruded was like the clash of sword-blades. His myopic gaze as he spoke was turned within, looking into the darkness, where, as he himself said, 'there is always something'.

The only overt reference to a memory from these tours is in 'His Phœnix' (*CP*, p.170), a poem written some years later. Here, among a list of attractive and beautiful women, he remembers a certain Miss Marlowe, an actress whom he had seen as Juliet. But she, with all the others, is not equal to the proud, lonely Maud Gonne.

I knew a phœnix in my youth, so let them have their day.

France

Paris

Compared with T. S. Eliot, who spoke French fluently, Yeats was little influenced by visits to Paris and meeting French writers. He went in 1894, '95, '96 and '99, usually to see Maud Gonne or MacGregor Mathers. The meeting with Synge was by chance. In 1894 he was taken by Arthur Symons to see Verlaine who died in January 1896 and was then considered *the* poet of the day, who fortunately spoke English. But, as far as I can find, he never went to the *mardis* of Stephane Mallarmé in the rue de Rome, though he heard all about them from Symons, and later copied the idea at Woburn Buildings. On his final visit in 1921 he was the delegate of Sinn Féin at the Irish Race Congress.

Normandy

Yeats often visited Maud Gonne MacBride, her adopted daughter Iseult, and her son, Seán, at her house at Coleville, near Calvados in the summers of 1910, '12, '16, and '17. It was on the beach there that he read her 'Easter 1916'.

Cap Martin and Roquebrune, Alpes-Maritime

Yeats and his wife spent part of the winter of 1937–38, when he was recuperating from his illness, at the Carlton Hotel on the sea-front at Menton, in the south of France. Then, after moving round in Ireland and England in the spring, summer and autumn of 1938, they again went to the French Riviera in late November 1938, to the small Hôtel Idéal Séjour above Cap Martin, two kilometres from Menton, amid pine trees and olive groves, very different from cosmopolitan cities like Menton. He was mentally active right up to his death, writing some of his *Last Poems*, correcting proofs of *The Death of Cuchulain*, and corresponding with friends. He died on Saturday 28 January and was buried in the cemetery of the Chapel of St Pancrace at Roquebrune, a small town clinging to a terraced and rocky hillside, overlooking the sea and Cap Martin. Not until 1948 was his body brought home to Drumcliffe.

Places referred to either directly or by inference in the poems

The Glen at Alt, Co. Sligo	The Man and the Echo
Ballinaford, Co. Sligo	The Ballad of Father O'Hart
Ballisodare, Co. Sligo	Down by the Salley Gardens
Ballygawley, Co. Sligo	Red Hanrahan's Curse
Beltra Strand, Co. Sligo	The Valley of the Black Pig
Ben Bulben, Co. Sligo	Towards Break of Day
	Under Ben Bulben
	The Mountain Tomb
	The Tower, 1
	Alternative Song for the Severed Head
Carrowmore, Co. Sligo	The Wanderings of Oisin

Castle Dargan, Co. Sligo	Red Hanrahan's Curse
Cumeen (Cummen) Strand, Co. Sligo	Red Hanrahan's Song about Ireland
Cloone, Co. Kilkenny	The Tower, II
Cashel, Co. Tipperary	The Grey Rock
	The Double Vision of Michael Robartes
Collooney, Co. Sligo	The Ballad of Father O'Hart
Cloyne, Co. Cork	The Seven Sages
Coole Park, Co. Galway	In the Seven Woods
	Upon a House shaken by the Land Agitation
	The Wild Swans at Coole
	Shepherd and Goatherd
	To a Squirrel at Kyle-na-No
	A Prayer for my Daughter
	The New Faces
	Coole Park, 1929
	Coole Park and Ballylee
	The Man and the Echo
	Beautiful Lofty Things
Croagh Patrick, Co. Mayo	The Dancer at Cruachan and Cro-Patrick
Croghan (Cruachan), Co. Roscommon	The Hour before Dawn
	Tom at Cruachan
	The Old Age of Queen Maeve
Dooney Rock, Lough Gill, Co. Sligo	The Fiddler of Dooney
Dromahair, Co. Sligo	The Man who dreamed of Faeryland
Drumcliffe, Co. Sligo	Are you Content?
	Under Ben Bulben
Dublin, The Abbey Theatre	Beautiful Lofty Things
Dublin, the General Post Office	Three Songs to the One Burden, III
	The Statues
Dublin, Glasnevin Cemetery	To a Shade
	Parnell's Funeral
Dublin, Kilmainham Gaol	On a Political Prisoner
Dublin, St Patrick's Cathedral	The Seven Sages
	Swift's Epitaph
Dublin, various streets	The Three Monuments
	In the Seven Woods
	Easter, 1916
	The O'Rahilly
Ferrara, Emilia-Romagna, Italy	The People
Glencar, Co. Sligo	The Stolen Child

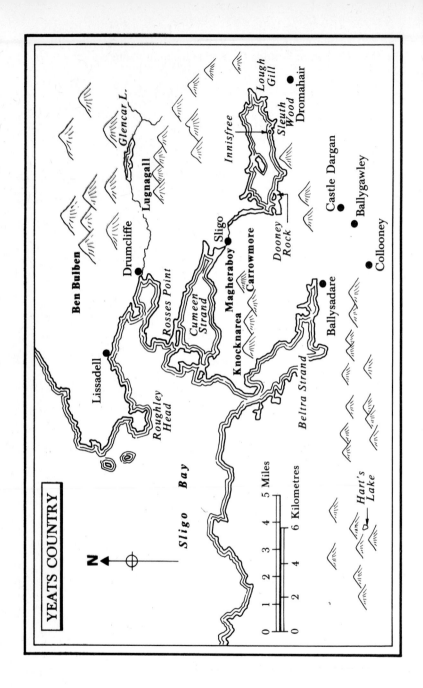

YEATS COUNTRY

Sligo Bay

N

Ben Bulben

Glencar L.
Lugnagall
Drumcliffe
Rosses Point
Lissadell
Roughley Head

Cumeen Strand
Sligo
Magheraboy
Knocknarea
Carrowmore
Beltra Strand

Innisfree
Lough Gill
Sleuth Wood
Dromahair
Castle Dargan
Ballygawley
Colooney
Dooney Rock
Ballysadare

Hart's Lake

5 Miles
6 Kilometres
0 1 2 3 4 5
0 2 4 6

199

Sligo	Under Saturn
	Are you content?
	In Memory of Alfred Pollexfen
	The Meditation of the Old Fisherman
Tara, Co. Meath	The Two Kings
	Tara's Halls
Thoor Ballylee, Co. Galway	The Tower
	In Memory of Robert Gregory
	A Prayer for my Daughter
	A Dialogue of Self and Soul
	Blood and the Moon
	To be carved on a Stone at Thoor Ballylee
	A Prayer on going into my House
	Meditations in Time of Civil War II, V, VI, VII
Tiraragh, Co. Sligo	The Ballad of Father O'Hart
Urbino, The Marches, Italy	The People
	To a Wealthy Man ...
Venice	To a Wealthy Man ...

Yeats's spelling is often erratic. 'Magheraboy' above is an example of this.

Yeats's Symbols

SYMBOL	ORIGIN	CONNECTIONS	ATTRIBUTES
I			
Tower	Babylon	Aspiration to Heaven	Isolation
	Alexandria	Gyres (winding stair)	Security
	Ballylee	Norman Conquest	Night
	Milton	Crumbling roof	Scholar
	Shelley	Battlements	Warfare
	Samuel Palmer		
Troy	Homer	Leda	Cyclic periods
	Virgil	Destruction	Burning of a city
		Achilles	'femme fatale'
		Helen	
		Deirdre	
		Maud Gonne	
Annunciation	Myth	Leda	Origins of love and war
	Iconography	Logos	Cyclic reversals of civilization
	New Testament	Swan	
		Dove	Arrow
II			
Swan	Myth	Soul	'Free from all elements'
	Iconography	Purity	Woman-bird-spirit
	Irish folk lore	Fidelity	
	Coole	Death song	Subjective man
		Leda	
Falcon and Hawk	Egyptian and Irish folk-lore	Soul Guardian	Spirit
			Immortality
			Freedom
			Strength
			Nobility (heroic)
			Subjective man
			Ferocity

Heron *(Herne,* *Crane)*	Iconography Myth Folklore Visual experience	Solitary fisher Metamorphosis Hunchback	Solitary man
Curlew	Experience	Loneliness Moorland Sea	'Crystalline cry' Souls in Company
Crow and Raven	Myth Folklore	Omens Blackness and death	Morrigu

III

Hare	Myth Folklore	Soul Metamorphosis	Hunter/Hunted Pursuit of female Pity Magic (of collarbone)
Cat	Myth Folklore Egyptology	Woman Moon	Grace Influence of moon Grimalkin Witchcraft Eyes
Dolphin	Myth Iconography	'Love-beast' Man's rescuer Arion Fidelity	Rescuer from sea Life Sex Joy Vitality
Serpent	Old Testament Myth Hindu Iconography		
Cherub	Iconography	Innocence	Man's return to innocence

IV

Phidias	Greek sculpture	Perfection of Greek art	Creator of perfect human form
Michelangelo	History Iconography	Last synthesis of Renaissance Ending of gyre	Creator of perfect human form

SYMBOL	ORIGIN	CONNECTIONS	ATTRIBUTES
Locke	History	'Mechanized' mind (with Newton)	Mind bound to mechanic world

V

SYMBOL	ORIGIN	CONNECTIONS	ATTRIBUTES
Fire	Arrow	Hound Dance	Sea voyage
Sword	Spear	Horn	Climbing of the hill
Forge	Cave Well Fountain	Deer Boar Bell	

Irish (Gaelic) place names

Derivations

As these are often given anglicized spelling by Yeats and by the Ordnance Survey it leads to confusion.

Bal, balla, bally, baile	town, settlement, e.g. *Ballisodare*
beg(g) beag	small
ben, bin	peak, mountain, e.g. *Ben Bulben*
carrow	a district or quarter, e.g. *Carrowmore*
cashel, castle	fort or castle, e.g. *Cashel*
clon, cloon	meadow, e.g. *Clonmel*
cool(e)	back, e.g. *Coole*
croagh	a rick or rick-like hill, e.g. *Croagh Patrick*
croaghan, cruachan	diminutive of above
curragh, currach	a marsh, e.g. *Curraghmore*
drom, drum	a ridge, e.g. *Drumcliffe*
glan, glen, glin	a valley, e.g. *Glendalough*
inch, inis(h), ennis	island, e.g. *Inishmaan*
kil, cill	cell, church, e.g. *Kilcolman*
knock	hill, e.g. *Knocknarea*
lough, loch	lake, sea-inlet, e.g. *Lough Gill*
more, mir	big, great
rath	ringfort, e.g. *Rathmines*
slieve, slew, sliabh	mountain, e.g. *Slieve-Da-Ein*
tibber, tipper	a well, e.g. *Tipperary*
tir	country, territory, e.g. *Tiraragh*
toor, tore, thoor	a milking enclosure, e.g. *Thoor ballylee*

Pronunciation

'C' is always hard. 'Ch' is guttural as in Scottish 'loch'. The spelling varies even in the best Irish authorities.

Aedh (anglicized Hugh)	Ay (as in 'day')
Almhuin	Alloon
Aoife	Ee-fa
Aughrim	Ochrim
Baile	Boi-la
Beltaine	Bal-tinna

Caoilte	Cweelta
Conchubar	Conn-ahar
Cruachan	Croc-han
Cuchulain	Cu-hoolin or Cu-hullin
Cumhal	Coo-al
Dail Éireann	Dau-il-Ayrun
Danaan	Donnan
Diarmid (anglicized Dermot)	Dee-armid
Emir	Aevir
Eochan	Eohee
Eoghan	Owen
Fianna	Fee-anna
Guiare	Gorey
Knocknarea	Knock-na-ray
Maeve	May-va
Muirthemne	Muir-ev-na
Naoise	Nee-sha
Niamh	Nee-av
Oisín	Usheen
Ribh	Ree-v
Robartes	Ro-bart-ees
Samhain	Sou-in
Sinn Féin	Shinn Fayn
Sidhe	Shee
Usna	Ushna

F. 8r: V

What stalked through the Post office at his side

When Pearse cried out Cuchulain? What intellect,
    What
Numbers measurement replied?
                into
We Irish born ~~to~~ that ancient sect

~~And (.   .   .   .   .   .)~~

~~And thrown up thrown on this vulgar empty emptying modern tide~~
                But
~~Thrown upon this And~~ thrown upon this filthy modern tide

And by its formless spawning ~~fury~~ fury wrecked

Climb to our proper dark that we may trace

The lineaments of a plummet measured face

Yeats's MS of The Statues. Transcription by Jon Stallworthy.
206

Further Reading and References

Further Reading

Much of Yeats's writing depends on his experiences—Ireland, his family and friends, public life, his reading and the theatre. Yeats himself wrote (*E & I*): 'The first Principle is that a poet writes of his personal life, in his work out of its tragedy, whatever it be, remorse, lost love or mere loneliness . . .' Just an analysis of either his symbols, his philosophy or his imagery, though important, is not adequate. One must bring to bear on the poems a wider knowledge, for though there are not more than about 450 in all, the time span is long and their development extensive.

His own prose works give much background to the poems, especially *A Vision* (revised 1937). No definitive biography comparable to Richard Ellmann's *James Joyce* has yet been written, nor will it be in the near future. Covering most aspects of the poet's life and work, if put together, the following, especially the first three, are almost essential. Joseph Hone, *W. B. Yeats* (1942), the standard biography, full of information, though the quotations are sometimes inaccurate, and the index incomplete. A. N. Jeffares, *W. B. Yeats: Man and Poet* (1949) very scholarly and full, but perhaps over-emphasizing the influence on the poet of Maud Gonne. T. R. Henn, *The Lonely Tower* (1950) especially valuable for an explanation of *A Vision*, and for the influences on the poet of the world of art, as well as an incomparable appreciation of the heroic aspects of the poet's thought, expressed with a wealth of scholarship and an insight into Yeats's Anglo-Irish heritage. Richard Ellmann's *Yeats. The Man and the Masks* (1949) and *The Identity of Yeats* (1954) are useful criticism, but are less easy to read than the first three books on this list. George Saul, *Prolegomena to the Study of Yeats's Poems* (1957) is already out of date, nevertheless is irreplaceable. F. A. C. Wilson, *Yeats and Tradition* (1958), analyzing neo-Platonic influences and occult mysteries; and his *Yeats's Iconography* (1960), dealing with Yeats's Nöh plays and twelve related poems, are valuable, though difficult reading on account of the depth of Dr Wilson's reading.

At equal depth, Jon Stallworthy's textual studies are fascinating to follow: *Between the Lines* (2nd impression) (1965) and *Vision and Revision in Yeats's Last Poems* (1969). He sometimes disagrees with Curtis Bradford, *Yeats at Work* (1965) after examination of the same MSS. However, Bradford reveals much about the MSS: how difficult the writing of verse was for Yeats; his illegible writing, erratic spelling and eccentric punctuation; how mistakes are still printed in the final printed text because of Yeats's method—dictating to a secretary, who often misheard or misread Yeats's texts, and finally because of

Yeats's own proof reading errors.

There are numerous collections of critical essays, one of the best being edited by John Unterecker (1963), which contains fourteen essays, totalling 170pp. of which nearly a quarter is taken up by an analysis of the text of the Byzantium poems by Curtis Bradford. In this same collection, T. S. Eliot's essay is especially valuable as revealing a poet writing about a poet. In the same class, an Irish poet about an Irish poet, is Louis MacNeice's *The Poetry of W. B. Yeats* (1941) which discusses Yeats's versification uniquely. For the visual influences on Yeats, with particular reference to the Byzantium poems, *Images of a Poet* (1961) by D. J. Gordon and R. S. Fletcher, shows much scholarly and sensitive investigation. *W. B. Yeats* by Harold Bloom (1970) has some interesting judgments on the value of Yeats's early work, and of the lifelong influence of Blake and Shelley; but is spoilt by extravagant critical overstatement and a prolix prose style.

Yeats's position is now universally established, so it is amusing to look back at Yvor Winters's extraordinary criticisms in *The Poetry of W. B. Yeats* (1960). Winters contrives to choose some of Yeats's incomparable and memorable poetic phrases such as 'A terrible beauty is born', and abruptly dismiss them, in this case with 'one can understand the sentiment, but the diction is pure Yeatsian fustian'.

Certain collections of letters to and from the poet are also helpful: *The Letters of W. B. Yeats*, edited by Allan Wade, is definitive as yet and important; *Letters on Poetry from W. B. Yeats to Dorothy Wellesley* with an introduction by Kathleen Raine; J. B. Yeats, *Letters to his Son, W. B. Yeats and others* and Lady Gregory's *Journals 1916-1930* may help to complete the background.

References

YEATS, WILLIAM BUTLER
A Vision (Werner Laurie, 1925), 2nd edn, Macmillan, 1937.
Dramatis Personae, Macmillan, 1936.
The Collected Poems of W. B. Yeats, 2nd edn, Macmillan, 1950.
The Collected Plays, Macmillan, 1952.
Essays and Introductions, Macmillan, 1961.
Explorations, Macmillan, 1962.
Mythologies, Macmillan, 1962.
Autobiographies, 2nd edn, Macmillan, 1965.
The Letters of W. B. Yeats, ed. Allan Wade, Hart-Davis, 1954.
Letters on Poetry from W. B. Yeats to Dorothy Wellesley, ed. Kathleen Raine, Oxford University Press, 1964.
Memoirs W. B. Yeats. Ed. D. Donoghue, Macmillan, 1972.
The Senate Speeches of W. B. Yeats. Ed. D. R. Pearse. Faber, 1961.

SECONDARY SOURCES

BAX, CLIFFORD, ed. *Florence Farr, Bernard Shaw and W. B. Yeats*, Dublin, Cuala Press, 1941.

BLAKE, WILLIAM, *The Complete Writings of William Blake*, ed. Geoffrey Keynes, Oxford University Press, 1966.

BLAVATSKY, HELEN P., *Isis Unveiled*, 1877.

BRADFORD, CURTIS, *Yeats at Work*, Illinois University Press, 1965.

CAULFIELD, MAX, *The Easter Rebellion*, Muller, 1964.

ELIOT, T. S., *After Strange Gods*, Faber, 1934.

——*Four Quartets*, Faber, 1944.

ELLMANN, RICHARD, *The Identity of Yeats*, Faber, 1954.

——*Eminent Domain*, New York, Oxford University Press, 1967.

——*Yeats: the Man and the Masks*, Faber, 1961.

ENGELBERG, EDWARD, *The Vast Design: patterns in W. B. Yeats's aesthetic*, University of Toronto Press, 1964.

GOLDRING, DOUGLAS, *South Lodge, reminiscences of Violet Hunt, Ford Madox Ford and the 'English Review' Circle*, Constable, 1943.

GOGARTY, O. ST JOHN, *Memoir of W. B. Yeats*, Dublin, Dolmen Press, 1963.

GORDON, D. J. and FLETCHER, IAN, *Images of a Poet, Exhibition Catalogue*, Manchester, 1961.

GREGORY, ANNE, *Me and Nu*, Colin Smythe, 1970.

GREGORY, LADY, *Lady Gregory's Journals, 1916–1930*, ed. Lennox Robinson, 1946.

——*Cuchulain of Muirthemne*, Colin Smythe, 1970.

——*Gods and Fighting Men*, Colin Smythe, 1970.

——*Kiltartan Books*, Colin Smythe, 1972.

——*Visions and Beliefs in the West of Ireland*, Colin Smythe, 1970.

——*Collected Plays*, 4 vols, Colin Smythe, 1971–72.

——*Selected Plays*, Colin Smythe, 1972.

——*Journals, 1916–1930*, Colin Smythe, 1972.

HENN, T. R., *The Lonely Tower*, Methuen, 1965.

HOLT, EDGAR, *Protest in Arms*, Putnam, 1960.

HONE, JOSEPH, *W. B. Yeats, 1865–1939*, Macmillan, 1942.

JEFFARES, A. N., *W. B. Yeats: Man and Poet*, Routledge, 1949.

——*W. B. Yeats: The Poems*, E. Arnold, Routledge, 1961.

JUNG, C. G., *Psychology and Alchemy*, 2nd edition, 1968.

KERMODE, FRANK, *The Romantic Image*, Routledge, 1957.

KIRBY, SHEELAH, *The Yeats Country*, Dolmen Press, 1962

LYONS, F. S., *Ireland since the Famine*, Weidenfeld & Nicolson, 1971.

MCHUGH, ROGER, ed. *Ah, Sweet Dancer: W. B. Yeats and Margot Ruddock, a correspondence*, Macmillan, 1970.

MACMANUS, FRANCIS, ed. *The Yeats We Knew*, Cork, The Merrier Press, 1965.

MACNEICE, LOUIS, *The Poetry of W. B. Yeats*, Oxford University Press, 1941.

——'Yeats's Epitaph', in *New Republic*, CII, 26, June 24th, 1940, pp.862–3.

MANNING, MAURICE, *The Blueshirts*, University of Toronto Press, 1970.

MARRECO, ANNE, *The Rebel Countess* [Markievicz], Weidenfeld & Nicolson, 1967; paperback, Corgi, 1969.

MASEFIELD, JOHN, *Some Memories of W. B. Yeats*, Dublin, Cuala Press, 1940.

MELCHIORI, G., *The Whole Mystery of Art: pattern into poetry in the work of W. B. Yeats*, Routledge, 1960.

MILLER, LIAM, ed., *Yeats Centenary Papers*, Dolmen Press, 1965.

MOORE, VIRGINIA, *The Unicorn: William Butler Yeats's search for reality*, Macmillan of New York, 1954.

O'CASEY, SEAN, *Inishfallen, Fare Thee Well* (vol 4 Autobiography), Macmillan, 1949.

O'CONNOR, FRANK, ed. *Fountain of Magic*, Macmillan, 1939.

O'FAOLÁIN, SEÁN, *Constance Markievicz*, Cape, 1934; rev. edn, Sphere paperback, 1967.

OSHIMO, SHOTARO, *W. B. Yeats and Japan*, Luzac, 1965.

PRITCHETT, V. S., *Midnight Oil*, Chatto, 1971.

RAINE, KATHLEEN, *Blake and Tradition*, Routledge, 1969, 2 vols.

RICHARDS, I. A., *Practical Criticism*, Routledge and Kegan Paul, 1929.

——*Science and Poetry*, Kegan Paul, 1924, 1926.

ROTHENSTEIN, SIR WILLIAM, *Since Fifty. Men and Memories, 1922–28*, Faber, 1939.

SAUL, GEORGE, *Prolegomena to the Study of Yeats's Poems*, Oxford University Press, 1957.

SPENDER, STEPHEN, *The Destructive Element*, Cape, 1935.

STALLWORTHY, JON, *Between the Lines*, Oxford University Press, 1963.

——*Vision and Revision in Yeats's Last Poems*, Oxford University Press, 1969.

——*Yeats: Last Poems*, Macmillan, 1968.

STOCK, A. G., *W. B. Yeats: His Poetry and Thought*, Cambridge University Press, 1964.

TORCHIANA, DONALD, *W. B. Yeats and Georgian Ireland*, Oxford University Press, 1966.

UNTERECKER, JOHN, ed. *Yeats: a collection of critical essays*, Prentice-Hall, Spectrum Books, 1963.

WILSON, F. A. C., *W. B. Yeats and Tradition*, Methuen, 1958.

——*Yeats's Iconography*, Gollancz, 1960.

YEATS, J. B., *Letters to his son, W. B. Yeats and others*, ed. with a Memoir by Joseph Hone, Faber, 1944.

ZWERDLING, ALEX, *Yeats and the Heroic Ideal*, Owen, 1965.

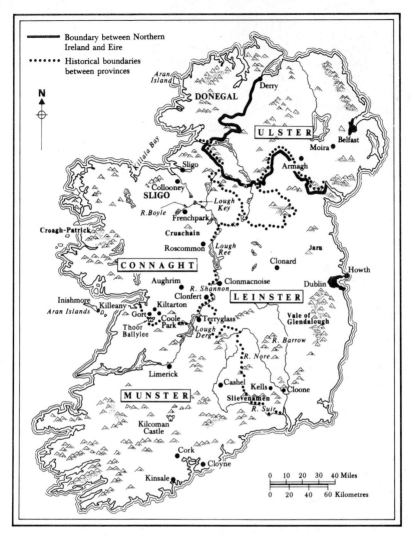

Map of Ireland.

Acknowledgements

The author and publisher are grateful to Senator M. B. Yeats and the Macmillan Company of London and Basingstoke, the Macmillan Company of Canada and Macmillan Publishing Company Inc, New York, for permission to reprint poems by W. B. Yeats all of which are from the *Collected Poems* of W. B. Yeats:

'To the Rose Upon the Rood of Time' Copyright 1906 by Macmillan Publishing Co., Inc., renewed 1934 by William Butler Yeats; 'The Players Ask for a Blessing on The Psalteries and On Themselves', 'The Fascination of What's Difficult' Copyright 1912 by Macmillan Publishing Co., Inc., renewed 1940 by Bertha Georgie Yeats, 'An Irish Airman Foresees His Death', Copyright 1919 by Macmillan Publishing Co., Inc., renewed 1947 by Bertha Georgie Yeats, 'Two Songs from a Play' and 'Leda and the Swan' Copyright 1928 by Macmillan Publishing Co., Inc., renewed 1956 by Bertha Georgie Yeats, 'After Long Silence' and 'Her Vision in the Wood' Copyright 1933 by Macmillan Publishing Co., Inc., renewed 1961 by Bertha Georgie Yeats, 'The Three Bushes' Copyright 1940 by Bertha Georgie Yeats, renewed 1968 by Bertha Georgie Yeats, Anne Yeats and Michael Butler Yeats, 'Under Ben Bulben' Copyright 1940 by Georgie Yeats, renewed 1968 by Bertha Georgie Yeats, Anne Yeats and Michael Butler Yeats and for an extract from *Autobiography* by William Butler Yeats, reprinted by permission of Macmillan Publishing Co., Inc., Copyright 1916, 1935 by Macmillan Publishing Co., Inc., renewed 1944, 1963 by Bertha Georgie Yeats.

The author and publisher are grateful to the following for permission to reproduce photographs:

Lady Albery, *frontispiece* and page 18; Alinar, page 190; Ashmolean Museum, Oxford, page 108; Fitzwilliam Museum, Cambridge, page 60; Giraudon, page 54; Major R. G. Gregory and Colin Smythe Ltd., page 21; Rupert Hart-Davis, *Letters of W. B. Yeats* by Allan Wade, page 154; Hokuseido Press, *W. B. Yeats and Japan* by Joseph Hone, 1942, page 66; Methuen *The Lonely Tower* by T. R. Henn, 2nd edition 1963, page 68; National Gallery of Canada, Ottowa, and Anne Yeats, page 175; National Library of Ireland and Michael Yeats, pages 12, 119, 136 and 206; Earl of Pembroke's Collection at Wilton House, near Salisbury, page 90; Phaidon Press, *Mantegna* by Tietze-Conrat, page 94; Press Association Ltd., page 144; Edwin Smith, page 180; Henriette Sturge-Moore, page 77; Syndics of Cambridge University Library, pages 44 and 45; Tate Gallery, page 16; Thames and Hudson, *W. B. Yeats and His World* by Michael Macliammoir, 1971, page 166.

The cover picture is by courtesy of Anne and Michael Yeats and J. Richards, Orpen.